The Voice of
the Turtledove

New Catholic Women
in Europe

EDITED BY

Anne Brotherton, sfcc

Paulist Press
New York / Mahwah, N.J.

Book design by Nighthawk Design.

Library of Congress Cataloging-in-Publication Data

The Voice of the turtledove: new Catholic women in Europe/edited by
   Anne Brotherton.
      p.   cm.
   Includes bibliographical references.
   ISBN 0-8091-3307-5 (pbk.)
   1. Women in the Catholic Church—History—20th century.
I. Brotherton, Anne, 1927–
BX2347.8.W6V65   1992
282′.4′082—dc20   92-9442
                                                              CIP

Published by Paulist Press
997 Macarthur Boulevard
Mahwah, New Jersey 07430

Printed and bound in the
United States of America

For My Mom
Annie Lenz Brotherton
A New Catholic Woman Before Her Time

My beloved speaks and says to me:
"Arise, my love, my fair one,
    and come away;
for lo, the winter is past,
    the rain is over and gone.
The flowers appear on the earth,
    the time of singing has come,
and the voice of the turtledove
    is heard in our land."

SONG OF SOLOMON 2:10–12

Contents

Introduction

TO PUT IT mildly, these are, in many ways, not "the best of times" to be a member of the Roman Catholic Church. We live in a world which is changing by quantum leaps; no more the gentle, almost imperceptible evolution of past ages. We are often elated, frequently fearful, and sometimes confused by the developments in science, technology, and politics and in sheer human knowledge. Yet, with all the risks involved, the human community, if it so chooses, has greater potential today than ever before in its history to learn from past mistakes, to build a better world, and to dignify ourselves, as human beings, in the process. To do so, we must be free to embrace all that is good and just, and courageous in resisting all forms of evil and oppression, whether of the old order or of the so-called "new world order." Regardless, we must act—there is no alternative—in the *context of our times.* Yet, sadly, the Roman Catholic Church, *as institution,* does not currently seem to be up to the task of modeling this for us in its own behaviors with the faithful. The present institutional church[1] does not seem to recognize the obsolescence of its censoring, censuring and silencing behaviors in an age when wisdom arises from myriad sources, or the ossification of an all-male hierarchy which clearly implies that some human beings are innately worthier than others in God's own design. To those who ask for bread, the institutional church today too often offers a stone.

However, the amazing thing about Catholic people themselves—most of us, anyway—is that, through all this, we keep a tenacious hold on the virtue of Christian hope. Perhaps it is one of the unsung gifts of our baptism, this hope. It enables us, for example, to make an important distinction between our faith, which we know, somehow, is eternal and abiding, and its current institutional manifestation, which is, after all, both temporal and transient. And we never rule out the possibility of conversion, either of persons or of institutions. Moreover, we are assured by our scriptural and traditional heritage as well as by our personal religious experiences that God is indeed among us and that we are God's people, come what may. Indeed, we Catholics are a hopeful lot, and we know, in faith, that, ultimately, our hope is not in vain.

Women in the Roman Catholic Church have had to become especially adept at Christian hope in the past several decades. While a new awareness and appreciation of our specifically feminine identity and of our rightful role in the human community are lately being realized by women the world over, this awareness and appreciation have been especially acute among Catholic women, who have for so long, and often only subconsciously, been painfully sensitive to the pervasive disjunction between the Catholic faith that we freely embrace and the Catholic faith as it is institutionally described and mandated to us as women. Granted, some Catholic women have found the nurturing of hope in such dark times too great a price to pay and have chosen to abandon, if not their elemental faith, at least their attachment to the institutional church. And their numbers may be more legion than we would wish to admit. Still, most have remained in the relationship and have committed themselves to the prophetic task of challenge and of re-creation. These are the women who, to me, notably exemplify the virtue of Christian hope. These are the women whose stories I wish to share in the following pages.

In the several years in which I have been engaged in this project, one of the questions I heard most frequently from colleagues and friends was, "What do you mean by 'new' Catholic women?" A fair question, even if the answer seemed to me rather obvious. I am indebted for the phrase itself to Mary Jo Weaver, who coined it for her 1985 publication, *New Catholic Women: A Contemporary Challenge to Traditional Religious Authority* (Harper & Row, 1985). New Catholic women, as I see them, are women who have come to a new realization and appreciation of what are surely some fundamental truths, however cleverly these may have been distorted through time: that women are as worthy a component as men in the human community, that women have full human dignity and full human value, and that their roles, their rights, *and* their voices merit full recognition—equal to that of their brothers—in all human affairs. For new Catholic women, these human affairs clearly include the affairs of the Catholic Church as the institutional representative of their faith, and it is the institutional church which they especially call to conversion, even as they live out their new freedom in the faith that is their heritage.

Almost invariably, the second question I heard was, "Why new Catholic women in *Europe*? Why not Latin America, Africa, or the Far East?" This, of course, is a characteristically U.S. question. There is a tendency in liberal theological circles in the United States (in which circles I generally enjoy spinning) to always strain toward the new frontier, the as-yet-unexplored wilderness of religious experience and theological reflection. About Europe, we in the U.S. tend, unfortunately, toward something of a "Nazareth complex." "Can anything good. . . ?" Or worse: "Forget Europe. The church in Europe is all but dead!" Yet somewhat to my surprise—and greatly to my excitement—I discovered —in Africa!—that the Catholic Church in Europe is neither dead nor dying. Once we accept that every-Sunday mass attendance can no longer be taken as *the* index of a vigorous Catholic faith, in the United States or elsewhere, we are able to look more carefully and to recognize the many other signs of fidelity with which the faith, even in seemingly dark days and dark places, is blessed. I found this to be especially true of western Europe. And I found it to be true especially because of Europe's new Catholic women, women who are bringing a "new flowering" of the faith to the very scene of Christianity's "first flowering" so many centuries ago. It is clearly through these women that "the voice of the turtledove" is being heard in Europe today, calling the institutional church to conversion as it heralds the disintegration of old battlements, the healing of old wounds, and the ultimate reconciliation of women and of men to one another and to their lover-God. It is, therefore, the stories of Europe's new Catholic women, stories of hope amid adversity, which I have chosen to chronicle here.

Admittedly, my own engagement in this project was not unbiased. I wonder, in fact, to what extent any such endeavor can be, in good sociological jargon, "value-free," for the very fact that we give our time and energy to an undertaking suggests that we already have some convictions—or even (God forbid!) some "feelings"—about it. As a "cradle Catholic," I care deeply about the Catholic Church. She is my spiritual mother. And I care just as deeply about how she is institutionalized and how, through this institution, she embraces her children, both women and men. Thus, in the absence of detached neutrality, I have chosen simply to be as accurate as I can be in presenting and as honest as I can be in reflecting on the experiences of the women who speak in these pages. I, also, live in Christian hope, and I invite our readers to share in this hope, to hear the "voice of the turtledove" announcing the springtime of the Catholic Church which surely lies ahead.

Many people have had a hand in, and have given heart to, this volume, and I am deeply indebted to them all. Europe's new Catholic women, who opened their homes and their lives to me, have been a continuing source of inspiration. Those who have contributed the essays which follow have given far more than their time and their considerable talents and will never know how much their encouragement, patience, and faith in our collaborative project have meant to me. My lasting gratitude, as well, to all the translators for their excellent and painstaking work, to Valerie Lesniak, C.S.J., for her skilled research assistance, to Charlotte Pace for her superb final editing of the manuscript, and to Lawrence Boadt, C.S.P., who welcomed *New Catholic Women in Europe* to Paulist Press. My project would never have gotten underway without the generosity of President Thomas Gleeson, S.J., and Dean David Stagaman, S.J., of the Jesuit School of Theology at Berkeley, who granted needed sabbatical time and research support, supplemented by a research grant from the Association of Theological Schools. Colleagues at JSTB, especially Mary Ann Donovan, S.C., Gloria Loya, P.B.V.M., Clare Ronzani, S.N.D., and Sandra Schneiders, I.H.M., have continued to enliven me as a new Catholic woman. Allan Deck, S.J., and Joseph Powers, S.J., were never too busy to help me with a quick translation, nor were Carmichael Peters, S.J., or George Greiner, S.J., to rescue me from an impasse with my word processor. My Sisters for Christian Community and friends in the Sisters of St. Joseph of Carondelet were always there when I needed them. Special kudos go to Elizabeth Byrne, Luis Calero, S.J., Joseph P. Fitzpatrick, S.J., Barbara Hazzard, O.S.B., Dan McDonald, S.J., Mary Murphy, Marie Studer, and Mary Trinitas, P.C., for their prayers and presence in my life, and to Mary Moore, C.S.J., who has kept me both chuckling and honest through the years, and who made me promise that her name would be in the book. Last, and above all, my family, Dick and Ann Brotherton and a host of wonderful nieces and nephews, have sustained me with their love, and I am ever grateful.

Note

1. When I use the term "institutional church," I am referring to the present hierarchical governing *structure* of the church, a quite different concept from that of church as community of faith or as people of God.

1

Catholic Women at the Close of the Millennium: Focus on Western Europe

There are four periods in human history, after which nothing was ever the same again, and those times are the period of evolution, the period of the ice-age, the period of industrialization and the period of the women's movement.

—MARGARET MEAD[1]

Genesis of the Project

STRANGELY ENOUGH, this story does not begin in Europe—or even in the U.S.—but in Africa, fifteen years before the close of the second millennium.

It was the morning of July 5, 1985, and we were on our last hop, airborne from Athens to our final destination, Nairobi, Kenya. Peering down through the miniscule, double-glass windows of Olympic's flight 105, we gazed on a silvery sheet of Mediterranean Sea, occasionally pocked by a small fishing boat or a larger freighter. And then, at last, the coast of North Africa! Still more hours over barren, sandy stretches of Egypt and the Sudan, changing ever so gradually to the greening valleys and elevations of Kenya, where the closing events of the United Nations Decade for Women were about to begin.[2]

The Kenya airport swarmed with women, a dizzying montage of costumes and colors with multi-lingual audio accompaniment. The energy of the historic occasion was palpable. A struggle through customs, then a jubilant welcome by our Kenyan "contact," Sister Mary Paul Thomas

1

(Margie) Maertz, a cloistered Dominican nun and an old college friend whom I had not seen in forty years. It was Margie who had arranged our housing in Karen, an outlying district near her monastery of Corpus Christi, and had negotiated for us the rental of a car, a small Italian Celeste, for navigating the tricky round-abouts to and from the city.

We were a delegation of six: Mary Ellen Gaylord, Chris Smith, Ida Thornton, Sandee Yarlott and myself, representing the Center for Women and Religion of the Graduate Theological Union in Berkeley, and Monica Clark, a reporter (soon to be editor) of the *Catholic Voice,* the diocesan newspaper in Oakland. Together we constituted one of the hundreds of NGO's (Non-Governmental Organizations) attending, not the U.N. Conference, which was restricted to official delegates of the various countries, but the FORUM, which was open to all who could get themselves there. Months of creative fund-raising had made our own trip possible.

FORUM planners had anticipated the participation of some three thousand women. The final count of those attending the FORUM was in excess of fourteen thousand, possibly the largest international assembly of women in history. Over one thousand workshops and informal gatherings spilled out of the lecture halls and specially erected tents on the campus of the University of Nairobi to grassy knolls and neighboring churches and cafes, where everything from female circumcision to the feminization of poverty, from polygamy to single parenting, from peace to politics, was discussed and debated. No woman who experienced those ten days in July could have left Nairobi without having been profoundly moved and fiercely challenged—and none more so than women from the so-called "developed" nations, for, as one of our "emerging nation" sisters soon suggested to us, we might more accurately describe our own nations as "*over*-developed." To which we could only respond by reflecting: "Over-developed? Well—yes." But, more to the point, "over-developed at whose expense?" During the days which followed, I found myself frequently recalling the words of our own U.S. prophet of non-violence, Martin Luther King, Jr., and applying them to our "worlds" today: "Injustice anywhere is a threat to justice everywhere."

I had gone to Nairobi as a Catholic woman, a woman religious, and a sociologist of religion, and many of the questions that I took to the FORUM with me were, understandably, religious questions. What part did religion play in the lives of women around the world? To what extent could religion offer some solutions to women's problems? To what extent was religion a cause of the problems? How would I perceive myself as a *Catholic* woman in Nairobi? To my dismay, religion, as such, was largely ignored by the scheduled workshops, a fact which, in itself, was food for thought. For so many women in the world today, sheer survival is preliminary to all other considerations; though religion often plays a role in their oppression, this is not always immediately clear. What, then, did religion have to say in a setting such as this?

Happily for me, other Catholic women had also noted the religious vacuum within the FORUM. I was clearly not alone in my struggle to reconcile my Catholic faith with my feminist sensitivities and issues of justice for women. A day or so into the meetings, hand-lettered signs began to appear on bulletin boards and assorted tree trunks, inviting interested Catholic women to an informal gathering "on the grass by the refreshment stands." Some sixty women, representing every continent, responded to the notices. On three consecutive days we assembled for lively and sometimes intense exchange, each woman speaking from her own cultural perspective of what it means to be "woman" and "Catholic" in her own situation and in the world today. It was here, on a sunny sward in Nairobi, that I first met the dynamic woman from Belgium, Denise Peeters, who would encourage my study, be a vital resource for me in contacting other European women, and later provide the excellent essay on Belgium's new Catholic women.

The meetings with this international group of Catholic women confirmed both of my still-untested pre-FORUM hypotheses about women in the Catholic Church worldwide. My first hypothesis was that there is indeed a new self-awareness emerging among Catholic women, *wherever they may be,* about their own identities as women, and about their roles—*and their rights*—not only in society but in the institutional Catholic Church. The truth of this was clearly evident as these women introduced themselves to one another and as many spoke—some hesitantly, at first—of their frustrations with institutional absolutism, of their sense of "voicelessness" in the church, and of the many religious settings in which they, as women, experience a "holy" oppression—all this despite their acknowledged loyalty to the Catholic faith and to the gospel message. And recent attention given us by Rome had led us Catholic women in the U.S. to believe that we alone were the refractory, the "trouble-makers" in the church![3]

My second hypothesis was likewise supported: that the specific issues and concerns of Catholic women, in spite of their unanimous call for justice in the church, tend to be culture-bound as well. That is, the more specific issues of women in the church arise from the unique circumstances which maintain in each country or culture, and are very much related to a particular history and to a national hierarchical character and cultural tradition. For example, separation of church and state is not the issue in the U.S. that it is in Ireland, where divorce is still proscribed both legally and religiously. Nor is the opportunity for earning a licentiate degree in theology the issue in The Netherlands that it is in Spain, where "theology is for priests." Being a minority, women, within a minority, Catholics, constitutes much of the suffering of women in India, while the culture of machismo is especially painful for women in predominantly Catholic Latin America.

FORUM 85 provided a rare—perhaps a first—opportunity for Catholic women from around the world to meet and to exchange with one another freely, *on their own terms,* without the usual institutional constraints. Our three days together as Catholic women in Nairobi brought each of us to a new level of respect and appreciation for our sisters from so many diverse cultures. Simply hearing one another sharpened our sensitivities and stretched our categories. Yet, amid the diversity, we found ourselves on a solid, common ground. Whatever our country or our culture, we all sought basic justice in our church, and we agreed that such justice will be realized only when our voices are fully heard, when our gifts are truly celebrated, and when we stand as equals with our brothers in the community of faith which is the Catholic Church.

The single corporate action which emerged from this gathering of Catholic women was instructive regarding both our common commitment and the problems that we face. We agreed that a representative group of us would formulate a simple statement, with a request for dialogue, which would be personally delivered to Bishop Paul Josef Cordes, appointed by the Vatican to head its delegation to the official U.N. Conference which was meeting across the city at Nairobi's Kenyatta Center.[4] Our statement read as follows:

> *To the Vatican Delegation to the United Nations*
> *Conference for Women, July, 1985*

> At FORUM 85, Roman Catholic women from every continent have participated in workshops, dialogues and informal gatherings in order to examine the themes of the Decade on Women: Equality, Development,

and Peace. In this process, we shared a common experience of discrimination against women in our Church. We are of the same mind on the following points:

—The Church encourages women to take their place in the world but not in the Church: women are not allowed to preach; women are excluded from decision-making, especially when the issues affect women directly; women theologians are not invited to serve equally with men on theological commissions.

—We, women of the Church, can speak for ourselves. It is offensive that the head of our Church's delegation to the U.N. concluding Conference on the Decade for Women is a man.

—We ask that women be included, equally with men, in the synod scheduled for this fall and in the Synod on the Laity in 1987.

—We ask the Vatican to join those nations that have already ratified the Declaration on the Elimination of All Forms of Discrimination Against Women.

We concur that the failure of the Roman Catholic Church to uphold the human rights of women within its own structures and practices undermines the call of the Church for justice in our world.

> A Statement by Forty-Five Roman Catholic
> Women attending a three-session workshop
> on Catholic Women and the Church, July
> 18, 1985. Nairobi, Kenya.

Bishop Cordes received the statement from the two women who presented it to him at a reception for delegates, but he declined to allow it to be read aloud as this would be "inappropriate for a social occasion" (though the official Vatican delegation, as such, was not otherwise accessible to Catholic women from the FORUM). The bishop likewise declined to meet with the FORUM women at another time, pleading his busy schedule and reminding the petitioners that he was in Nairobi "to represent the holy see, not women," and that, in any case, Catholic women's organizations had already been consulted in preparation for the Conference.

We subsequently published our statement in the July 22 issue of the special daily newspaper, *FORUM 85*, where it was accompanied by an editorial, "Vatican Questioned."[5] This did elicit a response from Bishop

Cordes and the Vatican delegation, not addressed, however, to the women who had formulated the statement and had asked to discuss it with the Vatican delegation, but to the *FORUM 85* newspaper, where it was published several days later:

> In *FORUM 85* of July 22, page 3, a statement "by Roman Catholic partici-pants in FORUM 85" was published. We request that you publish in your next edition the following text in order to correct the wrong information given by the statement.
>
> It is erroneous to affirm that "the Church encourages women to take their place in the world but not in the Church"; on the contrary, the guidelines of the Church's life underline that every Christian female and male has to commit herself/himself to proclaim the Gospel in Church and society. (See, for example, the "lineament" issued in 1985 to prepare the Synod of Bishops 1987.)
>
> It is erroneous to affirm that "women are not allowed to preach"; on the contrary, the guidelines of Church life gave permission for women to preach in many circumstances and occasions. (See, for example, the prac-tice in Germany, Brazil, Zambia, etc.)
>
> It is erroneous to affirm that "women are excluded from decision-making especially when the issues affect women directly"; on the contrary, women are members of the pastoral councils on different levels of parish, deanery and diocese.
>
> (Signed) Paul Cordes (German) Head of the Delegation, Lucienne Salle (French), Martha Mugambi (Kenya), Clare Chibesakunda (Zambia), Suz-zane Nye (Belgium), Janet Davis Richardson (American); Advisers Gus-man Carriquiri (Uruguayan), James McHugh (American).

The bishop's response was vintage "Vaticanese," ignoring the essen-tial point which the women were making, a call for the elimination of discrimination against women in the church, to focus on a few rare "permissions" given to women and on certain lower-echelon positions available to them. This is an institutional strategy with which Catholic women are more than a little familiar, one in which the major point that they are making is somehow "missed" in favor of argumentation over minor points and the citing of token "exceptions to the rule." The women, then, were not so much surprised at the bishop's response as they were disappointed; his willingness to dialogue directly with Catholic women at the FORUM might have signaled a breakthrough, a significant Catholic witness of ecclesial openness to thousands of women around the world.

The great value of Nairobi for Catholic women was that it enabled them to speak freely to one another across many national and cultural boundaries, and to discover an authentic sisterhood in their shared faith and in their call for full participation in the exercise of that faith. My questions then became: How can such stories continue to be told—and heard—so that they might give affirmation and courage to other Catholic women, cross-culturally? How can the institutional church be enabled, through such a telling, to realize that women throughout the world are united in these concerns, and that women so deeply rooted in their faith and so committed to its service are not to be feared but only to be heard? Are not to be merely "allowed" but to be embraced? Are no longer to be ministered "to" but to be welcomed as partners in ministry? How can these new Catholic women, so evident since Vatican II—since Nairobi—find a hearing for their voices?[6]

The Project

Nairobi proved beyond the shadow of a doubt that there are new Catholic women on every continent, however otherwise "developed" their countries may or may not be. I have chosen through this volume to give voice to some of these new Catholic women in western Europe, the "cradle of Christianity," which seemed to me a likely place to begin. I hope that other such works will follow, chronicling the similar-yet-different experiences, struggles and aspirations of new Catholic women in Africa, in Latin America, in Asia, and beyond. Thus, in time, the global story can be told to the glory of all that is authentically "Catholic" in our world today.

My initial plan was to write of new Catholic women in eight of the major countries of western Europe, basing the work on personal interviews with capable and representative spokespersons of such women in Belgium, England, France, Germany, Ireland, Italy, The Netherlands and Spain. Accordingly, in two separate visits, in 1986 and 1988, I spent some six months in western Europe, meeting and speaking with such women, taping more than one hundred hours of interviews, participating in their gatherings and religious celebrations, and visiting in their homes and churches. However, while this research netted much valuable information and rich insights which have contributed significantly to the present volume, it soon became evident to me that the stories of these new Catholic women needed to be told directly by the women themselves, to avoid the risk of their being filtered through my own undoubtedly culture-bound lenses. So lest I myself be guilty of attempting to speak "for" women, I determined that *The Voice of the Turtledove* should be primarily first-person accounts, a collection of essays written by European women who were both knowledgeable of the historical and cultural stories of their Catholic countrywomen and committed to the vision of the project at hand.

I was successful in recruiting outstanding women essayists in all of the eight countries visited. In soliciting the essays, as with the interviews, I found myself consistently impressed with the tremendous generosity of these women with their time and talents and with their profound commitment to the cause of women in the church, which they see as clearly related to the very future of the church itself. Though their stories often speak of the frustration, disenchantment and pain of Catholic women in their respective countries, all are undergirded by a tenacious and pervasive spirit of hope, the hope of those who, despite all, remain firm in their commitments to that community of faith which is the church universal. Through these women, if one has ears to hear, one can clearly recognize "the voice of the turtledove," which sings its promise of the justice and reconciliation to be ultimately realized in the Catholic Church.

It should be clarified that none of the essayists is an "official" spokesperson for the Catholic women in her country. That is, none has been formally delegated, either by the institutional church (which would be more a disadvantage than an advantage at this point, in any case!) or by some institutionalized voice of her women compatriots. Each of the essayists makes this clear (as each also speaks of the ideological diversity among the women in her own country, not all of whom can be described as new Catholic women). Yet each of the writers here is uniquely qualified for the task of description and commentary by virtue of her training, experience and commitment. Each has "walked the walk" with her sisters in the church and knows whereof she speaks.

My taped interviews were informal and open-ended, and most of them were one-on-one, though several were with two or more women. All were assured anonymity. Where necessary—and this was rare—I used interpreters. To assure some consistency in my data-gathering, I followed specific guidelines in conducting the interviews.[7] Surprisingly, the interview question which was most provocative and provided the most significant insights was question VI, which I had included almost as a "throw-away," to enable us to end the sessions on something of a lighter note: "If Pope John Paul II agreed to grant you three wishes, what would those wishes be?" The women's responses here ranged from comic to sardonic to quite serious; all were tremendously telling. I share some of them in my conclusions in Chapter 10.

Guidelines similar to those used for the interviews were provided to the essayists.[8] I stressed to the essayists that, while statistical data would be welcomed, facts and figures are readily available from other sources for those who desire them.[9] I was much more interested in Catholic women's untold stories and in their personal and collective experiences as women in the church in their respective countries. To this end, I suggested that the essayists focus on the *participation* of women in the church in terms of church attendance, ministry, theological education and scholarship, and membership in religious communities, on the *attitudes* of Catholic women with regard to the institutional church, on the institutional *changes* most desired, and on *organizations* working to bring about such changes. I urged the essayists' own additions to these categories, as well as their personal comments and reflections. I have been more than gratified by the thoroughness and honesty of their responses, which are shared in the following essays.

Notes

1. Quoted by Joan Chittister in *Women in the Church I,* Madonna Kolbenschlag, ed. (Washington, D.C.: The Pastoral Press, 1987), 215.

2. The U.N. Decade for Women, 1975–1985, had as its theme "Equality, Development and Peace"; its focus was on "issues that are of concern to women in all parts of the world." The Decade opened in 1975 with a Conference and Forum in Mexico City. An interim Conference/Forum met in 1980 in Copenhagen. The 1985 Conference/Forum in Nairobi marked the close of the De-

cade for Women. While participation in *conferences* sponsored by the United Nations is restricted to official delegates of the governments of member nations, the U.N. also sponsors accompanying non-official *forums* to which the general public is invited. Our delegation was to represent the Center for Women and Religion in Berkeley at FORUM 85.

3. The attention bestowed by the Vatican on U.S. Catholic women in the 1980s did little to disabuse us of the perception that we were under special papal scrutiny. U.S. women religious, whose canonical status makes them especially vulnerable to papal intervention, were especially targeted. In 1983 the Vatican issued a directive to U.S. bishops to open a detailed investigation of U.S. religious congregations, and a year later U.S. religious superiors were ordered to seek recantations from their members who had signed an October 7, 1984, full-page statement in the *New York Times* asking that the complexity of the abortion issue be fully recognized.

4. Since the FORUM (July 10–19) began several days before the Conference (July 15–26), registration and some initial activities of the FORUM took place at the Kenyatta Conference Center, an attractive, modern facility just southeast of the Nairobi downtown area. When the Conference began at the Kenyatta Center, FORUM activities moved to the spacious campus of the University of Nairobi, just northwest of downtown. Since the two sites were within easy walking distance of one another, many of the Conference delegates were seen in attendance at FORUM workshops, though FORUM delegates were not generally admitted to Conference sessions.

5. The *FORUM 85* editorial of July 22 read as follows:

> The Vatican should put an ear to the ground. A strong group of Roman Catholic women at the FORUM has given their church a surprise with a very clear criticism of the policy of the delegation of the Holy See to the U.N. Conference.
>
> In the FORUM newspaper of today, the reader will find the statement given by Roman Catholic participants at the FORUM showing that the time is apparently ripe to press the Church to give women equal opportunities with men.
>
> Women Catholics from every continent share the opinion that the Vatican should ratify the Declaration on the Elimination of All Forms of Discrimination against Women.
>
> There is a whole host of "laws" and attitudes within the Vatican which have to be changed before it is able to ratify the convention. Catholic women mention some of them: women should be allowed to preach; women should not be excluded from decision-making; women should be included in the Synod.
>
> It is some sort of divine irony that the Catholic Church, which is so strongly supported by women, the majority taking part in the mass and

the broad humanitarian workshop of the church, should be among the last Christian churches to give equality to women.

Many Catholic priests have been fighters for liberty, defeating exploitation of human beings. Some have even turned into guerrilla fighters in the liberation movements. How long shall we wait until Catholic priests start fighting for true equality for women?

The Vatican has a special position within the U.N. system, being recognized as a "member state." That makes the question of the Vatican even more burning. The question is put to the Vatican by their own sisters. The Vatican should give an answer.

6. This is not to ignore the papal encyclical *Mulieris Dignitatem,* other episcopal documents relating to women, or the current struggle of the U.S. bishops to formulate a pastoral on "women's concerns." Consistently, however, and in spite of "consultation" with women, such documents have come through as patronizing and unsatisfactory, praising the "dignity and uniqueness" of women at the expense of their equal rights in the church.

7. GUIDELINES FOR INTERVIEW:

    I. Name and background/organization of interviewee(s).

    II. How would you describe the relationship of Catholic women in your country to the Institutional Church?

        A. Membership in the Church, i.e., how many identify themselves as "Catholic"?

        B. Level of participation, i.e., how many attend Church regularly?

        C. How many are actively involved in traditional Church service, organizations, etc?

        D. Is there involvement of women in Church ministry, i.e., teaching, counseling, liturgy, etc?

        E. Are women involved in theological education at seminary or university level: as professors, students?

        F. To what extent are women entering religious communities (as Sisters)?

    III. How would you describe the attitudes of Catholic women in your country to the Institutional Church?

        A. With what are they satisfied?

        B. With what are they dissatisfied?

    IV. If Catholic women in your country could bring about changes in the Institutional Church, what would those changes be?

    V. Are Catholic women in your country working for such changes in an organized way?

    VI. If Pope John Paul II agreed to grant you three wishes, what would those wishes be?

VII. What nurtures (feeds) your own personal spirituality, spiritual life? ANYTHING ELSE?

8. GUIDELINES FOR ESSAY:

Defining "Catholic Feminism" as "a new consciousness among Catholic women regarding their rightful role in the Institutional Church," the essay should address, in your own words and from your own perspective:

I. The current *participation* of women in your country in the Institutional Church.
   A. Membership.
   B. Regular Church attendance.
   C. Ministry. What kinds? Full time or part time? Paid or volunteer?
   D. Theological education at seminary or university level. As professors? Students?
   E. Members of religious communities (Sisters).
   F. Scholarship in theology.

II. Current *attitudes* of women in your country to the Institutional Church.
   A. With what are they satisfied?
   B. With what are they dissatisfied?

III. *Changes* in the Institutional Church most desired by Catholic women in your country.

IV. *Organizations* through which Catholic women in your country are working for such changes.

   Please do not be limited by the above categories. You might also wish to address such topics as hope for the future, feminist spirituality, women's ordination, the role of the laity, etc. Statistics are helpful, but the *spirit* of Catholic Feminism in your country is more important.

9. Most dioceses and national bishops' conferences have current data on church membership and participation, current numbers of women religious, etc. Pro Mundi Vita in Louvain is an excellent source of religious research, internationally, and was of tremendous assistance to me during the course of this project. For further information, contact Pro Mundi Vita, Louvain, Belgium.

2

New Catholic Women in Belgium

Denise Peeters*

In all humility, I am more Catholic than the pope. If Catholic means "universal," the pope doesn't accept the universe of women, who are half of humanity, while I accept the universe of men. I accept men to be equal to me. At the same time, we must be the Catholic Church born again. Naming ourselves as Catholic is much bigger than the popes and bishops.

—A CATHOLIC WOMAN IN BRUSSELS

French-Speaking Belgium

THIS CONTRIBUTION from French-speaking Belgium was among replies from participants in a "mini-poll" which I conducted in October and November 1988 based on Anne Brotherton's interview questions and addressed to fifty Catholic women. Thirty-five replies were received, some from individuals, others from women's movements such as Catholic Action, still others from family movements and research and reflection groups, teams from working-class milieux, base communities, the alumnae association of a religious educational institution, renewal movements, etc. The ages of the respondents range from twenty-six to sixty-eight, including married women, single women, women religious and members of secular institutes.

It is not easy to give an accurate total of the women represented by

* Translated by Mary Elvinger.

these replies. For instance, taking into consideration only one of the women's movements which has a membership of approximately 100,000, it can be said without doubt that the replies expressed the opinions of an important part of the Catholic female population of French-speaking Belgium.

In respect of truth, quotations given are the actual words of the women who responded to the survey. The origin of all the replies is not given because of the discretion requested by several correspondents.

Women and Church Attendance

For many respondents, "belonging to the church" can no longer be measured by attendance at Sunday mass or receiving the sacraments. Participation in Catholic feminine movements does not necessarily mean "regular church attendance":

> First of all, we do not participate in the church in terms of attendance. The manner in which this question is worded raised my hackles. I would like to turn the question around. It is my own faith in the good news of Jesus Christ which prompts me to accept being a member of an assembly which recognizes the gospel message and is based on it. Then follows participation and an action of faith.

This personal reaction confirms the perceptions of a group which points out that, although attendance is constantly on the decline, the faithful who still attend nowadays have a more profound awareness and a less formal commitment.

The replies also mention a distancing from the traditional parish. Committed persons are searching for more meaningful celebrations which are less anonymous. They seek communities where they find more affinity. One woman religious points out that for her and her community "attendance" is obviously on a regular daily basis, but she adds:

> It is sometimes tedious to participate in a eucharistic celebration because there is so little fervor and a lack of inspiration, as the priest celebrating the mass is so often a stranger to the community. We listen to a homily

which is not relevant to community life. I regret that a voice is not given to someone in the congregation, possibly a woman, and that the priest would simply preside. In this way the church would gain vitality.

In one *doyenné*,[1] a way to establish religious statistics is to count the "celebrants," that is to say, the persons who attend Sunday mass (ten percent), and those who ask for the rites of passage, or sacraments (seventy-eight percent). Pastoral work covers the seventy-eight percent of the baptized and not just the ten percent of the "celebrants."

To give a more global figure of Sunday attendance, the most recent figures (1985) show a continued decline, but this would seem to have stabilized after the spectacular drop in the period between 1967 and 1979.[2] For the whole of Belgium, there are almost twenty-five percent practicing Catholics (26.9 percent in Flanders, 17.7 percent in French-speaking Wallonie and 28.5 percent in Brussels). In 1967, the figures were 42.5 percent in Flanders, 28.3 percent in Wallonie and 28.5 percent in Brussels. Statistics do not give a breakdown by gender, but it is easy to point out that non-practice among the young is equally divided between girls and boys. Insofar as adults and older people are concerned, women are in the majority at both Sunday and weekday masses.

Women in Ministry

The Facts About Women in Ministry

According to the 1972 papal encyclical *Ministeria Quaedam,* no "ordained" or "institutional" ministry is accessible to women in the Catholic Church. (One of the answers received through the poll underlines this decision of the Vatican.) What name can then be given to the many services performed by an increasing number of women in the Belgian church today? For some of these services, there does exist a mandate given by the hierarchy. But it is seldom that the new assignments of pastoral assistants or teams is accompanied by a "sign" or solemnized by a gesture or a celebration in the community concerned.

In the French-speaking church of Belgium today, one finds women, both religious and lay, working in a variety of ministerial roles: as cate-

chists in parishes and schools (in fact, the majority are women); in continuing education for young people and adults; in animation[3] at parish,
vicariate and diocesan levels; on a team directing a seminary; in charge of
psycho-sociological "accompaniment"[4] of diocesan seminarians; in the
celebration of some of the sacraments; as eucharistic ministers—even,
although very exceptionally, as homilists; in chaplaincy teams in hospitals; in leadership, though at a lower institutional level, of Catholic movements (such as Vie Féminine, Action Catholique Rurale Féminine, Action Catholique en Milieu Indépendant, etc.).

Furthermore, in one diocese a woman directs the pastorate of health;
in another a woman heads the Committee on Religious. Finally, one
woman is chairperson of the National Justice and Peace Committee.
This is unprecedented in Europe, where justice and peace committees
are usually presided over by bishops.

Mention should also be made of committed Catholic women who
often have great responsibilities in pluralist movements and actions
without any direct connection to the church. In the eyes of these
women, their actions are in direct reference to the gospel.

Most of these services are volunteer and therefore unpaid. When
remuneration is made, it is almost always at a salary inferior to that given
to a man doing the same service and not in proportion to the efforts
expended.

Experiences of Women in Ministry

Judging from current opinions expressed at meetings and from some of
the replies received from the poll, it would appear that:

> Although women are more numerous in participation in the life of the
> church, they do not hold power . . . or very little. They feel that they are
> being "used" by the church, but not "recognized."

The women who work in teams at either the parish, diocesan or
vicariate level do not appear to have difficulties in their relations to their
priest partners, with one or two exceptions where older priests were
concerned. The principle of equality is acknowledged. However, some
women are aware that their education in theology is at a higher level and
more advanced than that of their priest partners; this is especially true in

rural milieux. But, finally, as admitted by one of the respondents, "Priests lay claim to supreme superiority; they can *consecrate!*"

Most women are aware that they must be twice as competent as their male partners if they are to be taken seriously, a phenomenon which also prevails in the society at large. These women are also aware that they are not being listened to or understood, as explained by one of the respondents:

> When I affirm something at team meetings, I must be twice as convincing as the men present, who, after all, are in the minority. Does the priest instinctively have more faith in the word of a man?

With the public, "the faithful," everything is fairly smooth, and women are accepted without hesitation. However—and once again in a rural milieu—women in ministry experience a certain amount of jealousy and envy on the part of other women. In one parish, some parishioners show a certain "hostility" toward two women employed and paid by the parish (at the same rate as a sacristan!). These women are accused of trying to "manipulate" the pastor.

In small groups and base communities, groups that are more homogeneous and less traditional, there are certainly fewer problems than in a parish:

> Small groups and communities set up new practices and this is essential. It enables their members to find their place in the group, to collaborate, to experience the conflicts and, together, to find the solutions. Women are more aware and have the courage to speak out. But we must always remain vigilant, so that men do not take over the initiative in the group, and this is especially true when dealing with secular clergy.

In one community involved in renewal, the ministries and services—such as group animation, singing, decoration of altars, teaching, prophecy, etc.—are shared by men and women in accordance with their charisms and availability. However, men are predominant "at the summit."

In summing up these responses, we find few women entering the institution without being aware of its patriarchal character, yet many do not question the institution. Undoubtedly there are women who question but who allow themselves to be co-opted by the institution. There are also those who reply that:

There is no such thing as a strictly institutional church. The church is a mystery made up, at one and the same time, of the risen Christ truly living today and of the visible element which is the people of God.

This theological reminder can prove useful for those whose existential reality is far removed from ecclesiological theory.

On the whole, however, the responses show that the women who are committed to the institutional church today have a new awareness of their role in the church and perceive it with great lucidity. They have accepted their responsibilities in the church because they feel that this itself is a strategy for change. They feel that the changes will be long in coming because they see so many obstacles:

When one is part of the hierarchy, one has the impression that it is "the faithful" who are slow to accept change. When one is outside the hierarchy, one accuses the hierarchy of slowing down the movement.

The majority of these women are convinced that change is irreversible; there is no going back. Figures showing the numbers of priests today and predictions for the future lend credence to this conviction.

The women refuse, however, to see co-responsibility and sharing of tasks as a mere solution to the shortage of priests. For them their engagement is, above all, a recognition of the equality of all the baptized. But, in the eyes of these women committed to the institution, there is a complete lack of concern on the part of the institution to face this problem of declining numbers of priests. There is no realistic plan on either a short-term or a long-term basis. For the present, church authorities appear simply to "overload," that is to say, to add to the responsibilities of priests who are already overworked, and this without much consideration of their availability or their personal well-being.

Women also say that a study should be made of the financial aspect of the declining-priests problem. If one wishes to employ more people, of whom the majority will be women, as members of pastoral teams, these people must be offered an equitable salary. The institution lacks realism in this matter.

Criticism is also voiced over the fact that no overall pastoral planning exists at any level, from parish to diocese. In parishes, services very often are limited to the approximately ten percent of those who are "practicing" or those who request the sacraments. The rest are ignored. New initiatives are not taken, such as research groups, prayer groups, sharing of the gospel, and other ideas stemming from the grass roots, all of which are "of the church" but not recognized as such by the parish. As one woman says:

> I think that parish projects should be reexamined. I see this through my contacts with persons far removed from the church and with immigrants in my neighborhood.

Another has this to say:

> In parishes which seem to be "neglected" by the church, the faithful must live with the pastor they have been given. The dynamism of Christians is basically rejected, and one wonders how the church of Jesus Christ can even retain its visibility! We should not be surprised that the integrists are making headway! One often hears it said: "Things were much better before, when we were young!"

What many committed persons, priests as well as the laity, miss is a systematic, regular evaluation of the pastoral enterprise. One animator, during her time of commitment in the parish, set up a yearly evaluation of her own work and that of her team by an outside animator. Rare is the parish animator who has the courage to assess his or her work and rectify it for the future.

Do these women aspire to the priesthood or the diaconate? Nothing in their responses leads to such a belief. Those who do bring up the question tend to have a negative approach:

> As a woman I do not aspire to ordained priesthood because I consider that under present circumstances this would entail a renouncement of my own vocation as a "woman in the church." This would also mean entering into a ready-made and totally masculinized framework.

> Obviously, I do hope that one day women will have access to ordained ministry, but certainly not in its present form. What is the role of a priest today? His specificity appears to be limited to the sacred character of his role and he is "distributor" of the sacraments, especially that of the eucharist. Is this "sacred" power not a perversion? The eucharist, which is the

symbol of the ultimate gift and of total grace, has become the sign of exclusion!

However, another respondent says:

> I desire to be an ordained priest if it is possible. But, alas, for the moment there is no sign of change, and I doubt if there is any hope of change in the near future. Therefore I do my best to invest my efforts in the pastoral team, hoping to pave the way for others.

Concerning ordained priesthood and the feeling of exclusion, another woman writes:

> It is especially during ordination ceremonies that I experience this exclusion. My feelings are deep and almost physical. As a member of the laity and as a woman (twofold exclusion), it is at the moment when all the ordained priests lay their hands on the new priest that I feel exclusion.

As far as the diaconate is concerned, the experience of permanent male deacons in the Belgian church is not all positive. What is the true status of the deacon? "Is he a priest of a lesser order? Or a super layman?" asks one woman. And another:

> Women do not really want this poisoned gift. At best, naming women deacons could be a way to break the lock which denies access to women to ordained ministries. And at worst, there is a risk that the magisterium would stop at this gesture, feeling that it had already fulfilled its duty.

This being said, another woman suggests that:

> Theological and pastoral research must continue in this field and should not be limited to the diaconate for married men, but should also be extended to men and women, married or single, on the same level.

Christian women committed in movements or actions in a pluralistic milieu feel that they are little or not at all recognized by the institutional church. There is no provision enabling them to report to the church on the basis of their work and actions; material or financial support is not available to them. The women are perfectly aware of the importance of their role and of what is at stake for the church: Christian presence manifesting the existence and vitality of the Catholic Church in a secular society.

Women in Theological Education

While only theological education given in seminaries and universities will be dealt with here, there are courses in every diocese—regular classes, weekend sessions, colloquies, etc.—in which women are the majority. Various movements also organize, for their own members and for others, study days or weekends.

The Catholic University of Louvain (the only Catholic university which has a faculty of theology in the French-speaking region of Belgium) had in the academic year 1988–89 a total student population of one hundred and seventy-one—fifty-nine of whom were women. In the last ten years, four women (two lay and two religious) have obtained doctorates in theology from Louvain. Before this date, only one doctorate was granted to a woman, in 1974. There are two women teaching on the faculty of theology and canon law; one is a guest lecturer and the other an assistant professor.

Regarding seminaries: In Brussels, sixteen men and two women follow the regular course. Of forty-four "free" students, three-fourths are women.[5] There is one woman professor. In Liège, there are fifteen men and no women in the seminary courses, and there are no women professors. However, there are many women studying in Liège's *l'Institut Supérieur de Catéchèse,* in which there is one female professor of philosophy. In Tournai, there are eighteen seminarians and ten women free students; there is one woman professor in the sociology of religion. In Namur, seven seminarians follow theology courses in an institute totaling one hundred and ten students, including sixty-five women; there is one woman professor in the sociology of religion.

Women in Religious Congregations

As of January 1, 1987 there were 5,906 women religious in French-speaking Belgium. In general, communities are aging, with the exception of some contemplative cloisters; in other orders, average age is retirement age, sixty years. But there has been a slight increase of religious vocations after the "desert" of fifteen to twenty years ago. There are more late vocations (more or less thirty years old) than before, and these often come from charismatic communities, prayer groups, etc.

Like their sisters in other countries, the life of Belgian women religious following the Second Vatican Council has been marked by less isolation and by more diversity. Said one respondent:

> At a given moment in history, religious institutions and their works constituted a response to a real need in the church and society, but they had a tendency to become constraining per se compared to the dynamism of religious life, and no longer corresponded to the needs of today's men, women and children. Therefore it is in fidelity to their profound inspiration that many women religious passed from "doing for" (we exist because we "do") to a "being with," by their presence and action to promote life.

The respondent continued with a comment on the future of religious life:

> At the present moment we are seeing an irreversible phenomenon: the aging process and the unlikelihood of new vocations, at least in western Europe, means that sooner or later most of the existing religious congregations as we know them today will die out. What form will religious life take in the church of tomorrow? Certainly not as large institutions, but rather as smaller units marked by a simplicity of lifestyle, quality of relationships and discreteness of actions.

As to relations with the institutional church, the time has passed when a hierarchical and male authority can govern the organization of the daily life of women religious. In the past, women religious were considered minors, unable to manage their lives and their relationship with God. Today, autonomy has been achieved, and relations between diocesan congregations and representatives of the bishops are in general very fraternal. But this is less simple for papal congregations, which are dependent on the Vatican's Congregation for Religious. However, as one woman religious shrewdly suggests, "As often in the church, dictates are one thing, but life at the grass roots is something else."

Another feels that there is "a sad lack of understanding on the part of the hierarchy, even when there is evidence of good will." She sees this as a reason "to move forward by doing things, moving like the tide, imperturbably, rather than offering theoretical protest." She feels that it is important to:

—Form community groups which are liberating.
—Say what we mean when talking to the young and others.
—Set up micro-projects of all kinds.

Today we find women religious actively committed in a variety of ministerial roles. For women religious the situation is the same as that of other women committed to the institutional church: they are found more often in a consultative capacity rather than in decision-making posts. And they are sometimes met with suspicion and mistrust, but more often with impassivity and immobility.

Some women religious in Belgium are living their commitments with communities of faith and celebration that are outside the traditional structures of the church. Many religious communities are havens of refuge for the materially and humanly destitute. Here the needy find someone to listen to them. Friendships are formed and there is an offer of companionship which often reveals something comparable to God's tenderness as revealed by Jesus.

Yet one religious speaks of her uneasiness concerning present tendencies of certain religious communities. She sees "a certain return to the institution, toward structures in the traditional model similar to present trends in the institutional church." "Does this represent a need for security in the face of old age?" asks another. "Or is it simply a repetition of what is going on in the church at large? Is it the influence of movements such as the charismatic movement? Or even the personality cult of Pope John Paul II?"

Still another religious writes:

Women religious are doubly isolated: as women and as single women. In parishes, in schools, they were often recognized for their services. Today they are recognized for what they are. Their human, biblical and theological education is more advanced.

Religious congregations are no longer dependent on a canonical visitor. This has been replaced by a vicariate (diocesan) for the religious, composed of a majority of sisters and nuns.

Laywomen questioned about women religious had little or nothing to say, probably stemming from a lack of communication between the two groups. Specific occasions do not exist for this type of meeting. However, comments by several lay respondents are notable:

> Small groups living in community gave rise to hopes. But the chapters of the various religious orders curbed this momentum. This does not prevent some religious from continuing their in-depth questioning, their orientation, their options and their policies.

> I think that in public opinion religious are much more appreciated today, especially by the fact that they have come out of their convents and have taken their place in society, and also due to the fact that they are no longer catalogued by a uniform or a habit, often unadapted to the needs of daily life.

Women's Attitudes Toward the Church

Obviously, there are differences of opinion and attitude among Catholic women in Belgium today toward the institutional church. There are also varying degrees of acknowledgment and reflection concerning women's status in the church.

With What Are Women Satisfied?

Several replies made evident the existence of a category of "traditional" women of an older age—and sometimes even younger women—who find that they are comfortable in today's church and suggest that "we should continue to go along as in the past." One might ask if this attitude corresponds to the truth, if it signifies only a desire for security and comfort, or if some women simply prefer to ignore the problems.

It is said that many women do not see the utility or the need of "claiming a place in the church." Some are content to continue in subaltern domestic tasks. There are also a great number of women who do not feel "of the church," even though they still call themselves Catholic; it would not occur to these women to raise the question of whether or not they are satisfied with the church!

At the other end of the pole of "satisfied" women can be found committed women, especially from the newer movements in the church, who are fully aware of what is still to be done but who objectively recognize that progress is being made. One such woman sees:

> ... [a] Church of human dimension where, together, we recognize and listen to one another and discover the word, and where there is mutual respect for what we are in our commitments: women, priests, religious and laity.

And others:

> Women are the equal of men in our community. Celebrations of the eucharist are carried out in a circle, the table in the middle. Everyone pronounces the words of consecration and everyone is permitted to speak out or comment on the word.

> In my community (a secular institute), I feel that I belong to the church, which puts me at ease, and I have the desire for involvement and commitment. I think this is true for all of us in our institute. I can explain this by the fact that insertion in this community "of the church" allows us the opportunity to experience the church; it gives us a spirituality that enables us to find our rightful place as Christians today, in the world and in the church.

The respondent added that "the church gives us an education in theology which is helpful when we are called upon to proclaim our faith in a pluralistic world. . . . On the whole, I think I can say that we love our church!"

One woman religious wrote:

> There exist places where we find open minds. [There are groups], especially at the level of movements, where with others—whether they be priests, laity or religious—we reflect together. Let us not minimize the role of these groups which dare to speak out, to challenge and question, when wealth and power take precedence over the values of the gospel, when the institutional church is inaccessible, when the door (of the institutional church) is scarcely open or is deaf to the problems of today's society. In these groups, the sisters speak out boldly.

The women brought up other areas with which they were satisfied, such as the follow-up to Vatican II, changes in canon law, the interventions by Belgian Cardinal Danneels at the 1986–87 Synod of Bishops, more equality between women and priests, the pressure on the institution by feminist movements in the United States and Canada, male catechists in groups which, up to the present time, were exclusively female, and a theological education that is more accessible to women (though without any prospect of a career).

Finally, women are satisfied "when the church reminds the faithful of the contents of the gospel. This happens when the church speaks out on situations of injustice and poverty in the world."

With What Are Women Dissatisfied?

The women's replies here tended to fall within four basic categories:

1. CHURCH LANGUAGE

. . . rigidity, self-sufficient, esoteric official language. For example, Vatican documents do contain good elements, but are absolutely indigestible for the poor lay people that we are! Finally, for whom are these documents written?

. . . the "macho" language of the church; women are confined to the roles of "spouse," "mother," and as complementary to men.

Church language is full of discrimination in many official texts. Among others: the Constitution on the Liturgy, "Inter Insignores," "Ministeria Quaedam" and the new Code of Canon Law. There is also a non-existence of women in many liturgical translations in the canon of the mass and in the language of many priests (during the homilies).

2. CHURCH TEACHINGS

The discourse continues to convey an over-evaluation of maternity. The latest example of this is the pope's letter "On the Dignity of Women," where the stand on equality in the first part of the letter is nullified by the vision of "maternity" in the second part. This exaltation is in fact a way of subordinating all else to the function of maternity. This discursive reasoning does not take into account the evolution in our countries marked by the determination of women to live their motherhood and at the same time accept many different responsibilities in society: professional work, socio-political participation, etc.

This type of thinking often betrays ignorance of the true economic condition of women today. Women are the first to be affected by crises and unemployment. The feminization of poverty the world over is not taken into consideration in the official church statements on economic questions and social justice.

There are repeated declarations concerning methods of contraception. This reasoning no longer has any effect on the practices of couples who believe that this is a personal choice. . . . There is a lack of openness in the thinking of the church about everything that concerns the life of couples (procreation, divorce, abortion). Both men and women experience this type of deception.

3. CHURCH PRACTICES

Many respondents referred to discrepancies existing between the teaching and the practice of the institutional church in areas of male/ female equality, human rights and justice. What women do not appreciate in the practices of the church are:

The display of wealth (buildings, resources, etc.) and the fact that riches are not shared.

The importance given to the administration and to the management of these Christian institutions which absorb available energies.

Political lobbying when the question of legislation on abortion is concerned. Even if the question remains controversial for the public, a majority of women resent this intrusion of the church institution as abusive in the present understanding of a pluralist state.

An increasing number of women are irked by the fact that the hierarchy takes stands in areas that directly concern women without associating women in the reflection.

We believe that the church's attitude toward sexuality has provoked rupture, and that many women reject the church's teaching on this subject. Vatican proclamations are no longer convincing (concerning contraception, masturbation, marriage relationships, artificial insemination, divorce and remarriage, priestly celibacy, etc.).

Causes of dissatisfaction go far beyond questions which affect the women's daily lives. Women are concerned as well with the fundamental questions facing the church today. They deplore:

The condemnation of some bishops participating in trends of liberation theology.

The nominations, in Latin America and especially in Brazil, of bishops who represent the "right wing." This parallels the recent appointments in France, in Germany and even in Belgium.

In a wider sense, the concept running through the pope's declarations about "recruiting Christianity." This idea is a step backwards and runs counter to the policies of Christians in western nations.

The "enhancement of European values" gives rise to suspicion on the part of certain Christians ... an increasing suspicion when the same trend appears in recent speeches by the pope.

On this last point, suspicion and discontent are also expressed concerning some Belgian dioceses in particular:

What women—especially those who have followed a continuing education in the faith or in group reflection—resent is seeing the parishes in our dioceses directed by our pastors toward objectives described as "essential," but which, in fact, are a "cover" for a kind of "restoration." These include "new evangelization," the Marian Year, the Year of the Family, and the multiplication of devotions such as pilgrimages. Other signs of "restoration" are the over-stressing of the role of pastor, the promotion of faith based on certitudes, and the espousal of charismatic and other "spiritual" movements.

It is a source of irritation that in the institutional church there is no room for questioning, and doubts are never taken into consideration.

4. CHURCH ORGANIZATION

Finally, there are expressions of dissatisfaction about the institutional church as an organization:

A church of and for men.

A hierarchical church reluctant to dialogue with the grass roots.

Men hold the reins of power in the church. This explains why women are not recognized.

Women are absent from the platforms at conferences or debates, whether it be for the Year of Peace or the Year of the Family. Key speakers are male and, very often, priests. One would think that women had nothing to say about peace and no competence in matters concerning the family!

Internal divisions among the hierarchy, between priests and bishops, among priests themselves, between priests and lay people, between French-speaking and Flemish-speaking people, between Catholics and Protestants.

Young people are scarcely at ease in the church and care little about its functioning. A part of their trouble stems from the fact that this hierarchical church is strictly male and celibate.

One can only be uneasy in a church which is organized on such a centralized and hierarchical basis that the laity are excluded from all important responsibilities and reflections. To us, it would seem important to integrate the analysis of feminine reality into the global subordination of the laity.

Changes Most Desired by Women

Most participants in this survey felt that they had already replied to this question by having listed dissatisfactions earlier. However, some of the respondents wished to specify certain points:

Women aspire to a recognition of their difference in relation to the institutional church. They do not feel like partners; they feel that they have been deliberately left out. They note that often it is the women who are "uncomplaining" who are entrusted with tasks by the clergy.

It is important to give women the opportunity to speak out (and to listen to what they have to say) because women represent fifty percent of humanity, and they have a right to a voice in the church as well as in other bodies. Women are absent from the higher spheres of power: the entourages of the bishops, the Roman curia, etc. Under these conditions, how can we conceive of the institution as other than "macho" and paternalistic?

[There needs to be a] capacity on the part of the bishops to reflect, work and collaborate with Catholic women in a more informal, more natural and more consistent manner. It is only in this way that we can attain an in-depth dialogue in a relaxed fashion, that is to say, in a different way than that which now exists because we do not meet often enough.

The voice of women in the church is still *insolite*[6] and is perceived as *insolent,* as mentioned by M. de L. Pintasilgo in her book, *Les Nouveaux Féminismes.*[7]

Many women wonder how much longer the church will continue to deprive itself of the source of richness represented by women's thinking and of women's contributions in the sphere of responsibilities. How much longer can the church deprive itself of married priests, male or female? How long will the remarried divorced be kept aloof from the church?

It would appear important that women be associated in the formation of future priests and that the latter be given an appropriate psychological training, especially as long as celibacy remains obligatory.

Mariology in today's church also bothers many Catholic women, and they hope for change:

The place of Mary in the Church should be reexamined. Today she is seen as "the first lady of good works." It is indispensable that she be given her true place in theology and spirituality.

Finally, women are well aware that all these changes cannot be brought about by the institution alone, but that they themselves must accept their share of responsibility:

There is likewise a need for change in the laity, both men and women, who should also reassess their attitudes and behavior.

A great number of women, even young women, are still passive and/or ignorant of the true situation. Too many of them are still incapable of analyzing the situation as it affects them.

Bolder women are needed (faith is the opposite of fear), women who will not hesitate to accept the few posts of responsibility which are proposed to them; above all, they must be prepared to set up the necessary strategies to widen the possible field of action which will result from change.

Women's Organizations Working for Change

There were few replies to this question. Must we therefore conclude that few efforts are being made through women's organizations to bring

about changes in the institutional church affecting the role of women—
or that what efforts there are are very discreet? As one respondent wrote:

> The real work lies elsewhere. There is an urgency of certain questions
> which take precedence over our own claims or this "dialogue with the
> deaf" with regard to the church. What is truly urgent is to work for
> justice, the humanization of sexuality and the improvement of economic
> and social relations.

Several specific organizations and groups which were mentioned by
the respondents include:

Femmes et Hommes Dans l'Eglise (Women and Men in the Church). This
is an international group which publishes a trimestrial bulletin in French.
Among other objectives, the aim of this group is to react publicly to
declarations or positions taken by the institutional church which are seen
as discriminatory toward women.

Femmes Chrétiennes de Belgique (Christian Women of Belgium). This is
an ecumenical women's group affiliated with the Ecumenical Forum of
Christian Women of Europe, which, among other activities, organizes
workshops devoted to the study of feminist theology published abroad
and to Bible study. The group has also published a file on "Femmes et
Eglises" ("Women and Churches") to conscientize women.

L'Association Européenne des Femmes pour la Recherche Théologique (European Association of Women for Research in Theology). This is a new
European group which is ecumenical in the widest sense of the term,
including both Jewish and "post-Christian" women theologians. The
group recently began a branch in Belgium.

Dialogue Caucus of Catholic Women's Organizations in Belgium. This
caucus was created with the aim of establishing dialogue between Catholic women and bishops. Its members meet regularly and prepare papers on
urgent matters. From time to time they meet with Cardinal Danneels.
"But," say the participants, "we cannot talk of real dialogue yet. We
would like to see a real dialogue *with* the bishops."

Beyond the above groups, it can be said that all the women's movements of Catholic Action include in their programs the same sorts of
questions. Mention must also be made of the existing "open spaces"

and, especially, the base communities, which are truly places where changes are being demonstrated.

Will these dispersed efforts be vigorous enough to overcome the indifference and immobility of an ossified institution? In any case, it is in this hope that the efforts are being made, with an openness to the Spirit to receive "all things new" which *she* will accomplish in us.

Notes

1. A *doyenné* is a deanship which covers several parishes under the responsibility of a dean. Similar to the U.S. "deanery."

2. Statistics from the Interdiocesan Center, Brussels, *Le Soir,* June 14, 1988.

3. "Animation" is similar to the U.S. "facilitation." An animator is co-equal with but responsible for the facilitation of a group.

4. In French, *accompagnement,* the "going along with" or "being beside" a person on his or her journey.

5. "Free" students are men and women of all ages who follow the studies but are not "seminarians."

6. In French *insolite* means "unusual" or "strange." It is used here as a play on words.

7. Maria de Lourdes Pintasilgo, ed., *Les Nouveaux Féminismes* (Paris: du Cerf, 1980).

Denise Peeters, who resides in Brussels, has been involved in women's groups, both in the church and in society, for many years. She is an active member of Femmes et Hommes Dans L'Eglise (Women and Men in the Church), which is a French-based network publishing a quarterly magazine in French. She is also a member of various ecumenical groups as well as the National Council of Women, the Ministerial Council for Social Emancipation, Pax Christi, and the theological committee of the Justice and Peace Commission. M. Peeters has written, lectured and traveled widely in Europe, Africa, the USSR and the United States.

Dutch-Speaking Belgium

Caroline Vander Stichele

Our wildest imaginings? We wish that the pope could revise his own anthropology [to espouse] the notion of full humanity for all men and women, even though it's hard. The people don't seem to be too afraid, but the pope seems to be terrified.

—A CATHOLIC WOMAN IN BRUSSELS

THAT THERE ARE two contributions from Belgium in this book dealing with the situation of new Catholic women might seem a bit odd. But this reflects the reality of our country. Belgium is now a nation with two distinct communities, Flanders, the Dutch-speaking, and Wallonia, the French-speaking. Besides this linguistic differentiation, there are political, cultural and social differences. Not surprisingly, the religious situation also has its own particularities. It is therefore sensible and fair to look at both situations, women in Flanders and in Wallonia, in order to get a more complete picture of Catholic women in Belgium.

The Catholic Church in Flanders

Firmly rooted in the past, the Catholic Church is still the dominating influence on the religious scene in Flanders. There are few other Christian denominations, and the presence of Islam and Judaism is mostly related to certain ethnic groups. The influence of the Catholic Church is not limited to the personal sphere; it also has a large impact on political, cultural and social life.

To understand the link between religion and politics, some explanation concerning the political situation in Flanders is necessary. There are three major political parties in Flanders: the Liberal Party (PVV), the Socialist Party (SP), and the Christian Democratic Party (CVP), which is situated in the political center. Typical of the Belgian situation is the

33

phenomenon of political segregation, or "Verzuiling." This means that the three political parties also provide certain services for their members in other than strictly political fields. They provide, among other things, social and health services, education, and cultural and formation programs.

Although the CVP is not formally linked with the Catholic Church as such, most of its members are Catholic. The same people often partici-pate in one or another of the many existing Catholic organizations, which give the church its important social dimension.

In the network of Catholic organizations, three traditional Catholic women's organizations are found: the KAV (Katholieke Arbeidersvrou-wen Beweging) traditionally has been the organization of working-class women, the CMBV (Christelijke Beweging voor Vrouwen uit de Mid-dengroepen) the organization of middle-class women, and the KVLV (Katholiek Vormingswerk van Landelijke Vrouwen) the organization of agricultural women. Over time, social changes have made these class divisions less evident. Becoming a member of one or the other organiza-tion is now more a matter of personal choice than a matter of belonging to a certain social class.

The Catholic women's organizations are important in that they oper-ate in two directions. They provide formation for their members on the one hand and exercise important social and political influence on the other.

However, as a recent investigation of the KAV has made clear, the relation between their members and the church is not as close as it has been in the past. Although most members still adhere to Christian val-ues, church practice is decreasing. This is symptomatic of the loss of influence by the Catholic Church. Since political segregation is also less evident, the influence of the institutional church on society is constantly diminishing: Catholics, by definition, no longer adhere to the Christian Democratic Party.

Recent Changes in the Flemish Catholic Community

Vatican Council II was a milestone for the Catholic Church all over the world. So, too, the council has inspired many people in Flanders during the past two decades. It has been a starting point for both reflection and gradual change by Catholics trying to take seriously the ever changing "signs of the times." In discovering that the church is not limited to clergy, but rather that they themselves are "church," lay people have become aware of their responsibilities. However, this process of con-scientization as a discovery of one's own responsibility has also resulted in conflicts at all church levels.

Role models need to be changed. This applies to both clergy and laity, as well as to men and women. As the average age of the clergy has been rapidly increasing and their numbers have been decreasing, a sense of urgency has emerged to look for new ways to solve old problems. In practice, new functions have been created and old ministry models have been revived. To the latter category belong the (male) lay deacons. These are seldom full-time roles. In the former category are the parish assis-tants, whose formation is organized by the diocese. Both men and women are eligible. In most cases, parish assistants work together with a priest to form a parish team. In some parishes this formula has proved to be successful, while in others it has not. Much has depended upon the coordination of the team itself, as well as on its acceptance in the parish.

Lay men and women also sometimes engage in pastoral activities outside the parish, in the strict sense. They offer pastoral counseling in hospitals, in Catholic organizations, and in other settings. Since most of these activities are not officially recognized, they are poorly, if at all, paid. Most lay people, many of whom are women, engaged in the church still do their work on a volunteer basis.

In addition to lay people, there are also religious women engaged in parish work. But female as well as male religious communities face the same problem as the clergy—a lack of new candidates to fill the ever widening gap between their many responsibilities and the limited num-ber of people available. More and more religious communities are disap-pearing and their buildings are being sold. Many of their tasks could be taken over by competent lay people, but one of the major problems is financial. In Belgium, according to law, ministers of recognized religions are paid by the state. The only "recognized" ministers of the Catholic Church are priests. At the same time, there is in Belgium no tradition of parishes paying their own ministers. Therefore, in order to pay lay peo-ple for their services to the church, either the law or the parish mentality about financing its own ministry must change.

Another important issue is formation. Many lay people who take some responsibility in the church feel that they do not have sufficient preparation for their tasks. Consequently, they look for more (in)forma-tion. In response, grass roots initiatives have produced, for example, weekend sessions for pastoral training. On a diocesan level, one can participate in a three-year theological program at a catechetical center. Formation offered to the laity depends on the diocese. In some dioceses there are good opportunities at the grass roots level but not at the diocesan level, while in others only involvement at the diocesan level is possible. It is important to note that women may represent up to fifty percent or more of the participants at all levels of the programming. This is also the case at the only Catholic university in Flanders, the Katholieke Universiteit Leuven (Louvain). The Faculty of Theology there offers two types of programs: one for students studying to be high school teachers of religion and one for students interested in a more classical theological program. In the first instance half of the students are female, while in the second there are fewer women enrolled. In some areas lay people may also attend classes at diocesan seminaries, though each diocese is free to decide whether or not this opportunity is given and under what conditions.

The number of female professors in all programs (grass roots, cate-chetical and university) is very small. This is both a problem of qualifica-tion (only recently have women started to study theology) as well as a problem of institutional unwillingness to accept women in such posi-tions. Most professors of theology are still clergymen.

Women in the Church

The previous overview has shown that women are using the possibilities that have become available to them to play a more active role in the church. Besides these rather new and developing possibilities, there are also the previously existing ones, such as positions on pastoral and parish councils. Here, also, women are participating more than they have in the past.

But women are not only participating in the official church structure. They are also well represented in the base communities, which are often more critical of the church. Women also take initiatives of their own. Besides the classical women's organizations already mentioned, a less structured movement calling itself "Women and Faith" has recently emerged. This movement consists of small groups throughout Flanders who find their inspiration primarily in feminist theology.

All this might sound very positive, which it is. But it should be noted that the place of women in the church is closely linked with that of the laity in general. This means that the higher one looks in the ranks of church leadership, the fewer women one finds. Thus, as far as power is concerned, women are still at the bottom of the pyramid. Canon law and the current theology of the magisterium still define the role of women in such a way that women's possibilities within the church are very limited.

In Flanders, as in many other countries, women question the validity of the role definition of women by men. While the situation of women in society at large is improving and women are finding equal opportunities in all areas of their lives—education, business, politics, etc.—this is not the case in the church. Younger women feel this contrast more sharply than older women. They also more readily leave the church because they perceive this as injustice.

Although the question of women's ordination is considered important because of its structural significance, most women do not regard this as the key issue. First, they are well aware that any discussion on the question of women's ordination should focus on the perception of priesthood as such. Ecclesiology is the heart of the matter. Do women— or men, for that matter—want to participate in the priesthood as it is now practiced? What kind of priesthood do we actually want? Second, women are giving priority to more attainable goals, such as involving more women in the church's decision-making process, getting more opportunities to be pastorally active, using inclusive language in church services and documents, and caring about women in problematic situations such as divorce, abandonment, incest and unwanted pregnancy.

Prospects for the Future

There are reasons to be optimistic as well as pessimistic. As a strategy, women must exploit the possibilities they already have to strengthen their impact on the church. An important possibility is in the area of theology. As women have access to theological training at all levels, they are in a position to develop alternatives to the present situation. This is what feminist theology is doing. Such a theology, which is a theology from "below," needs to be developed in close contact with the everyday life of women. In Flanders such a process has just begun. Until recently, Christian women were not very involved in the feminist struggle. Hopefully, a strong movement of new Catholic women will emerge in the coming years. If women from traditional organizations as well as from the newer ones succeed in concentrating their forces, they can gain an important voice in the church.

But there are also reasons to be less optimistic. It is clear that theology today, and especially moral theology, is seen in Roman circles as a main source of trouble in the church. Efforts are being made to keep theologians "in line." Unity is once more being perceived as uniformity. The ideas that Vatican II promoted are now more tolerated than encouraged. Participation of the people is reduced. The roles of laity and clergy are again being strictly defined, and this role division turns out to be an especially negative one for women. It recalls the ancient dualism between church and world, clergy and laity, men and women, heaven and earth, good and evil.

One hopes, on the one hand, that reality itself, specifically the lack of priests, might create an opportunity for the laity to fully engage in the church. But, on the other hand, it would be tragic if only such a negative reason were to create this opportunity. However, the prevailing clerical response to the lack of priests, expressed as the constant hope for new candidates, paralyzes every other effort to try to cope with the new challenges of this situation. It is to be hoped that the well-being of the whole community, women and men, will finally prevail.

Conclusion

The future of the church is highly dependent on its capacity to deal with ever changing conditions. The local churches in Europe are facing a major challenge as they deal with the new self-understanding of women. One fears, however, that, if the official church is not ready to dialogue with women and to take them seriously as partners in the church, women will simply go their own way.

Caroline Vander Stichele is a married lay theologian. She is currently an assistant at the Faculty of Theology of the Katholieke Universiteit te Leuven (Belgium) and teaches New Testament exegesis at the Faculty of Theology of the Rijksuniversiteit Utrecht (The Netherlands). She edited *Het zwijgen doorbroken: Vrouwen over vrouwen en kerk (Breaking the Silence: Women on Women and Church)* (Tielt: Lannoo, 1989), a book on the situation of women in the Flemish Catholic Church.

3

New Catholic Women in England

Alexina Murphy

What I gather from the early church is that they were struggling against a secular world to hold on to a vision of church. Today the secular world is ahead of the church. It is the church that is resisting. The church has sacrificed its prophetic role.

—A CATHOLIC MOTHER IN OXFORD

I refuse to go. This is *my* church. Why should I go? I am working for change in the church that will benefit everyone. I do feel impatient. . . .

—A CATHOLIC MOTHER IN LONDON

I would hate to see women being ordained in this present system. Women do feel called to ministerial priesthood, especially celebrating eucharist and reconciling. However, the official church doesn't realize the many ways women already do these ministries.

—A CATHOLIC SISTER IN LONDON

THERE MUST BE many ways to tell the story of the changing consciousness in women in the Catholic Church in England. Young women tell it differently from older women. Women with a primary commitment to justice and social change have a different story from women caring primarily for the quality and development of women's spiritual life. Some would tell the story from their experience and skills acquired in the church's ministry. Their struggle in the church is for inclusion in leadership and decision-making, for parity of esteem and power-sharing with clergy. Others earn their living at work in the secular world, and so see the church and the believing community more from the outside. Their concern is for the credibility of the church's witness to truth, justice and love. They see the need and opportunity for the church beyond preoccupations with Catholic schools and controversy over birth control.

There must be many women who remain mystified as to what all the fuss is about. They have done their growing, as it were, in spite of being Catholic. They are not concerned with the connectedness of religion and culture, feel no responsibility that the influence of religion should be for the human well-being of persons and communities, do not see faith in Christ as food for the hungry, drink for the parched. And there are still other women who, as a result of changing consciousness, have walked away from the church. All these women have relevant stories to tell.

The Catholic Women's Network (CWN)

I have chosen to trace the changing consciousness in women of their role in the Catholic Church through the experience of a particular group of women who, between January 1983 and August 1984, identified a need to organize women, and set out to create a "Network." We think of the Network as a loose association of like-minded women who want to work together to achieve the full humanity of women and men, the full participation of all members of the church in all aspects of the church's life. The Network is for women who want to engage in this work, who think that the journey is as important as the destination, and that the way we search is as important as what we are looking for. We want to learn as we teach.

What is this consciousness of women, and what changes it? I think we are talking about certain assumptions which have to do with our value as persons, with the meaning of our lives, and with God's will for us, all of which tend to remain unexamined until, for some reason, they thrust themselves into our awareness. Then we have to pay attention. Most probably we are presented with difficult choices affecting our idea of ourselves and the course of our lives. We have to act; we certainly grow. And we cannot go back. In traditional spiritual language, this is called a "conversion." It is both sudden and lengthy. It is painful but also deeply satisfying. It happens in both individuals and in communities.

The Work of the Network

Our work has to do with individual needs of women to sort out information and attitudes toward religion, both belief and practice. It has to do with making choices about relationships and lifestyles. There are questions of authority: to do what you are told, or to think for yourself, to find a basis on which to be confident that one has discovered a working solution to values and their application to daily life. This work of personal growth and maturity involves a spiritual component, especially when we have had a Catholic upbringing. Our loyalty to Sunday mass-going, our instilled obedience to the voice of authority, our firm sense of what is right and wrong—these habits have to be reviewed and evaluated for their liberating quality. In order to grow, we have to be sure of our sense of joy and meaning, to know where these are coming from and how to nurture them.

In order to help individuals, we have to become community for each other. We become a believing community, a worshiping community, a reconciling community, a prophetic community, a learning community. We become a subversive community, a liberated and liberating community.

To build community we have four community days a year. We spend these days first in prayer and reflection, then in guided conversation with one another on specific themes. This guided conversation usually focuses on an area of the day's work, and is a way of ensuring that we always begin with women's experiences, that we always ground our argument and our theory in women's lives. Each woman is participating. Each woman is recognized as a resource for the day's work. Each woman's life is valued and affirmed. The input for the day might be a presentation by an informed speaker or a panel of two or three women sharing different experiences and points of view. It may be that we divide into groups to work on a learning task, for example, to work on a passage from scripture or to work directly from our experience. Liturgy, held usually at mid-day, amplifies the lesson of the day. In this circle of women, we have a precious opportunity to worship from women's experience of God present in our lives. We have the chance to present women's concerns to God, to celebrate women's gifts and achievements. Here women shape the worship and lead it. In doing so, we experience the power and the awe and sometimes the banality of leading the community before God. We learn new aspects of personal need and communal need. We grow in love.

In addition to these community days, a core group meets for a day once every other month. A newsletter explores ideas, communicates points of view, and gives information about meetings, resources and events. The circulation address list gives us an idea of our membership, which has increased from two hundred to more than four hundred.

We also have held several public meetings, drawing more than three hundred men and women, to hear such women as Rosemary Radford Ruether (September 1989), Mary Hunt, Ellen Leonard, and, on one occasion, both Rosemary and Daphne Hampson. The debate between Rosemary and Daphne addressing the issue "Can a feminist be a Christian?" was promoted jointly by the Network and Women in Theology and was subsequently published in *New Blackfriars*.[1]

By becoming community, we offer each other an alternative provision to that which is currently available. In the church as it stands, with a male-dominated leadership, women are not able to worship from their own experience of being human, from their own experience of the divine. The very language used excludes women. The celebrant is male, the homily is given by a man. Women are not able to learn through carrying the responsibility for worship. Becoming a community gives us visibility in the church. Other women can find us, can see what we stand for. Others in the church can see what we mean by what we say and that we mean what we say.

There were two events which led to the founding of the CWN in August 1984. In January 1983 in London, there was a large ecumenical conference called "Women, Men and Power." Rosemary Radford Ruether was the invited speaker. The important aspect of the conference from a Catholic point of view was a meeting on the Friday evening before the main event. Rosemary asked to meet with Catholic women in order that she might hear from them the kinds of activities that women are involved in on behalf of women in the Catholic Church in Britain. For the forty or so women who came to this meeting, it was the first time that we heard a number of women from different parts of the country talking about the work women are doing and about our position in the Catholic Church. As well as telling Rosemary, we were telling one another.

An earlier event occured in May 1982, when Pope John Paul II visited

Britain. Up until this time, Catholic women who were developing a feminist critique of church teaching and practice had been meeting with women of similar outlook from other churches in ecumenical groups. They met for experimental liturgies based on women's experience and led by women. They campaigned together for women's ordination in the Anglican Church. They began to read theology from a feminist perspective. They began to seek out and to gather the experiences of women in ministry as deaconesses, as students in training for ministry, as teachers of theology. As the time for the pope's visit drew near, one of the women in this circle telephoned one of the Catholic women and asked, "What are you women going to do when the pope comes? We will support you." This prompted the Catholic women in the ecumenical circle to contact one another and to meet one evening.

I recall several impressions from that evening. First, there was the sense that nothing we could do would make any difference, and there was a sense of heaviness. It took a little digging to surface why we felt so depressed that the pope was coming. The pope makes visible a church that is formal, hierarchical, male. The authority of the institution seems impregnable. The pope is such a credible "star" that maybe we were all a little nostalgic for an uncritical acceptance of this church. I think we were all aware of the effort going into preparing for his visit, and we were rather enjoying the sense of occasion. But the fact was that other projects were being shelved meanwhile. None of us relished the message we thought the pope might be bringing. We tried to think of the women who would be meeting with the pope, especially ones who, like Teresa Kane in the States, might speak some of the things we wanted the pope to hear. We assumed that the women chosen for their leadership and work in Catholic women's organizations would not have anything critical to say, otherwise they would not be chosen.

As we went around the circle, I realized that each woman had a complete but different plan of what we might do. I realized that Catholic women would need to go through a process of sharing our experience, or raising our consciousness, on the ways in which we are marginalized in the church. I realized that, if we were ever to achieve any significant change in the church, we would have to learn to work together and agree on our objectives. From that time, a group of women continued to meet regularly. There was quite a high turnover of members, with a small nucleus of six to eight women coming regularly. It was in the context of this group that the idea of the Network was hatched. We felt that it was important for all like-minded women to be in touch with one another. We needed to know what women in other parts of the country were up to. We needed to be in regular communication. We wanted to learn from each other and lend strength to each other.

Gradually it was decided that we should run a weekend conference so that there could be a communal and public decision about what we should do to work for change in the Catholic Church in Britain. The conference was entitled "Called to Full Humanity." Our venture was supported by Rosemary Radford Ruether and Catherina Halkes, who was scheduled to give a public lecture the evening before. Unfortunately, Catherina Halkes, at that time professor of feminist theology at the University of Nijmegen, had to cancel at the last minute, but the meeting went ahead.

More than sixty women came to this inaugural conference held August 24–26, 1984, at St. Mary's College, Strawberry Hill, Twickenham. At the first session we talked about our experience of growing up in the church. Next we "denounced" all the aspects of church teaching and practice which we felt to be false and un-Christian. Then we "announced" our vision of how we would like the church to be, all the things we longed for in the church but which seemed to be missing.[2] We worked at brainstorming a program of changes in the church which, by working together, we would like to bring about. Finally, we set up a core group of officers and agreed to begin a newsletter.

Other Events in Catholic Circles

It would be helpful to note the context of history which led up to the formation of the Network. During these times many women individually were coming to the point of recognizing that all was not well in the fit between faith and life, between theory and practice, between vision and custom.

Sometimes a shift in consciousness occurs because of a momentous event in one's personal history, such as desertion by or separation from a marriage partner, the death of a child, the loss of a job, or a crisis of identity over sexual orientation or religious vocation. This can then become a faith crisis, when women need spiritual counsel and practical advice. Not finding it because of the incomprehension of the parish priest, the indifference of the community or the insensitivity of official church pronouncements, the individual is pushed back on her own resources. She must think for herself. She must find nurture for herself wherever she can. In the light of her experience she develops a critique of religion as she has received it, and of the church which has handed it to her. At first this is a very lonely process. It is as if no one has ever before criticized the church, put angry questions to God, or doubted her own competence as a responsible person.

But when, in the course of time, we discover that other women are going through much the same process, encountering the same difficulties, then hope is born anew.

Humanae Vitae and Its Aftermath

For me and for many others of my generation, the publication of the encyclical *Humanae Vitae* was a turning point in consciousness. The encyclical was published in August 1968. I was three months pregnant with my fourth child. Although I had always envisaged myself as the mother of twelve children, all boys, I knew that, with three and another on the way, I had reached my personal limits of tolerance. In order to give proper attention to the baby, I was missing time with the older children. I could hire help, either with the baby or with the older children. But then I began to feel like a "baby machine," producing children I had no time or energy to enjoy and keep company with. These personal considerations were reinforced by the economic realities of housing and educating four children. My husband and I knew we had reached the limit of our family and we were considering ways of not conceiving another child. At this psychological moment *Humanae Vitae* was promulgated.

The publication of the encyclical was followed by a period of confusion. My first response was to do what I was told. I felt in loyalty that the questioning must stop and we must accept our fate—to continue, in all probability, to have a baby every other year for at least another ten years of fertile life. But our parish priest pointed out that we had a duty to follow our consciences that came before our duty of obedience to authority. This put me back to trying to discern what was right for me, for my husband, and for our family. I knew that for me it would be irresponsible to bring another child into the world when I had the knowledge to avoid conception. This became our decision in spite of the heavy moral pressure not to use artificial means to avoid conception.

The debate then became one of authority. What is a right course of action? How do we find out? Who can tell us we are right? I was just as eager to discuss these issues over the dinner table as I had previously discussed family size and methods of contraception. But, sadly, a silence grew in the whole area. Couples preferred to keep their decisions to themselves because knowing what other couples were doing caused uncertainty and conflict. The whole subject became too painful to discuss.

Some of us were able to grow through the experience and reach new maturity. But many people were confronted with a most difficult moral dilemma, compounded by insufficient personal knowledge of the issue and inadequate grounding in scripture and tradition to cope with the challenge to faith. Many lost their faith in dealing with the practicalities of safeguarding their marriage relationship, limiting their family, and maintaining some personal integrity. Others did what they were told, or followed their consciences and kept quiet. Still others, of course, became passionate and convinced advocates of the papal teaching.

For women the controversy around *Humanae Vitae* had further implications. Women are the ones who conceive, who carry new life to term, who nourish it in the early months, who have hour-by-hour care of pre-school children. Women often give up life outside the home to take on these responsibilities and make many of the financial sacrifices needed to accommodate children in the family unit. But the moral choice of when to have children and how many to have was taken out of our hands by the church's official teaching. This is destructive of a woman's self-image, since her life is shaped beyond her own choosing. She is told that the new baby is more important than her own physical, psychological and social well-being. She is not encouraged to trust her own informed judgment, to discern her own capabilities, and to look for the presence and revelation of God in her life. She is told from the outside and from a great distance what is right for her. And she is expected to comply.

In the wake of the furor over *Humanae Vitae,* the Catholic Renewal Movement in England sprang into being in 1968. The issues were birth control methods, freedom of conscience and the right exercise of authority. Among the married couples with young families who became involved were former university students from the mid-1950s, when the

Union of Catholic Students of Great Britain was active in the lay apostolate. I remember, as a student, the series of conferences, retreats and study weekends organized through the university chaplaincies in which we students had the opportunity to explore the meaning of our faith. We were exposed to a ferment of new ideas and the fervor of shared enthusiasm. The Dominican seminarians of the time shared their biblical, theological and historical knowledge at these meetings. We all shared in their liturgies and recitation of the divine office, particularly during Holy Week. I remember our strong sense of community, the excitement of discovering scripture and the unfolding history of the church through the centuries. I came to realize that the church was not only about personal holiness but also about changing society and influencing events. We followed closely the proceedings of the First and Second Congresses of the Lay Apostolate and understood ourselves to have a role in the world as lay Christians. When we later read the documents from the Second Vatican Council, we found there the ideas that had already become familiar to us as students. The Newman Association continued to hold together these former students, now young professionals.

Gradually, through official channels, the changing role of women was being put on the church's agenda. In 1966 the World Union of Catholic Women's Organizations had organized a vast inquiry "on the freedom of women in marriage, social and civic life and their participation in the life of the Church." At the receiving end of church ministry, women had sharp things to say about the church's lack of sensitivity to the reality of women's lives. The World Union of Catholic Women's Organizations followed up on this survey with a colloquium held in Paris in April 1969 called "Women in the Church and Canon Law." The findings of their 1966 survey were also influential at the Third Congress of the Lay Apostolate, which was held in Rome in 1967.

The Fifth Resolution of the Third World Congress for the Lay Apostolate called for an end to discrimination between "persons" in Christ, and pointed out that "women's role" is due to social and cultural factors and is evolving toward perfect equality of rights between men and women. The resolution expressed a wish to see women granted all the rights and all the responsibilities of the Christian within the Catholic Church and called for a serious doctrinal study on the place of women in the sacramental order and in the church.

Continuing Calls for Equality

The motion was actually drawn up at the initiative of St. Joan's International Alliance, which had begun in London in 1911 as The Catholic Women's Suffrage Society.[3] This group of women was always consciously feminist, working to secure legal equality for women and the acceptance and participation of women equally with men in all fields. Characteristically, the members of St. Joan's were professional women, educated women, women in public life, women earning their own living. Their focus was the contribution that Catholic women might make in society. They saw how the church's attitude toward women made it difficult for women to act on behalf of the church. They made themselves unpopular by being the first to ask the church to change its ways.

After becoming international, St. Joan's was granted status as a nongovernmental organization at the United Nations and has played its part in working for the liberation of women on such issues as the abolition of the traffic in women and the abolition of female circumcision, and through participation in the United Nations Decade for Women, 1975–85.

From the beginning, St. Joan's has recognized that the exclusion of women from ministerial priesthood was a fundamental discrimination against women, though it was not until the time of the Second Vatican Council that they were able to call upon the church to address this question.

It cannot be said, however, that St. Joan's was a typical understanding of women's role in the church. For me, as for most women in England at the time, the idea that women might be priests had the same probability as the notion that men might have babies. I never gave the idea of women priests a second thought, either for or against, until 1975. I can still remember the conversation in which the possibility was put to me, and my feelings of both instant recognition of its rightness and indignation that such an idea had been kept from me until that moment. In this I was well insulated from what was going on elsewhere.

In 1971 Cardinal Flahiff of Canada had insisted that the Synod of Bishops meeting in Rome should put the question of admitting women to the priesthood on its agenda. This led, in 1973, to the setting up of a

Study Commission on Women in Society and the Church. In 1975 this Study Commission compiled a questionnaire which it offered to local churches to help them assess the position of women. Pope Paul VI, in his address to the World Conference of Women during the International Women's Year in 1975, suggested that "local churches should use the occasion to examine themselves regarding the effective participation of women in the church's life."

In England there were two related developments. One, in an official context, was the Laity Commission's attempt to discover how Catholic women regarded themselves—"to discover the feelings of Catholic women"—to see if the church was justified in taking their loyalty for granted. During 1976–77, the Laity Commission asked a number of convenors to invite groups of parish women to discuss their role and place in the Catholic Church. The findings were then compared with what official Catholic women's organizations had to say about the views of their members. The report of the Laity Commission was published in 1981 and was called "Why Can't a Woman Be More Like a Man?" What emerged in the report with startling clarity was how strongly women felt about their role in the Catholic Church.

Women agreed for the most part that they should be the equals of men. This is not to say that women think they are the same as men, for they expressed pride in being different from men. But they felt that they had been taken for granted as far as domestic chores and childbearing were concerned, and had not been taken seriously when questions of morals, church administration or pastoral concerns had been considered. They felt as if they had been treated like children, too immature to take on responsibilities. Yet this was in marked contrast with every other aspect of their lives, whether they ran a home, went out to work or followed a professional career. The women spoke eloquently of the hurt they feel when the church seems to disregard and devalue them.

Education is another area where women feel they have an important role to play, but they complained of a complete lack of any meaningful participation in this process.

Observations about the clergy were an important part of these discussions as well. Women resented being patronized by the clergy. They felt that celibacy as a value and as a lifestyle puts a barrier between priests and women, making communication next to impossible.

There was a tendency in the Laity Commission's consultations for the women to respond at first with the "approved" view. Then, as confidence grew in the group, women felt free to express their own opinions based on their own experience. Thus the question of women's ordination, which met strong opposition at first, gradually changed to acceptance during the discussions. It seems that the low self-esteem which holds women back from becoming readers or special ministers of the eucharist causes women to reject any idea that women might be priests. But when women see their value and their contributions to the church, the idea that women should be ordained follows quite naturally. However, preventing girls from being altar servers was already well understood as discrimination on the grounds of sex. Some women recalled their chagrin at discovering that their brothers might serve on the altar though they themselves could not. Others spoke of how hard it is to explain this exclusion to their daughters. Abortion, contraception, divorce and remarriage were also discussed in this open-ended way. Women spoke about the suffering caused to members of their families and to close friends by an unyielding application of strict church teaching in these areas. The proscription against non-Catholics receiving the eucharist was another issue which might have directly touched their lives and offended their sense of justice and mercy.

The second important development for Catholic women in England at this time came in response to a brief notice in *The Tablet* in May 1972 stating that the Catholic bishops would discuss "the laity" at the Synod to be held in Rome in 1974. The bishops would also have to consider "the place of women in the church." From this notice, the idea grew that women themselves should think about their position in the church and thereby make a positive contribution to the thinking of the church. The women decided to hold a conference and, during the following year, groups of women, lay and religious, mostly living in and near Oxford but with one group in London, studied different aspects of the position of women in the church in preparation for the Synod.

The Newman Association also conducted a survey of its members, eliciting one hundred and fifty-three individual responses and a further one hundred and twenty-two from groups, covering one hundred and ten parishes distributed fairly evenly throughout the country. Seventy-five percent of the individual respondents thought that women should have the same role as men in the lay apostolate. Eighty-five percent agreed that there is discrimination against women in the church, and ninety percent thought such discrimination incompatible with justice.

Eighty-one percent of the Newman respondents were in favor of ordaining women who, in South American parishes, are doing the work of parish priests; seventy-one percent were in favor of ordained women working in ordinary parishes. Over ninety percent welcomed the idea that women be trained as pastoral workers to work alongside parish clergy. Group replies were broadly similar, except that only about one-third would accept women priests.

About one hundred women gathered in Oxford in September 1973 for the conference called "The Place of Women in the Church." Ten papers were presented covering such topics as women in the gospels and in St. Paul, women saints and prayer, family liturgy and Christian education, religion today, women in other churches, the position of women in the Catholic Church, theology and equality, the call of the baptized and the priesthood of the people of God, and, finally, women and the priesthood. During the final session of general discussion, the underlying feelings of discontent revealed by many of the replies to the Newman questionnaire became apparent. The women who had come to the conference from widely different parts of the country knew, first-hand, what the situation was and what improvements could be made. Accordingly, the following suggestions were forwarded to the Conference of Bishops for their next meeting in October 1973:

1. There should be more adequate representation by women at all levels of the life of the church, for instance, on national and diocesan commissions and on parish councils.
2. We regret that the terms of reference of the Commission meeting in Rome to study the position of women in the church do not include discussion of the possibility of ordaining women to the priesthood.
3. We are concerned that women are not allowed in all parishes to read at mass inside the sanctuary.
4. We would like to support the request that trained women religious be given permission to distribute holy communion wherever circumstances make this desirable.

These recommendations were deliberately kept modest so as not to provoke undue resistance. For example, a request that masculine phraseology for the Trinity be changed was not included.

The Rise of Christian Feminism

In the late 1970s a Christian feminist self-consciousness began to emerge in several groupings of women. One focus was a newsletter called "The Christian Feminist Newsletter," which began in 1977 and continues to be published four times a year. The newsletter was begun by a group of women who met sometimes in London, sometimes in Oxford. This group identified a number of tasks for women in relation to faith and to institutional Christian churches. One was to communicate information and keep contact among a number of otherwise isolated women and among a number of groups which were meeting in such centers as Bristol, Newcastle, Birmingham and Sheffield, as well as Oxford and London. The newsletter was produced in London.

Another task which the women identified was the collection of all the ephemeral writings as well as publications which explored or made reference to the position of women in the Christian churches in order to make these available to women. This task needed a place to lodge, and it came to rest in Oxford when, in 1979, the Dominicans at Blackfriars provided a room to be used as the Christian Women's Information and Resources Centre. Since 1980 the Centre has developed bibliographies, not only on Christian feminism but on related topics such as women and ministry, women in the early church, and sexuality. A lending library was begun in 1981. Though fund-raising was a constant headache, the Centre also began a newsletter to review books and to share some of the information and resources it was acquiring. As a way of meeting people and talking about the issues, women from the Centre also began to attend conferences with their materials. In 1977 a group who called themselves "Roman Catholic Feminists" began meeting to try to integrate feminism with theology and to deal with the specific denominational problems of women seeking equality in the Catholic Church. They collected information about discrimination against women in the church and published it in a newsletter. As a pioneering group in a difficult area, Roman Catholic Feminists suffered a great deal of abuse. Membership remained small, but they succeeded in attracting a fair share of attention. For example, at the bishops' Low Week meeting in April 1978, when the bishops gathered to concelebrate in Westminster Cathedral, RCF members sat in the front row wearing identical T-shirts proclaiming "Equal Rites for Women."

RCF's most successful involvement was in the National Pastoral Congress held in Liverpool in 1980. The list of resolutions which they drew up at the end of the Congress publicized the conscious demands of feminists in the Catholic Church. The twelve resolutions, significant for their repetition of the phrase, "as a matter of justice," asked for "adequate representation of women in all bodies capable of influencing decisions about the church's lifestyle," for example in the selection of seminary students and the appointment of bishops. The church was asked to admit that there is no basis in scripture or theology for refusing to allow women to celebrate the eucharist and to absolve sin. Sexist language in the liturgy was denounced. The resolutions asked that girls be allowed to serve on the altar and be admitted to choir schools equally with boys. One resolution spoke of nuns, deprecating any tendency to give them exalted status as compared with other women. Another deplored the low esteem in which single women are held. Another upheld the right of married women to work outside the home. Additional resolutions called for a study of marriage breakdown, for a condemnation of rape, both inside and outside marriage, and for consultation with women before any further church pronouncements on abortion. Finally, the church was asked to rescind the condemnation of artificial birth control expressed in *Humanae Vitae*.

For lack of time and resources, Roman Catholic Feminists discontinued its newsletter in 1983. The group, not surprisingly, failed to make the transition into a national movement for change for women in the Catholic Church. However, the Dorcas Group, which worked closely with RCF, continued. Dorcas was established to monitor the Catholic press and to write letters to editors upholding women's equal dignity and rights whenever these were slighted.

The National Pastoral Congress was a highly problematic experience for many who were involved. Many lay people put a great deal of work into the consultation process prior to the Congress, and many parishes took this opportunity very seriously. It was hoped that a greater involvement and participation of the laity in the leadership of the church would result. But these hopes were not realized, and laity subsequently have not been so willing to be consulted nor so confident that their opinions would be valued. In addition, many women refer to the Congress as the context in which they clearly realized that women are second-class members of the church, which led them to shift the focus of their activity from the empowerment of the laity to the empowerment of women.[5]

Other Influences from Outside the Catholic Church

The decade of 1975–85 was the United Nations Decade for Women. In 1976 the U.K. passed the Equal Opportunities Act, making it an offense to treat women differently from men simply because they are women. Religious groups were exempted from the provisions of the Act. An Equal Opportunities Commission was set up to deal with complaints and, where necessary, to prosecute offenders. Important precedents have since been established on such matters as equal pay for work of equal value.

The World Council of Churches, for its part, was developing a significant theme in preparation for its 6th General Assembly, to be held in Vancouver, Canada in July 1983. The theme was "The Community of Women and Men in the Church," and a conference on the theme was held in Sheffield in 1981. In preparation for Sheffield, the British Council of Churches initiated a consultation process which touched many of the parishes of England and Wales, Scotland and Northern Ireland.

In the mid-1960s, the Christian Parity Group, born of the vision of Una and Leo Kroll, was established. The stated aim of the Christian Parity Group was "to use and create opportunities for developing a true partnership between women and men, based on the acknowledgement of their equal worth, both throughout the whole church and in every part of the community." From 1974 until 1982 Una Kroll wrote a newsletter two or three times a year, connecting some two hundred members, mostly Anglican but including Free Church and Catholic, men as well as women. Retreats and conferences were organized and there was cooperation with other groups with similar aims, such as the Anglican Organisation for Women in Ministry and St. Joan's Alliance. Members met monthly, often in each other's homes, for shared worship. Parity Group members kept in step with developments leading up to the International Women's Year in 1975 and with activities in the World Council of Churches which culminated in the conference in Sheffield in 1982. A member of the Parity Group wrote the study outline for Sheffield, "Circles of Community," which was widely used. Parity lobbied Parliament and Synod in favor of the Equal Opportunities Act and of the ordination of women. In due course, Parity gave rise to other movements, founded by women and men who saw sexism as a contradiction of the gospel. Early members of the Christian Women's Information and Resource Centre, Women in Theology, the Movement for the Ordination of Women and the Network were all active in Parity Groups.

The Church of England and the Movement
for the Ordination of Women

Because of the process of government of the Church of England through the General Synod, which meets twice a year and consists of three chambers—bishops, clergy and laity—the Movement for the Ordination of Women (MOW) has a focus for its campaign to bring about change. The Movement had come into existence after a meeting of General Synod in November 1978 in which a motion before the synod meant to remove legal barriers to the ordination of women was lost in the House of Clergy. Following this, supporters of women's ordination organized a campaign to ensure the passage of the necessary legislation to bring about women's ordination through future General Synods. The organization gained momentum and members, and by September 1980 there were some two thousand men and women active in local branches in all the regions and most of the dioceses. Over the next few years a regular newsletter was circulated and a series of Kairos booklets treating aspects of the theological argument was produced. Members held vigils and acts of witness before and after ordinations and picketed at meetings of the General Synod, carrying the letters spelling out "STILL WAITING."

Between 1984 and 1989, motions and legislation for women's ordination seesawed between the General Synod and Parliament, which must approve any radical changes of practice in the Church of England. In July 1985, General Synod carried a motion enabling women to be ordained deacon, and thus enter holy orders. In October 1986 the House of Commons passed the Deacons (Ordination of Women) Measure with the largest majority—301 to 26—ever accorded any church measure in its history. The Measure was then carried in the House of Lords and received Royal Assent. In February 1987 the archbishop of Canterbury ordained fifteen women deacons, the first of seven hundred women to be ordained deacons that year. In July 1988 General Synod voted on draft legislation to enable women to be ordained priests. But the recommendations dealing with "conscience clauses" were rejected. The problem now is to agree on provision to be made for clergy who cannot, "in conscience," accept the ordination of women and so refuse to work in ministry with them.

The year 1988 was also the year of the Lambeth Conference, the gathering of representatives of all churches in communion with the Anglican Church. MOW sponsored a program of activities in Canterbury, where the Conference was held, to raise consciousness and support for women's ordination.

MOW now has 4,500 members and hopes to double that in the next several years. Both men and women belong to MOW, and they represent a broad spectrum of opinion from the radical to the conservative. Some are hoping that, by the ordination of women, an understanding of women as made in the image of God and improved relationships between women and men so that they can share leadership will become axiomatic, and that ministry itself will thereby be transformed. Others hope that women can be included with as little disturbance to the present order as possible. Some who are involved are consciously feminist, recognizing that the exclusion of women protects the privileges of men and devalues women's gifts. Others feel that women have different gifts, feminine gifts, which complement those of men and which the church needs to affirm for the sake of wholeness. There is also an awareness that the church must resolve the issue of the equality of women in its own house if it is to have anything to say to society at large about the dignity of women and their role in society, one of the most lively issues on the current political scene.

The Church of England has been pushed to deal with the desire among its members for women's ordination by the pressure coming from those churches in the worldwide Anglican communion who are already ordaining women. There has been a significant shift toward the acceptance of women in equal ministry, and heightened consciousness of the inherent demeaning of women by their exclusion from ordination. The hardliners are feeling more and more beleaguered, and as time goes by their arguments appear more and more threadbare. Their best publicized exponent, the bishop of London, seems to be resting his case on the symbolism of men and women for the male and female in creation and for humanity in relationship to the creator. Christ was a man, so only men can represent Christ. Women may represent the church. This is the cosmic myth which validates the subordination of women and which is so thoroughly discredited in feminist political theory. If religion is not to become an anachronism in our modern world, we need to reinvest the truth of salvation in a symbolic language that is intelligible to our contemporaries.

The burning question between Anglicans and Catholics is the ecumenical one: would the ordination of women in the Anglican Church postpone reconciliation between the two churches? The practicalities of this are hotly debated on both sides and in both churches. On the whole, the opponents of women's ordination claim that reconciliation will be irreparably harmed by women's ordination. Advocates insist that, as it is the right and just thing to do, it must be done; reconciliation must be based on truth. The findings of *The Times* MORI Poll, published November 14, 1988, suggest that those who want reconciliation with Rome are also those who want women's ordination. It is a wry paradox that the same group of Christians should want such seemingly contradictory changes.

The Network Continues

In December 1987 two members of the Catholic Women's Network conducted a survey of subscribers to the CWN Newsletter. They received one hundred and ninety-five replies, sixty-five percent of the total subscribers. Eighty-one percent of the respondents were Roman Catholic, seventy-two percent practicing. The researchers found that as a group we are white. Almost half are aged over forty-five and another third are aged between thirty and forty. We are highly educated, with just over thirty percent currently employed in some educational role such as teaching, lecturing or religious formation. Only eight percent of us are "housewife/mother/homemaker."

The Network data was then compared with that of the 1978 National Opinion Survey of Catholics (RCO), with data from a survey of delegates to the National Pastoral Congress held in Liverpool in 1980 (NPC), and with the British Social Attitudes Survey data from a national sample (SCPR). Compared with these other data, Network women are highly engaged in the institutional life of the Church, despite our dissatisfaction with it. Sixty-seven percent of Network replies were from women who go to mass weekly or more often. Fifty-three percent described themselves as "very" or "quite" involved in their parishes.

Compared with both the general population and the Catholic population as a whole, Network women are less likely to vote Conservative, which places us left of center as a group. A quarter of Network women are members of a political party, and half are members of pressure groups. Forty-one percent belong to trade unions. Network women, then, are active in many different arenas.

In 1987 the Catholic Women's Network joined the National Board of Catholic Women (NBCW), a fifty year old organization representing perhaps fifty thousand women in various organizations. The National Board of Catholic Women has always worked closely with the bishops, who have used the Board as a line of communication with Catholic women's organizations. The Board has sent delegates to many national women's bodies and government committees to speak on women's concerns in the Catholic Church; it has also sent delegates to ecumenical groups such as the Women's Interchurch Council. Throughout the years, notable NBCW women have made significant contributions to the life and work of the church. Catholic Action for Overseas Development (CAFOD), now the largest Catholic agency in the field, began as a result of a proposal put to the bishops by the Board. However, the Board suffers from the accusation that it is still not representative of the broad spectrum of Catholic women's opinion, certainly not of the critical voice of women. Nor is its existence widely enough known. Over the years, it has been seen as too much an instrument of the bishops and not enough a champion of women. Like all women's organizations, it is over-worked and under-resourced. The current effort to reorganize the Board may be able to overcome these limitations.

The Network has found membership in the Board a useful way of being in touch with women from a large number of diverse organizations. Until now, women's struggle for acceptance and recognition has been directed toward the bishops, and the mark of ecclesiastical approval has enabled an "approved" group to cast doubt on the value of another group, not so "approved." All too often, bishops resist women's demands on the grounds that women are asking for contradictory things, the stereotypical patriarchal device of dividing women and setting them against one another. What is needed is for women to spend enough time and effort to work out among themselves what is good for women and for the community of both women and men in the church. This requires of women that they first be women-centered in their self-definition and in their definition of community. And bishops must allow women to be self-defined in this way. Bishops cannot choose one kind of woman and refuse to deal with women who stand for other values. Bishops need to be firm about insisting that women work out together what women want. They must not, as so often in the past, short-circuit this process. This will not be easy, the journey. Most recently the Board has promoted a widespread discussion on "Women—Status and Role, Life and Missions," based on statements taken from "Christifideles Laici," as a first step in closer collaboration with bishops in attending to women's concerns in the church.[6] In the long term, it will be important for women working within the structures of the church to remain close, as well, to the daily struggles of all women searching to find meaning and to celebrate mystery in their lives.

Notes

1. "Is There A Place for Feminists in a Christian Church?" ("New Black-friars," January 1987).

2. See Walter Brueggemann, *The Prophetic Imagination* (Philadelphia: Fortress Press, 1978).

3. Archives lodged at Fawcett Library, City of London Polytechnic, Old Castle Street, London E1.

4. The Laity Commission, 38–40 Eccleston Sq., London, SWIV IPD.

5. For conclusions of the National Pastoral Congress, see *Easter People:* A Message from Roman Catholic Bishops of England and Wales in Light of the National Pastoral Congress (Middlegreen, Slough: St. Paul Publications, 1980).

6. See "Do Not Be Afraid," Report by the National Board of Catholic Women (Redemptorist Publications).

Alexina Murphy was Contact Secretary of the Catholic Women's Network from its beginning in 1984 until 1990. She worked on the planning team for the founding conference of the Network in August 1984 and on their Women's Celebration of Death and New Life, Easter 1990. She is presently one of the National Coordinators for the Ecumenical Forum of European

Christian Women in England. She was involved in planning the regional conference for the Ecumenical Forum of European Christian Women in Liverpool in 1988 and the Third Assembly of the Forum in New York in 1990. As a mature student, Alexina graduated in theology from the University of St. Michael's College in Toronto in 1981. She is married and is the mother of four young adults.

4

New Catholic Women in France

Marie-Thérèse van Lunen-Chenu*

> In France, we used to say that the traditional church passed over the worker's world, the working class, and I think that today the church is passing over the women's world.
> —A MEMBER OF ACTION CATHOLIQUE GÉNÉRALE FEMININE

> Ordination is not a big question for us. For a few, yes. The question is more when will they [the institutional church] take heed of our advice, of our life, of our experience. When can we decide *with* them?
> —A CATHOLIC WOMAN FROM A SMALL VILLAGE IN FRANCE

> A church with only one sex I find very odd.
> —A CATHOLIC WOMAN IN PARIS

APART FROM MY own involvement in the church[1] and a rather systematic collection of relevant information over thirty years,[2] I have, in preparing this essay, forwarded Anne Brotherton's questions[3] to a milieux beyond my usual circles.

I received only two formal refusals—which in themselves are very telling of new Catholic women. The first, a religious woman who is very involved in retreats and spiritual "camps" with young girls, sent me a friendly word and a prospectus from her congregation to justify her refusal: "Certainly a lack of time. Also, without doubt, a lack of passion for this subject, while others easily marshal all my energies!" The second refusal came to me from a woman teacher who has been very involved

* Translated by Anne Hennessy, C.S.J.

for several years on a diocesan commission and in the organization of discussions on women/church, all with the acquiescence of her bishop. She wrote to me:

> In fact, I am no longer interested in the questions you raise. I prefer to be involved in my work, where I feel more useful. I am too annoyed to confront the lack of intellectual rigor which usually characterizes the positions of the ecclesiastical hierarchy on "the place of women in the church." That is really why I opt for silence. Perhaps I am wrong, but I cannot do otherwise.

Respondents range from twenty-two to seventy years old. They are both lay and women religious (this is not always specified). Degrees of involvement or non-involvement in the church vary; most of the respondents simultaneously assume several tasks in both church and society. Their religious formation likewise is diverse: some of the women are theologians; most speak modestly of having taken courses in theological formation[4] (scripture, pastoral ministry, etc.); only a small minority, especially from the rural areas, confess to not having any specific religious formation.

Most of the responses are marked by an incommunicable tone which goes beyond the best-grounded intellectual argumentation to resonate with a profound personal experience of the faith. The letters range from one to twenty pages, and it is rare that the respondent does not voice, in her own terms, her attachment to Christ and to the gospel. These women are intense! And they become even more so in speaking of the church, of the transmission and the witness of the faith, than in speaking of the place given to women in the church. It seems clear that their care for evangelization surpasses all considerations of personal status, recognition or hardship.

Some respondents express reservations about the questionnaire itself, which "is centered only on the church/institution. The missionary basis, to which the institution is only relative, does not appear." Others reflect that, for the twenty years in which they have been considering the question of women in the church, nothing has evolved. They would rather see this problem give precedence to "a general reflection on the recognition of freedoms in the church." They would prefer that there be work at the anthropological, psychological, biblical and theological levels on notions such as "power" and "service."

Unfortunately some younger women, even with repeated requests, have not replied. I have consistently received from the young an impression of "spiritual enthusiasm" rather than of concern with precise questions about the faith. Settings of religious interest for French youth are foyers (hostels), retreat centers and charismatic gathering places.[5] But questions of "commitment," "the institutional church and its functions," or "the role of women" evoke few responses. "The question of structures does not interest me," one says, "but knowing where I can share with others my faith in the living Christ does. It is He who has changed my whole life."

Religious Practice

This was my only surprise. Three-fourths of the respondents simply bypassed my first question about religious practice without bothering to explain themselves.

Current statistics on religious practice in France are useful to see the French Catholic "feminist" in context. A 1984 poll for TFI and *La Vie*[6] underlines the astonishing degree of popular support which the Catholic Church in France continues to enjoy. According to other data, eighty-one percent of the French identify themselves as Catholic, meaning that they have been baptized. This number has declined only slightly, from eighty-six and a half percent in 1974 to eighty-three percent in 1983. In terms of actual practice, the decline has also been slow. In 1974 twenty-one percent of French Catholics practiced regularly; in 1986 fifteen percent, of whom the majority were women.[7]

It is clear that both age and class influence practice; the overwhelming majority of practicing women are over fifty years old and are from the middle class. One respondent from Versailles took the trouble to investigate further in her area. In a bourgeois-style residential community there, twenty percent of the women practice their religion, but only six percent of these are under thirty-five. In a more modest neighborhood of rent-controlled housing nearby, no more than one and a half percent of the women are practicing Catholics. And one young working woman commented: "The few working women in our parishes feel themselves doubly set apart."

Several respondents, well informed because of their own catechetical involvement, note that women tend to resume practicing when they have catechism-age children, participating in children's masses and their preparation for the profession of faith and confirmation, still a common practice in France. However, this little "jump in practice" does not last any longer among the mothers than among the children when they grow up.

Parish masses are often viewed as rather drab affairs. However, the parish is the logical place for women to become involved. Within ten years in my own small village in Bourgogne, I have seen a parish team developed, with half of the members women. Women have begun to speak at meetings and to take charge of activities in a way that they had never thought possible. They go to the microphone to do the welcoming[8] and compose some of the prayers, while the number of women readers, even for the most important occasions, has also increased. Some of my respondents expressed satisfaction with this, though others indicated some resistance on the part of both women and clergy. Still others noted that, though this "first step" fosters good will and commitment, it is often followed by a sense of frustration. "There, again, the priests remain the great decision-makers!" they say.

When there are "Sunday Assemblies in the Absence of a Priest," many are not satisfied with the liturgical model which is used; there is also a clear effort on the part of some bishops to limit such assemblies by regrouping parishes around itinerant priests, even at the expense of dissolving local congregations in which the laity had sought creative ways of making the celebrations truly communal.[9]

What discourages women—and many state this very strongly—are two serious and closely linked issues. The first is the ritual form of the celebrations, which makes them feel "cut off from reality." Such ritual does not take into account the cares of the people or their "human commitments, (especially) if they are not strictly in the church." The second is the fact that Sunday mass is no longer of spiritual interest to the family as such. This is a great concern for women who are mothers, aunts, and grandmothers of children, of whom the youngest are often no longer baptized.

What does "practice" mean to the women themselves? The few who spoke of this are fairly concrete. They do not look for either "grand manners or lovely formulas." Some cite, as their "practice," involvement in the community, in the service of human rights, "as a Christian." They go willingly, whenever they can, to those "places of life and of witness to life" which they themselves identify. Some, involved in the "Mission of

France"[10] or on workers' pastoral teams, prefer to pray spontaneously with the people of their tenements or with other communities of workers, and they note the gap which exists between these celebrations of life and the "official cult." They seldom try to recruit priests for these gatherings, in which celebration may arise from shared grief, suffering, anxiety, or a sense of solidarity, because "it is very rare that the clergy do not come bringing their 'devices,' sometimes doing more harm than good." The women have also been disappointed by the clergy's misunderstanding of them, even though the women themselves had gathered the community.

As for the so-called "base communities," only one respondent spoke of these, yet she asserted that such "celebrating communities," with or without a priest, are more and more numerous. This practice, which has been a subject of debate over the years, seems quite accepted as much by the laity as by priests who are members of the movement, though the movement itself cannot be said to be widespread in France.

Feminist liturgies simply do not exist, and the idea is seldom mentioned. Aside from a few small groups, discussion of this form of worship seems to evoke the same kind of reticence as the discussion of "feminist theology" itself. On March 8, 1985 a feminist liturgy was celebrated by a group of women who see themselves related to the "Women of Saint-Merri"[11] in the large Parisian parish of Halles-Beaubourg. The sponsoring group, which is somewhat ephemeral, called itself "Celles de la Terre" ("those of the earth"), a play on the words "sel de la terre" ("salt of the earth"). The liturgy, in the opinion of the secular media, was "very successful," indicating that public opinion, believing or not, saw the event as more important than the women themselves dared to imagine.

Commitment, Ministry, Office, Responsibility, Function, Service

Respondents used all of the words above to describe what they do in the church. However, only one, who has been in charge of a parish by herself for more than ten years, referred to "my ministry." None of the words suffices to describe a pastoral situation that is both complex and creative. The word "ministry" is not commonplace in France. Nor does it seem to describe the extent of the women's involvements or the mandates they claim and wish to have recognized.

The Grassroots: Catechetical and Parish Service

Teaching catechism is the initial ecclesial extension of the familial role of women. Women comprise eighty-five percent of the 200,000 catechists in France, though their situations are quite varied. Women catechists range from "catechist mothers," who are often, in fact, grandmothers and who themselves may have had no specific religious formation (and may quite distrust the "professionals"), to women who are called "Permanent,"[12] of whom there are now many dozens in France. These latter most often serve on a team with a priest, and they are involved in everything that relates to catechesis in a diocese, including the religious formation of adults. On the whole, the Permanents still seem to be perceived rather negatively, as "a battalion of foot soldiers," or "thoughtless repetitors under the 'cane' of the pastor." However, this negative image is being improved. Many of the women who began this involvement with little or no personal formation are now concerned about being better prepared. Catechists in some dioceses have asked for training courses and are using excellent catechetical materials for teachers.

"In the Absence of a Priest"

We must make particular mention of this situation, which has major consequences in France. In spite of the boasts of certain clergy, excessively rejoicing in "a renewal of vocations" (most often of a very traditional, "clerical" type), the situation is evolving irrevocably toward an increasing shortage of priests. And this situation creates, de facto, the mobilization of certain of the faithful: women are finding new roles in the church.

In a recent and well-documented article by Monique Brulin on "Sunday Assemblies in the Absence of Priests,"[13] we learn that, in 1988, there were more than 2,103 regular places of Sunday assembly without priests and more than 650 which have a priest only once or twice a month. The number of priestless parishes has tripled in the past ten years and will continue to grow. The proportion of women who are present at these assemblies is sixty-eight percent, almost all of whom tend to be actively involved. While Brulin's article refers to traditional attitudes of reserve about women and the marginalization of women with regard to liturgy, it is nonetheless important to note that the active, visible and competent participation of women in these celebrations is an important symbolic rupture with the past, one which simultaneously affects the consciousness of women themselves and their traditional double image in church and society.

Between Clericalism and Criticism

Most women are uneasy that they are "the main body of the troops," as this confirms the old idea that religion is essentially the "business" of "little old women in tennis shoes." Whether one goes to a church for registration, formation, a service or the sacraments, one is most likely to be met by women. As priest-sociologist Julien Potel[14] wrote to me:

> It is clear that the clergy and the bishops keep them [women] in secondary roles, while using them more and more, and hiring them more and more. The place of women in the church? We deplore the inertia, sometimes the docility, which makes them [women] accept abnormal situations. . . .

Still, it is from this female grass roots that the parish in France often takes shape, followed by the school and the neighborhood, where women have initiated what Monique Hebrard, a journalist and a well-known author, has called "a tranquil revolution."[15] It is here that women have found opportunities for consciousness-raising and religious formation, especially through the work of the "General Catholic Action of Women" (ACGF),[16] whose original focus was on the parish.

The experience of Arlette is an example; her growing participation in the life of the church was mediated by her membership in ACGF. She was the first lay woman catechist in her village, directly accountable to the parents of the students. Arlette was formed in various ACGF groups, and she founded still other groups before she became a diocesan ACGF leader. At the same time, she is a member of the Office of the Pastoral Council for her area, which includes several parishes, and for her region, which includes several areas. She participates in church movements such as the Catholic Committee against Hunger and for Development (CCFD),[17] and she has also initiated or participated in numerous local initiatives in support of neighborhood causes, divorcees and the disabled. And it is she who says that "everywhere and always, my passion is helping women to express themselves and to make their words heard."

Mandates and Recognition: The "Permanents"

In my own diocese of Autun there were, in April 1989, thirty-five Permanent church workers, of whom nineteen were women religious and sixteen were lay, including two lay men. In large letters in the local newspaper, we read that these Permanent workers "assure a service to the church, a recognized and salaried position," while deacons, often maintaining their secular professions, provide "a presence of the church." Clearly, with "the vocation crisis and the aging of the clergy, priests are no longer numerous enough to guarantee all the duties of their ministry."[18]

"I give you responsibility for the catechumenate. . . ." So begins the missioning letter which Genevieve received from her bishop in 1986. With Genevieve, three women religious share this responsibility, replacing a priest who resigned from the diocese of Grenoble. A lay woman in the diocese of Chartres had her duties described in this way:

> For a region, she is charged with promoting the pastoral ministry of adolescents, with organizing parish teams in the villages of the region, with animating (facilitating) liturgical life and with assuring the service of welcome to people requesting baptism, the registration of children for catechism, marriage, etc. . . .

Thus, Mme. D.L. is called "a Permanent woman in pastoral ministry." In the diocese of Lyons, one of the most advanced in the area, there are two hundred and fifty non-ordained Permanents in pastoral ministry, of whom eighty-five percent are women. These women, it is said, "have paved the way for the men." Together with these Permanents, there are six hundred diocesan priests and two hundred and fifty men religious. One woman, Claire Daurelle, has been named, with two priests, to be responsible for a parish. For ten years prior, Claire was entrusted with four chaplaincies in state schools. The commissioning of Claire and her priest associates was given by the bishop's delegate in a parish ceremony.[19] Marie-Louise Gondal, another lay woman, is responsible for the catechumenate office of the diocese. Of the nine part-time Permanents on Marie-Louise's team, four have master's degrees and one has a doctoral degree in theology.

In Savoy in 1985 there were thirty Permanents, of whom twenty were women religious and only one was male. Two-thirds of the group were assigned to catechetical ministry and school chaplaincies; the rest were assigned to formation, missionary animation, the pastoral care of tourists, and hospital chaplaincies. Most of them have contracts with their specific employers: diocese, parish or other. Only seven are unpaid; the rest receive stipends.

More Competent Women; Greater Responsibilities

In 1965 no woman among the already numerous women catechists was either a directress or an assistant in a diocesan office. By 1982, women comprised sixteen percent of the diocesan directors and sixty-five percent of the assistant directors, and several represented their regions on the National Commission for the Teaching of Religion.[20]

In the national offices for catechetics, pastoral ministry and liturgy, all appointed directors are still priests, but some women are recognized as the more qualified specialists in certain areas, able both to determine when matters have been processed as required by Rome and to recognize when matters have been "distorted by the theologians in the office who do not understand the question." The women are capable of intelligent argumentation and some are clearly superior to their male colleagues. They are inspired more by their sensitivity to contemporary life, to theology and to the human sciences than by the ins and outs of ecclesial bureaucracy.

Beyond Catechesis and the Parish

We have commented on catechesis and parish ministry in particular, but one meets women in other roles as well, roles less expected by the public, such as hospital chaplaincy and the conducting of funerals. In the dioceses of Nanterre and Grenoble, women are delegated to ecumenical work. There is a small increase in the number of women involved in religious broadcasts such as TV masses. Another surprise was to see a young mother, Jeanne Macherel, named president of the synod of the diocese of Grenoble. About twenty of the ninety-three dioceses of France have had synods since 1983 and, except for three lay men, all prior synod presidents had been priests. Jeanne Macherel, in a forthright first interview by the journal *La Croix*,[21] declared that she considered her task a service and that she was prepared to leave it when the synod concluded because "there is a manifest problem of power in the church.

[I await] something which does not revolve around the priest and authority."

Missioning letters, mandates and liturgies of commissioning and installation of lay church workers are becoming more common. However, the visibility and recognition of women are far from universal in France. In certain cases women are employed without a clear mandate or with missioning letters renewable at the good will of the bishop alone. Salary and clarity of role remain precarious. And, of course, some of the faithful themselves are more resistant than some of the clergy: "When will we have a *real* chaplain, Mademoiselle?"

New Questions for the Church

The new and intense participation of women in pastoral ministry is the most marked contemporary phenomenon of "new vocations" in France. The presence of women is identifying new needs and deepening the church's missionary vision. Several dioceses have commissions for discerning the hiring of full-time people in pastoral ministry, sometimes accompanied, as in Lyons, by a Committee for New Ministries. Under the direction of Georges Duperray, this Lyons Committee has done remarkable work on "the ministerial identity of women" and "men in ecclesial service."[22] The convictions of women themselves, and all that they have accomplished thus far, constitute a clear recognition of the missionary responsibilities of all the baptized. Also evident in several of my responses from women is their particular commitment to the accompaniment of adult catechumens and those who are "in the world" or on the fringes of unbelief.

The Issue of Women Priests

The theoretical question of women priests as such is seldom considered in France, and no group has been formed expressly to promote this cause. On the other hand, the issue is more and more often raised by the media, radio and television at times of major church events, and the question is asked in all major interviews with church leaders. The testimony of women aspiring to priestly ministry is treated with respect in all such forums as well as in daily newspapers and other print media.[23] The cause also gains credibility from the ministerial lives of women themselves and from their "ecclesial rootedness," says Marie-Francoise Giraud, a Dominican woman religious who for more than ten years has administered a parish.[24]

Special-Femmes (Women Only),[25] a publication of the catechumenate office of the diocese of Lyons, which is under the direction of a woman, illustrates the point quite well. Claire, a parish leader with two priests, found herself in an entirely new liturgical position at the time of her public ceremony of commissioning. She speaks of this:

> It was only a first step, even if I often tell myself that I have already taken the second and third steps. I just want to take them in the church. But when?

Women and Theology

Theological Education of Women

Jeannine is forty years old, a teacher, single. Since her youth she has held responsibilities in the church and she continues commitments which are of interest to her. Now she has begun studies for a licentiate in theology, studies which will involve six years of evening classes. Why this effort to do three days' work in every one: career, church service and study? Jeannine responds:

> It is necessary to give some stability to the various formations I have received. It is a means of being acknowledged a little, which is indispensable in order that the time I spend in meetings produces some efficacy. There is no way to do otherwise. One is a woman; it is necessary to prove one's capability.

Like Jeannine, most of the lay women who have degrees in theology complete them through long and often costly effort. Not surprisingly, then, such women are usually over forty-five years old and from the middle class!

It is fair to say that more and more women are being encouraged—by their own commitments, by their dioceses, and, if they are religious, by their congregations—to obtain diplomas through short courses in theology. There are also a number of diocesan institutes of theology, specializing in pastoral ministry, where current and future Permanents receive

financial aid for their studies. Many Permanent women, especially those
with positions of diocesan or national importance, are very well educated theologically, often holding doctorates or several specialized
diplomas.[26]

Women Theologians

Catholic France has experienced a certain delay vis-à-vis the United
States in the access of women to higher degrees in theology. The first
such degrees in France were doctorates from the U.S., from Paris and
from Strasbourg. The first women with theological doctorates from
Catholic institutions in France were a woman religious in Paris in 1966
(the second Paris doctorate was not granted until 1973) and another
woman in Lyons in 1968. No woman has yet received a doctorate
from Lille.

Despite the slow beginning, however, the number of women theologians in France has doubled in recent years. For example, on the theology faculty of Lyons, between 1968 and 1978, only thirteen percent of
the doctorates were earned by women. Yet in the last ten years, the
proportion of women earning doctorates is four women to seven men,
or fifty-seven percent of the total.

Still, very few women theologians are full professors in French institutions. The first woman to be appointed as a full professor is on the
Catholic faculty of Lille, where she also directs the Center of Medical
Ethics. There are also a woman Director of Studies for the First Course
at the Institut Catholique in Paris and a woman professor of canon law
in Strasbourg, both of whom say that they enjoy the same conditions as
their male colleagues. With few exceptions, however, most women
teaching theology are in subordinate positions and are overburdened
with courses, assistancies and substitutions.

Research and Feminist Theology

It must also be acknowledged that research by women on women as well
as research in feminist theology is still rare in France. In Lyons, where
there have been dissertations done on mystical theology and Marian
theology,[27] no doctoral dissertation has treated the question of women
as such. Out of eight doctoral dissertations written by women in Paris

between 1973 and 1986, only one, by a foreign woman religious, concerned a woman, Marie of the Incarnation.

There is much dispute about the very term "feminist theology."[28] Almost the only groups to deal overtly with feminist theology are Protestant women in the Groupe d'Orsay,[29] The Ecumenical Forum of Christian Women of Europe, the group Women and Men in the Church (FHE), and the French branch of The European Association of Women for Theological Research.[30] CERDIC of Strasbourg has published an excellent international bibliography on women from 1975 to 1982 (2,446 titles),[31] while the FHE has undertaken a remarkable thematic bibliography of French-language works from 1975 to 1987 and, in cooperation with the Catholic faculty of Lyons, has created the "Center for Research and Documentation on Women and Christianity."[32]

While a number of Protestant women theologians have received public attention through their involvement in literary, ethical and political arenas, this is not the case with Catholic women theologians. In the ecclesial sphere and in the Catholic press, however, the opinions of Catholic women theologians are more and more often solicited.

Women Religious

Respondents' impressions of women religious in France run the gamut: "Very present in life but absent from expression!" ". . . a blurred presence." "They rank sometimes with the pastors, sometimes with the laity." ". . . reserved in the church but radiant at the grass roots."

Apostolic Religious

Though they are eight or nine times more numerous than nuns (cloistered religious), half of all apostolic (active) religious in France are over sixty-five years old. And many of the some three hundred and seventy-two religious congregations of women are extremely small and have no novices in formation.

In one sense, women religious have become much less visible than in the past, yet many are witnessing to new signs of community and service.[33] They are less visible, perhaps, because they are no longer living in large, landmark convents, and many no longer wear traditional religious garb. They tend to speak little of themselves and rarely take public positions, even less a feminist position! The smaller congregations are sometimes affiliated with one another in unions, and some sisters individually belong to other groups such as those representing the teaching and health care professions.

"A crumbling presence," one might say, and sometimes an isolated one. Yet this is the price that sisters are paying for their new presence in small communities and at the grass roots of the church. Sisters are numerous in all the new pastoral ministries. Sometimes Permanent, full-time and salaried, at other times paid "a little," they are catechists, animators and chaplains in high schools, hospitals and prisons. And the sisters are still more readily accepted by the public than are the "simple" lay people.

Sisters are also found in the most impoverished settings: in neighborhoods and tenements, among immigrants and the imprisoned. They are present, too, on the fringes of unbelief and in groups committed to social justice. Though sisters collectively are absent from ecclesial and political life and from ethical and intellectual debate and are rarely represented in the media of radio and television, they are, as individuals, significant in French life. One is struck by the simple human presence of these women, by their competence, their availability, their interpersonal skills and, even more, by the spiritual intensity which seems to make them live "the more." It is, then, personally rather than corporately that sisters connect with other women.

As they age, some of the sisters spend their final years in secular retirement houses, since many congregations, lacking young religious, cannot assume independently the care of their elderly members. One should note, however, that women religious in France benefit from the same government support as do the clergy, making retirement costs less burdensome for them.

Contemplative Religious

The thirst among the laity for short spiritual retreats (*haltes spirituelles*) as well as a certain spiritual "tourism" attracts believers, those who do not practice the faith and even unbelievers to certain monasteries. And, astonishingly, the nuns in these monasteries have become hostesses par excellence! Guests are struck by the quality of their human, spiritual and communitarian integration and poise. The nuns work together at the realities of the common life: governance, finances, the sharing of tasks, the improvement of talents, and even the engagement in social support of those around them. In brief, they offer a witness to spiritual and community living that may well be the envy of monasteries and religious houses of men!

In addition to the cloistered nuns—and there is, of course, great variety among them—one finds today many who call themselves "contemplatives in the heart of the world." There are some twenty such institutes, some much older, others very new, united in a shared spirit and vision. There are also a number of charismatic renewal communities, in which consecrated lay people share in monastic traditions and practices and witness to a beautiful blending of men and women together. Two examples of such new creations are "The Monastic and Lay Fraternities of Jerusalem" and "The Monastic Family of Bethlehem," each composed of monks, nuns and committed lay people, both celibate and married. There are, as well, some sacerdotal fraternities of priests and some communities of young people which espouse the monastic and contemplative traditions. These have grown rapidly in a very few years and are experiencing an abundance of vocations.[34]

Women's Attitudes about the Church

Before the 1987 Synod on the Laity in Rome, Paul Valadier, S.J. commented in *La Croix* (September 30, 1987) on a recent SOFRES opinion poll. To the question "In your view can one speak of segregation vis-à-vis women in the church?" sixty-two percent of the respondents answered, "Yes, somewhat or entirely." Fifty-seven percent of the "occasional" Catholics and only thirteen percent of the practicing Catholics who responded felt that practicing Catholics are accepting of women in ministerial settings. And more women than men, we are told, are dissatisfied with this situation. Yet only seventeen percent of the French people in general and seventeen percent of French Catholics would accept the ordination of celibate women! "This is far from a feminist outburst," wrote Father Valadier.

A further reading on the subject comes from recent diocesan synods. The issue of women in the church does not appear among any of the major questions which the dioceses chose to consider. Monique Hebrard, author of a book on French synods, notes that ". . . the question of women is not a priority in its theoretical or its ideological aspects . . .

it is no longer of interest to discuss the question in terms of the access of
women to ministry; on the contrary, in all the synods, men and women
were naively astonished that one could not simply ignore this issue
(along with that of the ordination of married men)." Hebrard also tells
us that "the church continues to lose its women," and that "renewal can
even be seen more among young men than among young women, as the
men do not have the same negative experiences as the women."[35]

To my own question about what women most appreciate in the
church today, the women referred almost unanimously to the changes
brought about by Vatican II and then to the fact that "the role of
women is more and more important and recognized in tasks, responsibilities and services." Yet while the respondents cited "the recognition of
women's talents and abilities," not one noted this progress without
some accompanying reservations, and this even on the part of those
women who were most enthusiastic and even traditional in their remarks. From this I can only conclude that the dissatisfaction of these
women who are, for the most part, very committed to the Church clearly
prevails over any satisfaction they express.

The Dissatisfied

Fabienne is a single woman of twenty-nine, a Permanent part-time leader
in a school chaplaincy, with a missioning letter from her bishop and a
regular salary. She is happy about her good relations with the team of
priests, and she describes herself as "satisfied that women have a place in
the life of the church, that baptized people have places to speak and to
be formed and can participate in assemblies and liturgies which are no
longer the affairs of priests alone." But Fabienne's themes of dissatisfaction are serious: "When will there be women in areas of decision-
making? When will there be true diversity in ministries?"

Among my respondents, the most frequent criticisms of male-
misogynist clericalism in the institution were tied to authoritarianism:
"The church minimizes contemporary needs, values, realities and aspirations." "The bishops and the curia speak in an authoritarian and negative way." Almost all mentioned the problem of traditional teachings on
sexual morality and the fact that "some men pretend to speak for
women." The women's concerns extend to the rupture between the
church and youth, with the exception, perhaps, of the young charismat-
ics. "The institutional church is insignificant and a counter-witness to

the radical freedom of Christ," wrote a woman religious, while others commented that "the church is in a time lag as regards contemporary knowledge. Priests are not qualified to engage in any serious scientific discussions." "The curia foolishly stumbles and continues to feel compelled to respond immediately to everything, instead of being able sometimes, in areas of rapid change such as the role of women, sexual morality and the ethics of reproduction, to admit that she is searching *with* the Christian people."

I was even told that "the institutional church is closed to serious anthropological, exegetical and theological data, and has lost all credibility in the opinions of men and women who are open and searching."

Women and Bishops

Here, again, the situations are varied. First of all, there are those bishops who, convinced that something should be done regarding women, fall under the influence of a single woman or a single category of women in their dioceses. This, unfortunately, is a situation which ignores one of the most elementary rules of discernment at the heart of the presbyteral counsel, the inclusion of "the many" for the discernment of pastoral needs.

Some few bishops have gathered small consultative councils of women. In the diocese of Hauts de Seine, such a council prepared an outline for the reading of the pope's letter "On the Dignity of Women."[36] Two other commissions have had a somewhat more extensive existence, though not a great deal has been accomplished in this regard.[37]

In 1985, for the closing of the U.N. Decade of Women, the Social Commission of the Episcopate published a declaration entitled "Women and Men Partners," which, while it includes many excellent recommendations, suggests nothing that the bishops had not already committed themselves to earlier.[38]

Women's Movements in France

We have already discussed the promotion and the massive involvement of women in pastoral ministry which begins at the parish level. The organization "L'Action Catholic Générale des Femmes" (ACGF) has contributed greatly to this "feminism" (though it does not use the term) by focusing on the evolution and formation of women and the "conversion" of their spousal partners, even as it stresses uniquely feminine qualities and savoir-faire. For over twenty years, ACGF has maintained some fifty thousand members, and a congress which they sponsored in 1979 was attended by five thousand women and five hundred chaplains. For the women, this was a feast of their new identity, well symbolized by the standard of the congress, "Dare to live in the feminine; dare to say Jesus Christ in the feminine." The women expressed themselves so creatively and so successfully that some of the hierarchy was a little frightened and issued disavowals of certain publications. Since that time, ACGF has taken a broader approach, focusing less on the parish and seeking to unite women and their concerns in friendship groups or around specific themes. The movement continues to be effective in the conscientization and promotion of women and sees itself as a movement for evangelization. ACGF is less concerned with critical analyses and militant projects than it is with the "word of women" being supported and heard in the church.[39]

Other Catholic Action movements, both feminine and mixed, include some programs and specific courses in conscientization on the issue of women. These tend to be polarized, however, especially on the question of new partnership relations.

Le Groupe International Femmes et Hommes dans l'Eglise (The International Group of Women and Men in the Church) was founded in 1970 in France and Belgium and has since established contacts with other countries, including Canada and the United States. This group occupies an original position since it is both feminist and mixed and is close to other movements of critical and ecumenical Christians. It espouses not only the principle but the practice of partnership between the sexes (one-third of its members are very committed men) and among clergy, women religious and the laity. Its publications are influential and reach a large number of subscribers, men and women, both in Europe and abroad.[40]

In 1982 the Forum Oecuménique de Femmes Chrétiennes d'Europe was founded, following many years of contact and mutual exchanges among women in various Lutheran, Methodist, Catholic and Orthodox women's associations. The Forum seeks to identify and deepen the European identity common to Christian women from the Atlantic to the

Urals, putting movements, groups and isolated women in touch with one another.

For French Catholic women, both in organizations and isolated groups, the French section of the Forum has enabled an expansion of their ecumenical and international vision. French Catholic women have supported such Forum initiatives as the "Decade of Churches in Solidarity with Women" and the "Conciliar Process for Justice, Peace and the Protection of the Earth" in its two stages: the European at Basle in 1989 and the worldwide in Seoul in 1990. They have thus endorsed one of the first positions adopted by the Forum: affirming the determination and ecumenical action of Christian women and their concerns "in the face of ecumenical sluggishness."

"In Conclusion"

On the whole, it seems to me that the relationship which French women maintain with the Institution is a mature one, consonant with the quality of their commitment. Most are far removed from a "power trip." As Claire Daurelle, a Permanent in charge of a parish, wrote: "I am convinced that some women know that [our progress] is irreversible, and they are willing to advance the church without shedding light on themselves. They are patient to the extent that they are clear."[41] Brigitte, who is younger, is one who chooses to be quite clear. The mother of three children, Brigitte has always felt called to be a priest. She devotes her leisure time to writing, to grass roots pastoral work and to her theological studies. Brigitte believes that "women have been deprived of all apostolic images" and that "perhaps Jesus himself was poorly understood in his testament." And she adds, "I could not have any rest unless I awakened others to this aberration."

Not all are so ardent—or so lucid—as Brigitte, and the pastoral involvement of women in France, while it is rich, still contains many ambiguities. We have much to learn from American women, whose systematic analyses of their experiences have shaped a movement which has already known its apprenticeship, successes, deceptions, and corporate goals. While French women see their experience as closer to the feminine and ecclesial experiences of Quebec, I would nonetheless insist on a true international and interconfessional thesaurus of the experiences, research and Christian community of women. And not only of women but of all humanity.

French women are also very aware of the irrevocable ecumenism among us, which exceeds in practice any formal movements in this direction by the institutional church. It is their simple identity as Christians which unites French women in the rereading of the scriptures as a community of equal disciples.[42]

Finally, it is important to note that in France one has to deal with a feminism of evolution rather than of revolution, and the former is often common to both sexes. The uniqueness of women portrayed in French literature and cinema and the French will to defend by law the "right to difference" have both been assumed into France's Catholic feminism, which upholds *human* rights and also espouses feminism—"but not [a feminism] against men!" As it continues to affirm women's unique maternal qualities and values, their savoir faire, and their options *as women,* French feminism seeks to reform both attitudes and structures and to convince men to act with women *in partnership*—in the society—and in the church.

Notes

1. See author's biography.

2. Much of this collection, "Women and Christianity," is housed in the Center for Research and Documentation in Lyons. Readers may obtain information or copies of documents cited by writing to: Centre de Recherches et Documentation, "Femmes et Christianisme," Theology Faculty of Lyon, 25 rue du Plat, 69002 Lyon.

3. See Chapter 1, note 8, for this questionnaire under "Guidelines for Essay."

4. "Formation" is the term most commonly used in France for religious education, and may refer to both foundational and more specialized programs.

5. For excellent information on charismatic spirituality, centers and founders of groups as well as the influence of Marthe Robin and the foyers of charity on youth, I recommend Frédéric Lenoir, *Les Communautés Nouvelles* (Fayard, 1988) and Marie Aleth Trapet, *Pour l'Avenir des Nouvelles Communautés dans l'Eglise* (DDB, 1987).

6. TFI is a French television network: *La Vie* is a Catholic weekly. The poll mentioned is commented on in *La Croix* (June 7, 1984).

7. See Jacques Rollet, "Les Français et la religion," *Jésus* (No. 55, Dec. 1987) 8–13. A professor at l'Institut Catholique de Paris, Rollet compares and comments on four important national trends of 1986–87.

8. "Welcoming" refers to the greeting given at the beginning of the liturgy in France and is often done by a lay person.

9. Monique Brulin, "Les Assemblées Dominicales en l'Absence de Prêtre: Situation Française en 1987, les Résultats d'Une Enquête Nationale," in *La Maison-Dieu* (Paris: National Center for the Liturgical Pastorate, No. 175, 1988).

10. "Mission of France" is an association of secular priests, founded by Msgr. Suhard and the Assembly of French Bishops after World War II. Their specific mission is "to tear down the walls which separate the church from the people" and to do this in various settings.

11. "Women of Saint Merri" are a group of women from a very "open" parish in Paris who wanted to gather and to "be among women." In 1982 they organized, in the large Parisian church near Halles Beaubourg, an exposition on "Women in the Church." The event remains unique and has provoked considerable comment and reaction. One can read an account of the exposition in the monthly parish bulletin, *Aujourd'hui des Chrétiens* (June 1981), 76 Rue de la Verrerie, 75004 Paris.

12. The designation, "Permanent," common in France, refers to those who are officially appointed to a ministry as opposed to those who volunteer or serve without a specific commission by a bishop or local clergy.

13. See note 9.

14. See Julien Potel, ed., *Ils Se Sont Mariés . . . et Après? Essai sur les Prêtres Mariés* (Paris: L'Harmatan, 1986).

15. See Monique Hebrard, "Femmes Partenaires et Responsables dans l'Eglise," in *La Croix* (Etudes, No. 358/2, Feb. 1983) 263–274. Also Hebrard, *Les Femmes dans l'Eglise* (Centurion/Le Cerf, 1984).

16. ACGF, "Action Catholique Générale Féminine," publishes an excellent and widely read bi-monthly journal, *Le Gue*. Available from ACGF, 98 rue de l'Université, 75007, Paris.

17. CCFD, "Comité Catholique contre la Faim and pour le Dévelopment," is a charitable agency of the church of France which directs its aid primarily to developing countries in the third world. ("Le Secours Catholique" focuses more on aid within France.) The CCFD is the target of systematic slander campaigns on the part of certain publications on the Right, of which *Le Figaro* magazine is one.

18. *La Renaissance,* April 22, 1989.

19. See "Accueil et Liberté, Spécial-Femmes," in the *Bulletin du Service de Catechumenat de Lyon,* No. 54, Jan. 1988.

20. *Hommes et Femmes en Catéchése,* No. 94, Jan. 1984.

21. *La Croix,* Sept. 17, 1988.

22. The work of this committee is documented by the Antenne-Diocésaine-Formation, 2 rue Ste. Hélène, 69002 Lyon.

23. A report in *La Croix*, May 16, 1989, on the synod of the diocese of Beauvais quotes one of the delegates: "I have always wanted to be a priest. The proposal of the diaconate for women which has been formulated here is still not enough." For an excellent book on the subject by three women theologians, see Marie-Jeanne Bérère, Renée Dufourt and Donna Singles, *Et Si On Ordonnait des Femmes?* (Le Centurion, 1982).

24. This is an exceptional situation. For fifteen years Sister Marie-Francoise has functioned as pastor of a parish in a tourist area, where she provides welcome and pastoral ministry to visitors, good liturgies, guided tours and general spiritual availability. While her "personal charism is accepted by the diocese," and she is provided lodging, she is not paid. Her address, because she and her abbey in the Drome are worth visiting, is: Soeur M. F. Giraud, O.P., Leoncel, 26190 Saint Jean en Royan.

25. See note 19.

26. For a fuller treatment of women in theological studies, see Marie-Thérèse van Lunen Chenu, "Femmes, Féminisme et Théologie," in *Initiation à la Pratique de la Théologie* (Le Cerf, 1983). (Translations in German and Italian.)

27. In Lyons there is a remarkable doctoral dissertation by Marie-Jeanne Bérère, "Marie, l'Eglise, Deux Figures Symbolizatrices du Salut." There are other theses of interest in Lyons, about twenty of which were presented in non-Catholic universities.

28. See note 26. Also "Féminologie, Théologie Féministe" in the bulletin, *Femmes et Hommes dans l'Eglise* (No. 25, Dec. 1985). The bulletin, which includes both documents and bibliographies, is a publication of FHE ("Femmes et Hommes dans l'Eglise"), 14 rue St. Benoît, 75005 Paris.

29. "Groupe d'Orsay" also has Catholic members. Founded in 1984, it sponsors a Feminist Theology Group which has published a number of reports and bulletins, including a report on its seventh colloquium in 1989. Its address is: Groupe d'Orsay, Maison du Protestantisme, 47 rue de Clichy, 75009 Paris.

30. AFERT, the French branch of "The European Association of Women for Theological Research," was founded in 1982 in Switzerland. The third colloquium of the European Association, "Images of God," was held in September 1989. For further information, contact Marie-Thérèse van Lunen Chenu through "Femmes et Hommes dans l'Eglise." See note 28 for address.

31. See *RIC Supplément,* No. 70–71, "Bibliographie Internationale" (Strasbourg-Cedex: CERDIC, 1982). CERDIC, Palais Universitaire, 9 Place de l'Université, 67084 Strasbourg-Cedex.

32. Established in 1986, the Center has more than one thousand index cards of authors and a catalogue of more than one hundred subjects. Each year Maude Dillard adds a supplement of about eight hundred titles—books, articles and documents—to the thematic bibliography. The Center provides loans, consultation, and photocopies upon request. See note 2 for address.

33. See "Femmes Religieuses" in the bulletin, *Femmes et Hommes dans l'Eglise*, Nos. 16, 17, 18, 1984. See note 28 for address.

34. See note 5.

35. On diocesan synods in France, see Monique Hebrard, *Révolution Tranquille Chez les Catholiques* (Centurion, 1989).

36. *Mulieris Dignitatem (On the Dignity of Women)*, August 15, 1988.

37. See Collectif, *Femmes dan La Société et dans l'Eglise* (Paris: Le Cerf, 1980).

38. "Femmes et hommes partenaires, un espoir pour notre temps," *Femmes et Hommes dans l'Eglise* (No. 23), 25–28. Also published in *La Croix* (July 3, 1985).

39. On October 21–22, 1989, ACGF sponsored a conference in Bourget entitled "L'énergie des femmes, une force du monde" ("The energy of women, a world force"). It was a festive occasion, attended by some ten thousand women. Clearly, the awareness of French women about their difficulties in society and especially in the church has greatly increased. However, ACGF's primary aim for the conference was to enable women to share their personal experiences more than to engage in analysis of the larger picture, perspectives and strategies.

40. Since 1970, the quarterly Bulletin of FHE has committed itself to making the situations, actions and publications of women in other churches and in other countries more widely known. The Bulletin has included the work of Elisabeth Gossman, Suzanne Tunc, Mary Hunt and even Olivette Genest. Numerous articles, especially those by Denise Peeters and Donna Singles, concern the U.S.

41. See note 19.

42. The basic work which addresses such gatherings is Elisabeth Schüssler Fiorenza, *In mémoire d'elle: Essai de reconstruction des origines chrétiennes selon la théologie féministe (In Memory of Her: A Feminist Theological Reconstruction of Christian Origins)* (Paris: Le Cerf, 1987). Also the international review, *Concilium*, as well as major works from Canada by Elisabeth Lacelle and Monique Dumais and the review *L'Autre Parable*, to name a few. Finally, a beautiful little book which has just been published in France by Suzanne Tunc, *Brève Histoire des Femmes Chrétiennes* (Paris: Le Cerf, 1989).

Marie-Thérèse van Lunen-Chenu was born in Chalon-sur-Saône, Bourgogne, and currently makes her home in Matour and Paris. In 1970 she was among the initiators of the international group Femmes et Hommes dans l'Eglise (Women and Men in the Church), in which she remains active. She devotes much time as well to work in the Forum Oecuménique des Femmes

Chrétiennes d'Europe (Ecumenical Forum of Christian Women in Europe), the Centre Femmes et Christianisme (Center for Women and Christianity) in Lyons, and the Association Européenne des Femmes pour la Recherche Théologique (European Association of Women for Theological Research). She also remains much involved in her own parish in a small village near Cluny. It is important to Marie-Thérèse, who is married and a mother, that her feminist commitment and study in society not be separated from her feminist commitment and study in the church.

5

New Catholic Women in Germany

Hedwig Meyer-Wilmes*

Since Catholic women know they will never get a job in the church, they feel free to do theology. In an ironic sense, bad working conditions create good feminist theology.

—A WOMAN THEOLOGIAN IN HEIDELBERG

For every woman who begins to stand up, it is one step closer to a new church.

—A YOUNG MOTHER IN BRÜHL

The Christian Women's Rights Movement and Feminist Theology in Germany

DOING RESEARCH about women and theology is somewhat like the discovery of America. One expects a minor landfall and discovers a whole continent. Beginning with a simple question about the position of women in church and theology, a whole movement has emerged both within and outside the churches, leading eventually to developments in feminist theology that can no longer be easily dismissed by the churches or by theologians. In the following essay, I will focus primarily on these developments in West Germany (FRG), with some specific references to what we know of similar developments in East Germany (GDR), which developments, since reunification, are now of greater significance to Germany as a whole.

* Translated by Winfried Schmidt

85

Faculty positions in German universities for women in feminist theology are presently limited to research grants and other short-term projects. Still, the presence of such women in the universities is motivating
more and more German women to study theology. In addition, education centers and institutes which sponsor programs in feminist theology
have increasing numbers of participants, and parish women's groups
involved in studying the Bible together are less and less acquiescent to
that old mandate which women have for so long been given, "Serve and
listen." And even as feminist theology is still largely ignored by Catholic
Church leaders, it is significant that the activities and publications of the
largest church-related women's organization, Katholische Frauenge-
meinschaft Deutschlands, KFD (Catholic Union of German Women),[1]
manifest an increasing interest in feminist theology as well as the courage
to represent the organization as a feminist Christian women's rights
movement.[2] KFD is critical of "patriarchal patterns of thought and behavior,"[3] and it emphasizes openness to feminist theology and to theological women's studies.[4]

Early Development

Feminist theology emerged as a movement in West Germany through
the efforts of women in educational centers, ecumenical conferences,
and women's rights groups, as well as women on the peripheries of their
parish communities. That is, it developed by and large outside of the
university, becoming visible in Germany in the late 1970s. This is not to
say that there was no interest in feminist theology before that time, or
that there were no feminist publications in theology. Even before the
Second Vatican Council, women like Gertrud Heinzelmann (b. 1914),
no longer content to remain silent, courageously demanded ordination
for women in the Catholic Church.[5] Agnes von Zahn-Harnack (1884–
1950), whom theologians usually know only as the editor of a bibliography of her father's works, was a co-founder of the Deutscher Akademi-
kerinnen Bund (The German Union of Women Academicians) and the
first chairwoman of the Bund Deutscher Frauenvereine (The Union of
German Women). She also published the first important works on the
history of the women's movement at the beginning of the twentieth
century.[6] Elizabeth Gnauck-Kuehne (1850–1917), a convert to Catholicism, was the first woman allowed to study at a German university[7] and
wrote about the relationship between women's religiosity and politics.

However, an explicit feminist theology, a theology of women for women, emerged in Germany only in the late 1970s, at a time when a woman no longer had to blaze the trail alone but could speak as the voice of a whole movement.

In order to understand feminist theology in Germany, one needs to be aware of the three environments which have been most conducive to its development. The first is the ecumenical movement, with its impressive tradition of appeals for the liberation of women. The second is the Catholic laity movement which emerged after the Second Vatican Council. And the third is the women's movement within the universities. Feminist theology in the German context is a reflection on the questions initially formulated within these three movements, though it now goes far beyond the early questions.

From Women's Movements to Feminist Theology

Since feminist theology emerged within all three of the movements mentioned above, there is no single history of its origins in Germany; feminist writers have found their inspiration in one or another of these settings. Authors emerging from the women's liberation movement name the New Women's Movement[8] as the primary source of feminist theology and praxis.[9] Those involved in the movement for women's ordination in the Catholic Church have documented their struggles in this regard both before and after Vatican II. For example, Gertrud Heinzelmann regards her application to the council regarding women's ordination on May 23, 1962 as the "beginning" of feminist theology.[10] And Protestant theologians like Gerda Scharffenorth note the long tradition of seeking women's liberation from a Christian perspective within the ecumenical movement.[11] In all three settings—the women's liberation movement, the women's ordination movement in the Catholic Church, and the ecumenical movement—women have worked for concrete gains within their own particular context.

The Ecumenical Movement

When one looks at the history of emerging feminist theology, one must immediately appreciate the importance of the Weltkirchenrat (World Council of Churches) for the presentation and development of feminist theology in West Germany. An impressive tradition of appeals for the liberation of women can be read in the documents of this organization. As early as 1948, a WCC conference in Amsterdam affirmed that the church as the body of Christ consists of men and women, each created as persons with their own rights and responsibilities,[12] and urged that this conviction be incorporated into church practice. The conference then established a commission to oversee the churches' response to this mandate. It was this same commission which in 1974 organized the Berlin Conference on Sexism, the results of which enriched a variety of church-related women's movements.

The revolutionary character of the Berlin Conference was especially manifest in the posture of the women there. They no longer saw themselves as "beggars" but as activists in a movement that involved the church and Christianity. They protested their lack of representation in decision-making and administrative bodies, the underpayment of women pastors, and the absence of women in theological faculties, and they characterized the resistance to their demands as sexist. Charges of sexism became even more public at the WCC's General Congregation in 1975, giving rise in 1978 to the first International Consultation of Christian Women in Brussels, where the women's issues were acknowledged and further developed. Significantly enough, the Brussels Consultation chose for its title: "In Search of a Feminist Theology." Its two main speakers were Catharina J.M. Halkes of Nijmegen and Elisabeth Moltmann-Wendel of Tübingen, who were to become the leading feminist theologians in German-speaking countries.

The second Consultation of Christian Women, which was held in Gwatt, Switzerland, was attended by women from very diverse backgrounds and fields of activity. It soon became clear that, while this diversity greatly enriched the Consultation, it also introduced the problem of different expectations from the different women. Women whose work was in parish communities were looking for inspiration to take back to their groups and for other women who were willing to take official positions. Theologians who taught at universities sought theological exchange with other competent women. And women whose interest was primarily religious were interested in finding new and more appropriate forms for the expression of their spirituality. It became clear in Gwatt that subsequent Consultations should be more specifically focused.

In 1980 the Ecumenical Forum for Christian Women was founded and was attended primarily by women who worked in the church or in church-related institutions.[13] Five years later, in 1985, a conference was held in Boldern to found the European Association of Women for Research in Theology.[14] The work of this conference was coordinated by Marga Buehring, Catharina J.M. Halkes, and Elisabeth Moltmann-Wendel. The first constitutional conference of the European Association of Women for Research in Theology met in Magliaso, Switzerland in 1986, the second was held in Helvoirt, The Netherlands, and the most recent met in Arnoldsheim, Germany. All of these conferences were co-sponsored and staff-supported by the Ecumenical Forum for Christian Women.

More important than what happened during these conferences was what happened before and after them: women, as women, engaged in ongoing cooperation and dialogue. For Christian feminists in Germany, the ecumenical context was for a long time the only quasi-institutional forum which provided financing and an opportunity for them to be heard. For Catholic women, the ecumenical context was a place where women's issues, which were routinely ignored or considered taboo in the Catholic Church, could be fully explored, not only as "women's issues," but as problems concerning the entire Catholic Church and therefore as challenges to the Catholic Church.

Although Vatican II and the First General Synod of the Bishops Conference in Germany[15] had given Catholic women some hope, the Catholic Church in Germany reacted very negatively to the thematization of women's questions, to the infiltration of feminist ideas, and to any autonomous forms of Catholic women's organizations.

Post-Conciliar Reform Movements in the Catholic Church

The Second Vatican Council did bear fruit in West Germany. The council's greater esteem for the role of the laity opened the eyes of many women with regard to sexism in the church. For example, it seemed strange to women, whose work in the church was often of a "diaconal" nature, that the restoration by the council of the ancient office of lay deacon was restricted to men.[16] Many women, among them the first generation of theologically qualified academicians, saw this exclusion of women from all offices in the Catholic Church as a deep insult to their sex. These women included theologians Ida Raming and Iris Mueller and the lawyer Gertrud Heinzelmann, who persisted in making "apartheid at the altar,"[17] the exclusion of women from ordination, the test case for structural change in the Catholic Church.[18]

Raming notes that, as compared with the U.S., only a few of Germany's women theologians have publicly committed themselves to the goal of women's ordination.[19] Reasons for this, Raming maintains, include German deficiencies in the religious training and formation of its Catholic people and in the simple lack of numbers of committed women.[20] I myself believe that one of the reasons for Germany's not having an explicit women's ordination movement is the financially and ideologically secure position of the Catholic Church, which has not had to face much competition in these regards. A second reason, I think, is the lack of positions in the church and in the universities for qualified women theologians. And a final reason for Germany's lack of movement for women's ordination, I would suggest, is the "bad manners" of us Germans by which we address such issues according to theological principles, but do not deal with them politically. Of course, it cannot be denied that the office of ordained priesthood has lost much of its attractiveness, and this is true not only among women. The crisis of the ordained ministry in Germany can be attributed, at least partially, to a shrinking interest in religion generally, and this includes both men and women.[21]

In Germany today, it is primarily due to the three women mentioned above that the question of women's ordination remains an issue for the church and for feminist discourse.[22] However, it seems important to me that we do not isolate the ordination question, but that we locate it within the entire spectrum of our goals. The exclusion of women from the Catholic priesthood is not only theologically unsupportable and ecumenically critical, but it is also a catastrophe for theological education in Germany, cementing the image of the priest as the norm for the university professor of theology. This image not only degrades lay men, but it doubly discriminates against women, both as lay and as women. The discrimination is also in conflict with the constitutional law of West Germany, which insists on equal treatment of the sexes. Oddly enough, however, that same law, according to a 1933 concordat between Germany and the Vatican, gives the church veto power over all appointments to Catholic theological faculties, even though German universities are supported by the state.[23]

The Women's Rights Movement in the Universities

Much of the articulation of feminist theology in Germany can be credited to the women's movements within the universities. These movements have primarily been struggles for the increased representation of women on all levels of these institutions.

Since 1976, women have been applying for faculty openings in a variety of secular disciplines, and women have been attempting to connect these disciplines with feminist curricula. The latter effort has been carried out primarily by women students, as there are relatively few women instructors in German universities. Independent seminars for women, organized by students, are often their only opportunities to read women authors and to discuss woman-specific topics. Beginning in 1983, similar efforts have been made in theology faculties, where an initial phase of campaigning for and legitimizing feminist studies has been followed by efforts to institutionalize teaching grants, research projects, and job descriptions that are woman-friendly.

While feminist research in theology seldom finds as much support as projects in other disciplines, this research is an important expression of women's self-understanding. In June 1982 a special research project on Women and Christianity was begun within the Institute for Ecumenical Research at the University of Tübingen.[24] This was followed, in July 1986, by the establishment of a research program in feminist theology in the Catholic theology faculty of the University of Münster.[25]

The continuing debate over the specific form which the institutionalization of women's studies and women's research should take dates back to the movement's early beginnings. Should women's teaching and research become incorporated into existing disciplines or should they constitute their own discipline? This debate between integration and autonomy involves different understandings of women's questions as such, different ideas regarding the modification of existing disciplines, and different concepts of teaching and research among the teachers and researchers themselves. There are presently three models which can be roughly sketched as to the structural location of feminist theology in

German universities. Model A sees feminist theology as one of the perspectives taught within a traditional discipline (for example, feminist ethics is included in a course in general ethics). In Model B, feminist theology is presented, as its own course, but under the aegis of a traditional discipline, as is done at the University of Kassel.[26] In Model C, feminist theology is an independent discipline in teaching and research, as is currently being discussed in Berlin, Frankfurt and Münster.

As compared with other countries such as The Netherlands and the U.S., German feminist theology has no clear interdisciplinary status; for example, feminist theology is not necessarily a "given" in women's studies. This does not mean, however, that there are no interdisciplinary centers for women's studies in Germany. On the contrary, this fourth, interdisciplinary model, D (women's studies), is not only favored in Germany because it fits the self-understanding of women's studies, but also because, from the perspective of university administrations, it is less costly; all disciplines can be satisfied with a single instructor in women's studies. The disadvantage of this model is that, because of competition among the disciplines regarding who teaches women's studies, it becomes difficult to hire a theologian as primary instructor; subjects such as sociology, pedagogy and psychology are commonly preferred as being more relevant to society. Inasmuch as I know about The Netherlands,[27] I would say that the interdisciplinary structure there is not only formal, but it also requires a shift with regard to content at the cost of theological discussion, though it does favor feminist discourse in general.

In summary, the women's movement in German universities has ensured that the last bulwark of the patriarchy, the Catholic theological faculty, has not been spared its dose of feminist theology. On the other hand, the successful institutionalization of feminist theology and an adequate presence of women in West German universities are goals which are yet to be realized. In 1980 the percentage of women in university faculties in West Germany was just twelve and a half percent; in Catholic theology faculties, one can count no percentage at all unless one includes the women assistants. We are left with the hope that the power of the women's movement in the universities does not weaken and that the public conscience continues to be raised until the facts of discrimination on university campuses are finally acknowledged as a scandal. As I have indicated earlier, feminist theology in Germany first emerged outside of the universities. This means, "thank the Goddess," that its presence is not limited to the campus.

Women's Networks

Besides the ecumenical movement, the post-conciliar lay movement in the Catholic Church, and the university, there are other avenues in Germany in which religiously interested and active Christian feminists can articulate their self-understanding and their struggle and can formulate their critique of the patriarchy. These are the workshops for feminist theology which, since 1979, have provided forums for the exchange of ideas, reflection and communication[28] as well as a number of networks and groups, which I shall now describe in the chronological order of their founding and differentiating between those in West and East Germany.

Networks in West Germany (FRG)

In 1981 Ida Raming, mentioned previously, and Knut Walf, a canon lawyer at the University of Nijmegen, published in *Publik Forum,* a magazine for critical Christians, a description of the miserable situation of Catholic faculties in Germany as regards women and appealed to these women to unite in solidarity with one another. In that same year, interested women met and founded an action group which they called Catholic Women Theologians. Some felt, however, that the title would suggest a bias toward academic work and ordained office which did not represent all the members of the group. Accordingly, they decided, in 1984, to change the name to Action Group—Feminism and the Churches. They see themselves as a "group of feminist, religious and theologically engaged women who work in the field of feminism, Christianity and the churches as part of the women's movements."[29] The group meets twice a year, at one of which meetings there is a specially selected theme. Regional sub-groups and committees take on specific projects. The group responds publicly to episcopal statements such as papal encyclicals, papal and episcopal letters, and synods, and actively participates in the traditional public church conferences (Katholikentag, Kirchentag).[30] Most of the members are theologians, students, and laity under forty years of age, a population which is the group's most significant characteristic. Its target group is broad, including Catholic laity, students, academicians, and teachers of religion.

Even broader than the Action Group—Feminism and the Churches with regard to representing women's activities is the Frauennetzwerk

Kirche (Women's Network in the Church). The Network began with a congress of Catholic pastoral theologians from German-speaking countries in Vienna, Austria in 1982. The topic of the congress, "The Self-Understanding of Women Today," drew women from a variety of church-related fields who, desiring to remain in contact with one another, founded, in 1984, the Women's Network. The Network wished to address itself to all women, not only to those who explicitly described themselves as feminists. They saw themselves as a kind of experimental church, not hierarchically organized, valuing personal experience, and committed to formulating images of church for themselves.[31] Significant in the Network is its strong interest in liberation theology, namely in realizing the unity of theory and praxis. To this day, the Network, which remains predominantly Catholic, is still faithfully committed to the pastoral ideal of its founders, engaging students, academicians, and many women in church-related works.[32]

The Protestant counterpart to the groups mentioned above is the Netzwerk Feministische Theologie (Network for Feminist Theology).[33] Among this Network's founders are women pastors such as Eva Renate Schmidt, scientists such as Luise Schottroff, feminist theologians such as Elisabeth Moltmann-Wendel, and academicians such as Herta Leistner and Leonore Siegele-Wenschkewitz. The spectrum of the Network's membership is equally broad. In addition to annual meetings, the Network provides a constant exchange of information through its newsletters.

Slender Threads Make Strong Bonds: Networks in East Germany (GDR)

One might be tempted to assume that feminist theology and a Christian woman's movement would not be found in East Germany. The assumption would be incorrect. Both were in existence well before the November 8, 1989, fall of the Berlin Wall. When the Wall fell, scores of previously underground groups and movements came out into the open. Who would have guessed that on February 2, 1990, just three months after the Wall, some fifty women's groups would appear and, never having worked together before, would quickly merge into an Unabhaengiger Frauenverband (Independent Women's Organization).

For years there had been a lively exchange between Protestant women's groups in East Germany and feminist theologians in West Germany. Since 1985 a number of women's workshops have taken place in East Germany; the Erfurter Kirchentag, an annual Protestant church conference in the GDR, sponsored a woman's forum for the first time, and Protestant academies offer courses and special events focusing on the "origins and trends of feminist theology."[34]

Though the Christian women's movement in East Germany has yet to achieve any significant power or influence in politics or religion, the secular women's movement there has a public profile which is quite different from those of similar movements in western Europe. One of the reasons for this difference is that many of the demands of the western movements with regard to social programs and the rights of workers and families are already a part of official state policy in East Germany. For example, women's right to work is guaranteed; 91.3 percent of all East German women are involved in work beyond homemaking. Childcare is recognized as a social responsibility and is provided by a multitude of state-supported child-care centers. Women in leadership positions in the society are not considered the exception. In other words, there has long been in East Germany a social situation that is based on the compatibility of family and employment responsibilities, and women have not had to choose between children and career, as is still largely the case in western Europe. The social contradictions are less severe for the East German woman than they are in the west.

At the same time there is still room for improvement in the situation of women in East Germany. For example, even if children-plus-career is a familiar combination for women and is taken for granted in the society, the husband is still regarded, indisputably, as the full-time professional of the family. In education, too, though fifty percent of all East German students are women, the percentage of women holding teaching positions is far lower. And the experience of women in West Germany's Protestant churches is much like that of their sisters in East Germany. Even East German women in leadership positions in the churches have less access than their male colleagues to influential roles in pastoral planning and to university positions in faculties of theology.

It is clear that contact with women's organizations from the "outside" have been critical for the development of a religious-feminist consciousness by women in the GDR. Not surprisingly, the idea to found an Action Group for Feminist Theology in East Germany came from the west.[35] After participating in a conference of the European Association of Women for Research in Theology, Angelika Engelmann was inspired to do something similar in the East. "Our dilemma as women in the GDR arises, by and large, from the fact that we survive primarily on 'imports' from the west with regard to feminist theology."[36]

The GDR's Action Group for Feminist Theology was founded in 1985 during the first workshop in feminist theology there. Today the Action Group publishes an annual newsletter, "Das Netz" ("The Net"). By the Action Group's third workshop, it became clear that the interests and needs of the participants were quite diverse. While some wished to engage in serious theological discourse, others were more concerned about sharing their relationship and job problems. Accordingly, the Action Group decided to sponsor a variety of feminist workshops within the larger framework of the "Women's Decade"[37] of the World Council of Churches. This decision of the Action Group to locate and to "ground" its various concerns, whether political, church-related, or ecumenical, within an established, organizational framework is, I believe, rather typical of women's groups in East Germany. Women in the west are more inclined to work outside of established "umbrella" organizations, and they see the looser structure that this gives them as more of an opportunity than a problem. In this regard, the foundation of an independent organization of women in the east is qualitatively different than it is in the west.

Critical Areas of Dialogue

For quite a while the feminist-theological discussion in West Germany was dominated by reflections on translations of the works of American women theologians. Mary Daly's book, *Beyond Father, Son & Co.* (in the U.S., *Beyond God the Father*),[38] quickly became a classic among women interested in religion. Equally popular were translations of works by Rosemary Radford Ruether and Elisabeth Schüssler Fiorenza. Enthusiastic reception was also given to all publications by the Dutch theologian, Catharina J.M. Halkes,[39] and to new feminist interpretations of the Bible.[40]

Two of the most important discussions in Germany have centered around the "femininity" of God and around the issue of anti-Judaism in the Christian churches. The concept of "God as female" is often explored from Jungian,[41] exegetical-critical, and anthropological[42] perspectives. It is also treated in relation to the concept of matriarchy[43] and in the context of other theological disciplines.[44]

In contrast to the American focus on the conflict between the traditional Christian God-image and the matriarchal Goddess,[45] German feminist theologians have been more concerned with the antisemitic tendencies of Christianity, which manifest themselves in such works as those of avid matriarchialist and journalist Gerda Weiler. Weiler's book, *Ich Verwerfe im Lande Die Kriege: Das Verborgene Matriarchat im Alten Testament (I Ban War: The Hidden Matriarchy in the Old Testament),*[46] gave rise to a heated controversy over the patriarchialism in the Hebrew scriptures and the resulting sexism in Christianity.[47] Further, Weiler's theory of the murder of the mother (i.e. of the matriarchal goddesses) by the God of the Levite[48] priests reminded theologians like Marie-Theresa Wacker of the reproach of Christians against Jews for having murdered the Son of God.[49] The ensuing debate around the anti-Judaism of certain feminist theologians became highly polemical and extremely difficult, quite different from the debate in The Netherlands over this same issue.[50] Of course, the issue of antisemitism in Germany is always connected with the Nazi/Fascist holocaust and is, therefore, a debate which not only confronts us, as Christians, with our Jewish heritage but confronts us, as Germans, with our political burden. Last but not least, the issue confronts us feminists with our inheritance of patriarchy.

This discussion threw a light on what I see as a significant characteristic of German feminist theology: we lack a clear and common forum for dissent among women themselves. Conflicts among feminist theologians and religiously interested women are usually aired—though not always solved—in the public arena. Or they assume the character of intrigues, which go on behind the backs of those concerned and are rarely dealt with face to face. It seems that we have not yet developed a healthy tradition of feminist discussion and debate among ourselves. And we are still too isolated with regard to other socially relevant fields which might encourage and facilitate our self-critique. However, with the increasing feminist self-awareness among Christian women in Germany, it is our hope that dispute among the sisters will be engaged in more fruitfully and less destructively in the years to come.

"The Dispute between the Sisters": A Feminist Reading of Luke 10:38–42

As the disciples of Jesus continued their journey, they became tired. They entered a city and stopped at a place where some women lived together.

Martha, the owner of the house and well-known for her engagement in the liberation of women, welcomed them, Jesus in particular. Martha had a sister, Mary, who sat in a corner of the living room reading a book. When she saw Jesus, Mary got up, sat next to him, and talked to him. But Martha hastened to serve the Lord and his disciples. She set up the table, brought food and drink, and showed Jesus the recent flyers and posters from her last actions. Mary, however, remained seated, listening and talking to Jesus. After a while, Martha went to Jesus and said: "Lord, don't you care that my sister leaves me to do all the work alone? She prefers to converse with you while we others have to hurry. She likes to read her books while we have work to do. Please tell her that she should help me." But the Lord answered: "Martha, Martha, you care for many things, but only a little of it is necessary—as long as you don't leave behind those who are yours."

We all have hands to distribute justly the goods of the world. We all have feet to walk toward each other, to overcome separation and diversity, and to build a true community of women. We have eyes to see the light face to face. We can all experience the power that this vision gives us to create that divine spark which will dispel the darkness. With our minds, we can know those things which hinder us in our lives. One thing, however, is necessary: to know the part which is given to each of us.

Notes

1. It had 750,000 members in 1989.

2. For example, during the Katholikentag in Berlin in 1990, the KFD, Catholic Union of German Women, insisted on the foundation of its own center for women.

3. See KFD, Orientation and Program, 1979, 7.

4. KFD, ed. Impulse '87. Zum Orientierungs und Arbeitsprogramm, 1979, 11.

5. Gertrud Heinzelmann, Wir schweigen nicht länger, Zurich, 1964.

6. Agnes von Zahn-Harnack, Die Frauenbewegung-Geschichte, Probleme, Ziele, Berlin, 1928.

7. Vgl. Elizabeth Moltmann-Wendel, Die Sozialpolitikerin Gnauck-Kuhne, in Hermann Häring, Karl-Josef Kuschel, eds., Gegenentwürfe. 24 Lebensläufe für eine andere Theologie, Munchen, 1988, 255–267.

8. "New Women's Movement" is used here to indicate the women's movements since the 1960's. "Old Women's Movement" indicates those between 1840 and 1930.

9. So z.B. Rita Burrichter/Claudia Lueg. Aufbrüche und Umbrüche. Zur Entwicklung Feministischer Theologie in unserem Kontext, in Christine Schaumberger/Monika Maaben, eds., Handbuch Feministische Theologie, Münster, 1986, 14.

10. Gertrud Heinzelmann, Die geheiligte Diskriminierung. Beiträge zum kirchlichen Feminismus, Bonstetten 1986, 90.

11. Gerda Scharffenorth/Klaus Thraede, Freunde in Christus werden. Die Beziehung von Mann und Frau als Frage an Theologie und Kirche (Kennzeichen 1), Gelnhausen-Berlin 1977, 19.

12. Vgl. Una Sancta 29. Jg. (1974) 230–243.

13. Kontaktadresse: Präsidentin des Ökumenischen Forums für Christliche Frauen, Jean Mayland, 3, Minster Court, York Yo 1 2 JJ - England.

14. Kontaktfrau der Europäischen Gesellschaft für theologische Forschung von Frauen ist in der BRD Marietheres Wacker, Vor Hahn 25, 6257 Hunfelden-Nauheim.

15. Vgl. dazu den Synodenbeschlub VII "Die pastoralen Dienste in der Gemeinde," in: Gemeinsame Synode der Bistümer in der Bundesrepublik Deutschland, Freiburg-Basel-Wien 1976, 612.

16. Anneliese Lissner, Frau und Kirche, in: Barbara Leckel (Hg.), Erneuert Euch in Eurem Denken. Anneliese Lissner, Standpunkte von 1973 bis 1989, Dusseldorf 1989, 148.

17. Vgl. Monika Kringels-Kemen, Wider die Apartheid am Altar, in: Norbert Sommer (Hg.), Nennt uns nicht Brüder, Stuttgart 1985, 221–228.

18. In 1973, Ida Raming published an historical-dogmatic investigation of the foundations of Canon 986/1, CJC: "The Exclusion of Women from the Ordained Priesthood," Köln, 1973.

19. Ida Raming, Frauenbewegung und Kirche, Weinheim 1989, 83.

20. A.a.O. 95.

21. Vgl. zur Frauenordinationsbewegung Hedwig Meyer-Wilmes, Rebellion auf der Grenze. Ortsbestimmung feministischer Theologie, Freiburg 1990, 25–38.

22. Since 1987, in the FRG, there is a group called "Maria of Magdala" which is an initiative for the equality of women in the Church. It was founded by I. Mueller and I. Raming. Contact: Gertrud Tacke, Möllerstr. 36, 4790 Lippstadt.

23. This veto right of the Church has become an unfortunate practice which can leave positions in Catholic faculties vacant for years. Rather than hiring a lay person, the risk is taken of losing such a position altogether.

24. Begun under Hans Küng, Bernadette Brooten and Doris Kaufmann. Contact: Dr. Anne Jensen, Institut für ökemenische Forschung, Nauklerstr. 37a, 7400 Tübengen.

25. Kontaktadresse: Lucia Scherzberg, Arbeitsstelle feministische Theologie an der Katholisch-theologischen Fakultät, Pferdegasse 3, 4400 Munster.

26. Since 1987, feminist theology has been taught here by Luise Schottroff, a Protestant professor of New Testament, and Helen Schuengel-Straumann, a Catholic professor of Old Testament.

27. Since 1986, together with another theologian who is a member of the interdisciplinary Center for Women's Studies, I have been an instructor for feminist theology in the theological faculty of the Catholic University at Nijmegen.

28. Vgl. zu den Werkstätten feministischer Theologie entsprechende Informationsartikel in: Schaumberger/Maassen, Handbuch 1986, 142–156.

29. Zit. nach Grundsatzpapier der AG Feminismus und Kirchen. Kontaktadresse: Conny Schinzilarz, Nienkamp 20, 4400 Munster.

30. These conferences include public presentations by Catholic and Protestant churches for three days every other year.

31. Schaumberger/Maassen, Handbuch 1986, 164.

32. Kontaktadresse: Resi Bokmeier, Jahnstr. 30, 7000 Stuttgart 70.

33. Kontaktadresse: Maria Dietrich, Werderstr. 43, 6900 Heidelberg.

34. Wie z.B. 1989 die Evangelische Akademie Sachsen-Anhalt; vgl. zur Situation feministischer Theologie und christlicher Frauenbewegung das Themenheft "DDR" der Zeitschrift "Schlangenbrut" H. 29 (1990), besonders 21–33.

35. Kontaktadresse: Angelika Engelmann, Münzmeisterstr. 40, 8020 Dresden.

36. Schlangenbrut (1990) 28.

37. A.a.0.32.

38. Mary Daly, Jenseits von Gott Vater Sohn & Co, München, 1980.

39. Catharina J. M. Halkes, Gott hat nicht nur starke Söhne, Gütersloh 1980 sowie "Suchend was verloren ging," Gütersloh 1985.

40. z.B. Karin Walter (Hg.) Frauen entdecken die Bibel, Freiburg 1986 sowie "Zwischen Ohnmacht und Befreiung," Freiburg 1988; Eva Renate Schmidt u.a. (Hg.), Feministische gelesen (Bd.lu.2), Stuttgart 1988–89.

41. Christa Mulack, Die Weiblichkeit Gottes, Stuttgart 1983.

42. Elizabeth Moltmann-Wendel (Hg.), Weiblichkeit in der Theologie Gutersloh 1988.

43. Elga Sorge, Religion und Frau, Stuttgart 1985.

44. Marie-Theres Wacker (Hg.), Der Gott der Männer und die Frauen, Düsseldorf 1987.

45. By contrast with America, there are no major new spirituality movement in Germany. There are, however, many German publications which make these movements known.

46. München 1984.

47. Leonore Siegele-Wenschkewitz (Hg.), Verdrängte Vergangenheit, die uns bedrängt, München 1988.

48. Weiler 1984, 104.

49. Wacker 1987, 23–28.

50. Fokkelien van Dijk-Hemmes, In een nieuw feministisch jasje, in: Mara 3. Jg. (1990) H.3, 19–24.

Hedwig Meyer-Wilmes attended the Westfälische Wilhelms Universität in Münster, where she specialized in German studies, pedagogics, and theology. For three years she served on the pastoral staff of a community in Bielefeld, and for another three years she was academic consultant for the Katholisch-ökumenische Institut in Münster. For the past four years, she has lectured in Feminist Theology and has directed the Feminism and Christianity program at the Katholieke Universiteit in Nijmegen. Meyer-Wilmes is thirty-six years old and is the mother of one child.

6

New Catholic Women in Ireland

Ann Breslin

Nobody is going to define me out of my church. I am Catholic. Defining myself as a Catholic woman—but really a Christian woman—I believe the tradition is transformable. I feel that now, but I don't know if I'll feel it five years from now.

—A LAY WOMAN THEOLOGIAN IN IRELAND

I believe we are in the age of the Spirit. All the signs are there.

—A WOMAN RELIGIOUS IN DUBLIN

One of the most important challenges facing the church today is to develop a truly Christian feminism.

—IRISH BISHOPS' PASTORAL

THE LAST QUOTATION is taken from the Irish bishops' 1985 Lenten pastoral "Love Is for Life." The sentiment expressed would seem to augur well for the centrality of feminist issues in the deliberations and agenda of the Irish hierarchy, yet in the experience of many Irish women these words have yet to reach the fulfillment of their potential.

When we consider the question of Catholic feminists in Ireland, we are faced with the reality that few women's groups bear any denominational label, even though many of their members are Catholic. What is common to most, however, is the Catholic background which they share, the predominantly Catholic environment in which they live, and their struggle to challenge issues of inequality and injustice in a patriarchal society.

In order to understand the variations within the women's movement in Ireland, it will be useful to consider the different degrees of church affiliation found in the population at large. Of the Irish Republic population of three million, ninety-five percent are Roman Catholic, while the remaining five percent are Church of Ireland, Presbyterian, Methodist, Jewish and others.

Two further characteristics are relevant. The population of Ireland is the youngest in Europe, with fifty percent under age twenty-five.[1] In the capital, Dublin, fifty percent of the population are under twenty-one. In addition, a wave of urbanization has denuded rural areas, and has contributed to the growth of the one million people (a third of the population) who now live in Dublin. According to Jenny Beale:

> Rural life has all but disappeared, to be replaced by an urbanised culture, and a class structure more akin to that in other Western countries. Many aspects of these social and economic changes are reflected in women's lives. . . . The old and the new frequently rub shoulders, and there is tension between them.[2]

Indeed, the country has altered more in the last fifteen years than it did during the whole of the previous half-century.[3]

Church Affiliation and Church Practice

A National Survey, carried out for the Catholic bishops in 1984, showed that ninety-three percent of women (and eighty-four percent of men) agreed that membership in the Catholic Church was important to them. The most recent census data available (1981) show that, within the last ten years, a growing number of Irish people classify themselves as of "No religious affiliation": 8,000 in 1971, but five times that number, 40,000 ten years later.[4]

While it is possible to quantify church membership, it is difficult to assess the level of individuals' religious practice. However, "frequency of church attendance" has become an international yardstick by which to compare the practice rate from one country to another. Mass attendance in Ireland, with a national average of eighty-seven percent attending mass weekly or more often, is the highest in Europe.[5] It may, however, be queried whether this stability will persist in view of three relatively new phenomena to confront Irish society.

The first of these is emigration, by which between 35,000 and 70,000 Irish citizens leave the country annually. The majority of these are in the 18–30 age group. The 1984 national survey showed that, when Irish people emigrate, their level of mass attendance may be considerably eroded and their church affiliation diminished. The second factor is the anticipated incorporation of Ireland into a single European economic entity in 1992. Such a cultural transformation may be expected to have some effect on the traditional Irish religious values already alluded to: a strong level of church affiliation, a high level of weekly mass attendance, and a declared apprecia- tion of the importance of Catholic Church membership.

A third factor to be considered is the change in women's attitudes toward the Catholic Church's prohibition of divorce, pre-marital sex, contraception and abortion. The 1984 National Survey showed that some women's attitudes had, over the previous ten years, shifted away from strict adherence to the official church position. For example, whereas in the early 1970s thirty-eight percent of women were in favor of divorce, the percentage had grown to forty-seven percent in 1984. However, among women between the ages of 31–50 (a time of life when the issue of divorce might be most relevant) the percentage was fifty-nine percent "in favor."

The 1984 National Survey also showed an increase in the numbers of women who, when asked about the morality of pre-marital sex, abortion and contraception, chose the response "It depends on circumstances" rather than an expression of total disapproval. The increases were, in regard to "pre-marital sex": from seventeen percent in 1974 to thirty- nine percent ten years later; in regard to abortion: from nineteen percent to twenty-seven percent; in regard to the use of contraceptives: fifty-two percent "It depends on circumstances" (1984 figure only). As might be expected, the percentages opting for "It depends on circumstances" were higher in the younger age groups. These shifts appear to indicate a diminished support of orthodox a priori judgments, and a readiness to take into account some relevant and perhaps extenuating circumstances.

In view of the overall strength of Catholicism in Ireland, it may not be surprising to learn that the Irish Constitution and legal system reflect the ideology of the majority Roman Catholic Church. For example, divorce and abortion are entirely illegal, while the sale of contraceptives was legalized only in 1986. Although there was a strong women's lobby to support the legalization of divorce, and to have abortion permitted under certain circumstances, the views of the Roman Catholic hierarchy were widely publicized through sermons and pastorals. Eventually, on both issues (divorce and abortion), the Catholic position was upheld in national referenda, irrespective of the views of several substantial groups, including some of the minority churches.

The Story of Women in Ireland

In any account of feminism in Ireland, it is useful to refer to the oral narratives of women in Irish folklore, women who were presented as goddesses, queens, wise-women, poetesses, warriors and witches. These legends, important in the childhood socialization of Irish women, give us a glimpse of a society where women as well as men were students of the scriptures, and where the ancient Gaelic Brehon laws were relatively protective of women's rights. Only later, with the wisdom of adulthood, did we realize that even Celtic society had in many ways been heavily patriarchal, and that education and creativity had been the privilege of only a minority of women, usually those of royal lineage.[6]

During more than seven centuries of Ireland's occupation by invading powers, which ended only in 1921, the status of women was greatly diminished. English Common Law deprived women of political and property rights, and defined their role as subsidiary to that of males.[7]

However, toward the end of the nineteenth century, three great movements began to grow in strength, each with its women supporters, many of whom were working for all three causes: the Nationalist Movement, the Suffragist Movement, and the Labour Campaign.[8] In 1909 Countess Markievicz, heroine of the struggle for political independence, advised nationalists, "Fix your minds on the ideal of Ireland free, with her women enjoying the full rights of citizenship in their own nation."[9] Like the countess, many women were actively engaged in the 1916 Rebellion, which spearheaded the end of colonial power in Ireland.

However, once Ireland had gained independence, women did not retain the potential for political leadership which had seemed so promising in the years preceding the Rebellion. Dr. Margaret MacCurtain, feminist and historian, expresses the paradox:

> Irish women possessed the freedom to vote, the right to hold office—
> even to become cabinet ministers, as Markievicz demonstrated—the ex-
> pertise to set up and manage their own trade unions. . . . In many respects

it was a spectacular victory, but the paradox remains to be explained: Irish women were free in the areas they had struggled for. Why, then, were they content to remain subordinate in a society they had helped to create?[10]

The return of women to a state of subordination in a post-revolutionary era is not unique to the Irish situation. It has been noted in different countries which have engaged in and won a struggle for liberation and independence. Although women played an active part in the military operations and decision-making councils, after independence, "normality" returned, and with it the previous role distinctions between women and men.[11]

In a free Ireland, women's subordinate role was legitimized by the 1937 Constitution, which endorsed a patriarchal system of laws and culture, and which was closely allied to the ideals of the Catholic Church. Article 41 of the 1937 Constitution reads:

The State recognises that, by her life within the home, woman gives to the State a support without which the common good cannot be achieved. The state shall, therefore, endeavour to ensure that mothers shall not be obliged to engage in labour to the neglect of their duties in the home.[12]

This Article promoted the idea of the family as the foundation unit of the state, a view that coincided with Catholic social teaching, where "complementarity" implied that women were, by nature, best suited for a mothering role, to be carried out in the home, while the "real" business of the common good (legislation, government, financial management, to name a few) was the complementary duties of men. It will be noted that, in the above Article, the terms "woman" and "mother" are used interchangeably.

The sentiments expressed by a bishop of Clonfert were typical of the combined church and state position: "By nature and divine right, the father of the family is bound to maintain his home for himself, his wife and his family."[13]

In 1891, Pope Leo XIII wrote in *Rerum Novarum*:

Women are not suited for certain occupations; a woman is by nature fitted for home work, and it is that which is best adapted at once to preserve her modesty and to produce the good bringing up of children and the well-being of the family.[14]

And, over fifty years later, Pius XII stated that ". . . a true woman cannot see and fully understand all the problems of human life otherwise than under the family aspect."[15]

The sex-role stereotypes implied in such words were to have a profound effect on Catholic social teaching, particularly in the area of family life. Mary Cullen indicates the inherent constraints on women:

> The problem feminism sees with the stereotype is that it is based on a narrow, functionalist definition of woman's nature. Women as a group are assigned a strictly defined and limited role in society: that of wife and mother full-time in the home. Being a wife and mother is expanded into a vocation that should occupy a woman's time and energy to the exclusion of serious commitment to the development of other talents, or to other forms of contribution to society.[16]

The Role of Education

It was not only popes and bishops who expressed patriarchal viewpoints in the nineteenth century; such viewpoints were part of the prevailing outlook of the Victorian era. However, what made them particularly powerful and enduring in Ireland was the strong influence of the Catholic Church, particularly in the educational system.

As early as the 1770s, Nano Nagle, foundress of the Presentation Sisters, was active in Cork, providing education and social welfare for the poor. During the early nineteenth century, several other Irish religious orders were founded, and together they formed the nucleus of what was to provide a successful and influential system of education for Irish girls. It was, however, an education which was mainly intended to prepare them for their home-making role.

Dr. Tony Fahey writes:

> As champions of Catholicism, nuns entered into some conflict with anti-Catholic or simply non-Catholic social forces, but as disseminators of a particular form of social and personal discipline and manners, and as

champions of a particular form of femininity and women's place in society, they were very much in tune with the trends of their times.[17]

By the beginning of the twentieth century, however, under pressure of the ambitious middle classes, a system of career-oriented education for girls gradually began to emerge. Girls were prepared to compete with boys in the public service examinations, and to obtain civil service positions (even if for somewhat less remuneration than what males received).[18]

An inherent irony in this educational system was highlighted by Professor Joseph Lee:

> ...at a moment when educational opportunities increased for Irish women, the educational system began to be used to indoctrinate them into adopting as self-image the prevailing male image of women. . . . Dutiful women teachers, including many dedicated nuns, taught girls obedience, docility and resignation to the role assigned to them by a male providence.[19]

The influence of the church in education was endorsed by the government, as indicated by General Mulcahy, Minister for Education for almost ten years (1948–51 and 1954–57):

> The State accepts that the foundation and crown of youth's entire training is religion. It is the desire that its teachers, syllabuses and textbooks in every branch be informed by the spirit underlying this concept of education, and it is determined to see that such facilities as ecclesiastical authorities consider proper be provided in the school for the carrying on of the work of religious education.[20]

In 1967 a system of free secondary education was introduced, and, as a result, the number of adolescents attending second-level schools increased from one in four in 1964 to one in two in 1979. Despite the possibilities offered by the revised curriculum to teachers of girls to break the old sex-stereotyped choice of examination subjects, the patterns of a century were difficult to dismantle. A 1983 report, "Schooling and Sex Roles," stated:

> The extent of sex-differentiation is deeply institutionalised in the ideologi-

cal and cultural assumptions underlying the educational system. There are generally accepted assumptions as to what is considered to be appropriate to girls and boys on the basis of sex-stereotyped perceptions.[21]

However, within the last decade, there have been some signs of change, both in choice of subjects and in girls' high levels of achievement in what were traditionally boys' domains. One example is evident annually at the National Young Scientists' Exhibition, where girls' achievements equal and often surpass those of boys.

To those who are familiar with a dual system of education, organized along religious denominational lines, it must be pointed out that in Ireland there is no Catholic school system such as is known in the United States or in Australia. The government Department of Education pays salaries for qualified teachers in all schools, gives grants for capital and current expenditures and sets examinations which are taken by pupils in all schools throughout the Republic. However, because of the ninety-five percent Catholic identity of the population, and because the majority of educators in the nineteenth century were religious women and men, the Catholic Church influence is still strong in maintaining its ethos within the schools. Of the 3,500 elementary schools, 3,400 are under Catholic management, even though the majority of principals and teachers are lay people. Of the approximately six hundred post-primary schools in the Republic, five hundred are Catholic, and are managed by religious orders or dioceses. Until the 1950s these post-primary schools were almost entirely single-sex institutions, in keeping with the recommendations of the hierarchy:

> Apart altogether from moral considerations, we believe that the mixing of boys and girls in the same school is injurious to the delicacy of feeling, reserve and modesty of demeanour which should characterise young girls.[22]

The Modern Women's Movement in Ireland

The modern women's movement in Ireland dates from the early 1970s. Initially it grew from meetings of a small group of women who were concerned that, on issues of human rights, particularly in matters related to their sexuality, the position of women in the Republic compared very unfavorably with that of women in Europe. "Contraception was illegal, divorce was banned in the Constitution and abortion was a criminal act."[23]

In 1971 the first manifesto of the women's movement was published. This document, "Chains or Change," listed six demands: the removal of the marriage bar to employment, equal pay, equality before the law, equal education, the right to practice birth control other than by "natural means," and justice for deserted wives, unmarried mothers and widows. Of these demands, the call for contraceptives drew most attention, and the Catholic bishops and clergy pursued a campaign to oppose it.

This confrontation seemed to set a pattern which many were to follow. Interested churchmen would scrutinize women's demands for various rights under the law, but, despite the fact that women's demands were for justice and equality, the attention of churchmen was usually drawn to issues in the area of sexuality, and then usually in opposition to the current campaign for various aspects of human rights.

In 1970 the Irish government, in keeping with United Nations policy, established a Commission for the Status of Women. The Commission's first report, presented to the government in 1971, dealt mainly with women in employment, equal pay, and women and social welfare.[24] It is of interest to note that the Report on the Status of Women never once mentioned the words "religion" or "religious." The omission may have been prophetic in that many future feminist groups, seeking justice for women in Irish society, rarely considered it practical to turn to the churches for support. Indeed, women's access to social, political and economic equality, limited though it may be, has been achieved in the absence of campaigns organized or supported by the churches.

Since the early 1970s the women's movement has experienced "moments of high and low energy," as Ailbhe Smyth describes it.[25] "The Women's Movement is a creature of ebb and flow—a chameleon."[26]

Women's Groups

During this "ebb and flow," although no monolithic women's movement emerged, there developed a network of feminist groups, "some radical, and others reformist, some consciousness-raising and others actively campaigning," but with the general aim of liberating women and society from the tyranny of patriarchy and sexism.[27] As already indicated, many groups are not church-related, but form part of the network of women who are seeking to promote various conditions of women's equality in society.

Some groups, such as the Women's Political Association (WPA), have been successful in impressing on politicians the importance of the women's vote, and therefore in having women's issues raised in the government. Through the lobbying of the WPA, and of the Council for the Status of Women, the number of women government deputies had grown to an unprecedented fourteen in 1982, from only three just fifteen years earlier. In 1982, also, a new Ministry for Women's Affairs was created, headed by a Minister of State; however, this Ministry was not maintained by a subsequent government. An important Working Party on Women's Affairs and Family Law Reform continues to cooperate on an inter-party basis toward achieving rights for women in issues of housing, employment and protection of family rights.

There are several groups with a specific interest in assisting the marginalized in society, those caught in the poverty trap, victims of various kinds of abuse (battered wives, rape victims), and discrimination (single parents, travelers).[28] Several much-needed Rape Crisis Centers, with a twenty-four hour answering service, are staffed mainly by women volunteers who have undergone rigorous training, and who carry out a stressful mission to victimized callers.

One prominent group with an education agenda is the WSAI (Women's Studies Association of Ireland), with headquarters in Dublin and branches throughout the provinces. Each branch aims to provide a forum where women can share and acquire information in the general area of women's studies.[29] Two important parts of their program for action is a policy to eliminate sexism from school textbooks and curricula, and the setting up of women's studies as an academic discipline in universities.

Related special interest groups provide daytime education for women who are working in the home, but who can be free for a few hours to further their education. Many of these women come from disadvantaged backgrounds, and have had their education interrupted for various reasons. They are now given another chance to complete their second-level education or to follow other courses in personal development, such as creative writing, assertiveness training, drama, management skills and many others. In addition, some of these courses are focused on women's relationships with their churches. Dr. Margaret MacCurtain describes the women's reactions:

They announce simply and movingly what they want from their churches. Their laundry list runs all the way from resentment at the overpowering maleness of official ministry in the church to a request to be included in the decision-making processes of their local parish organisations.[30]

Religious Orders

In the context of this network of women's groups, one might ask where stand the very numerous members of female religious orders. Since the mid-nineteenth century, the increase in their strength had been remarkable: a growth from fifteen hundred in 1850 to over thirteen thousand a hundred years later.[31]

Although the number of vocations began to decline in the mid-1970s, nevertheless the number of sisters currently in Ireland represents fifty-three percent of the total number of "church personnel" (priests, sisters and brothers).[32] One might expect that these women would be a potentially powerful lobby for women's rights in general, and also for a more meaningful involvement in the church. However, despite the independence and vision of many of their foundresses, religious orders of women have largely been dominated by patriarchal influences.

Thus, patriarchal structure and their separation from lay women, as laid down by their rule, contributed to sisters' isolation from the stirrings of the women's movement in the 1970s. Even in the 1980s, although the total number of sisters is large, it must be noted that almost fifty percent of this number are over sixty years of age, while only one-sixth are under age forty. As the 1984 National Survey showed, conservative attitudes tend to cluster in the older age groups, and thus relatively few sisters over sixty would be likely to take an active role in promoting the aims of the feminist movement.

A Renewal of Religious Orders

However, even if few women religious became part of the mainstream feminist movement in the 1970s, sisters gradually became aware of the social justice issues involved. One might say that the growth had been initiated by the document *Perfectae Caritatis,* in which Vatican II invited religious orders to begin a process of renewal of religious life. In the search for a return to their founding charism, many sisters responded to a call to solidarity with the poor, both in Ireland and abroad. With this renewal of mission came a new critique of the causes of oppression in Irish society, and an identification of just who the "oppressed" were. Most of the oppressed were poor, most were women, and, even if many women were not materially poor, it was clear that most women had been oppressed by the structures of a patriarchal society, including its educational system. Many sisters also began to recognize the dualism inherent in their orders' rules which had kept them apart from other lay women.[33]

The pace of renewal of Irish sisters' orders in the 1970s may have been slower than in many other countries, due, perhaps, according to Jenny Beale, to a deference to clerical authority. She contrasts the Irish sisters' silence with the political activities and lobbying of sisters in the United States.[34] Dr. Donal Flanagan described sisters in Ireland as a "remarkably silent body."[35]

Gradually, however, in the 1980s, their voices began to be heard. One women religious wrote in the *Religious Life Review*:

> It is a sorry fact that clergy and laity look with mistrust and scepticism upon women religious as they begin to move into roles and opportunities that until recently have been reserved for ordained men.[36]

Parish Teams

For approximately ten years, sisters have been engaged as members of parish teams. Such an innovation was heavily endorsed by the respondents to the 1984 National Survey, with seventy-five percent agreeing that sisters should form part of such teams. Approximately one hundred sisters are trained for and are engaged full-time in this work, but there is no overall plan for a work contract or for remuneration. The matter is considered to be urgently in need of clarification, and is at present being monitored by the Association of Parish Sisters.

At the 1988 Annual General Meeting of this Association, opinions expressed by the members reflected various positions, from the impatient, to the fearful, to the prophetic:

> Adopting the parochial system, and accommodating to the wishes of clergy, has caused frustration, and even alienation, to many sisters. . . .

The very thought of criticising a parish structure, or confronting the parochial system, is something many sisters feel they just cannot do. . . .

As an Association, however, we feel that our challenges are: the need to
explore new and creative ways to dialogue with parish clergy and with the
rank and file of our Churches who often hanker for a return to the good
old days. . . .[37]

Finally, another innovation that promises to be influential for women
religious is the appointment of sister chaplains to second-level schools,
where they receive a professional salary from the Department of
Education.

Study of Theology

In the years since Vatican II, sisters and lay women began to study
theology, and many obtained post-graduate degrees and doctorates in
this subject. The Pontifical University at Maynooth, affiliated with the
Colleges of the National University of Ireland, offers a joint degree in
Arts and Theology (B.A. Theol.), which is a popular combination for
undergraduates.

However, despite the bishops' emphasis on the importance of developing a Christian feminism, it is significant that, except for "occasional
lecturers," no woman theologian has a teaching post on the faculty of
any of the diocesan seminaries in which future priests are being prepared
for their ministry to women as well as to men. Women theologians have,
however, been given teaching posts in institutes which are not under
diocesan trusteeship.

In an open letter to the Irish bishops, Eleanor Cunny comments:

It is an interesting fact that, as Leonard Doohan informs us in *The Lay
Centered Church*, there are now more theologically trained laity than are
priests in the world. Why is it then that, in Ireland at any rate, we find our
career prospects limited, our status within the church low, and our function undefined?[38]

As Dr. Margaret MacCurtain expressed it: "The Catholic Church in
Ireland, as in Rome, persists in retaining a male official teaching voice."[39]

Feminist Spirituality

Over the last decade a great deal of interest has been shown in various aspects of feminist spirituality. Much of this interest was generated on certain key occasions, such as workshops or seminars by prominent overseas feminists. Among these very influential theologians were Anne Carr, Madonna Kolbenschlag, Rosemary Radford Ruether and Mary Daly. Such was the enthusiasm sparked by these encounters that many Irish women, determined not to let the message die, organized various feminist spirituality groups throughout the country.

Parallel to the interest generated by these overseas women was the influence of a number of Irish women who organized numerous seminars and workshops on feminist theology and feminist spirituality. Prominent among these women are theologians Mary Condren, Ann Louise Gilligan, and "resident American" Katherine Zappone. Dr. Condren's most recent book is *The Serpent and the Goddess: Women's Religion and Power in Celtic Ireland,* which Rosemary Radford Ruether called "a powerful indictment of patriarchal consciousness."[40]

At the request of various religious orders, Drs. Zappone and Gilligan have organized weekend seminars for sisters and their lay colleagues in ministry, thus establishing a network of women religious with a heightened awareness of feminist issues. Katherine Zappone and Ann Louise Gilligan have also opened a Center for Feminist Spirituality, where groups of women, some from disadvantaged backgrounds, have opportunities to engage in meditation, sharing and personal development, and where many can experience healing through caring and bonding.

Gradually some fifty to sixty small groups of women have been formed throughout the country, with the broad aim of developing a feminist spirituality of bonding and connectedness, free from the hierarchical structures and thought-patterns of patriarchal devotional practices. Among the groups are:

The Cork Feminist Spirituality Group. "It aims to challenge the truth of traditional patriarchal beliefs and structures; to deepen and integrate women's experience of spirituality in their own lives; to create positive alternatives and to make connections with similar groups."[41]

The Sophia Group in Dublin describes itself as "a Christian feminist group who meet monthly to share with and listen to each other's experience on the journey towards wholeness." This is done through the selection of a book to be read in private, and later reflected upon by the group. Their vision is one in which women participate in the leadership and decision-making roles of the church. The Sophia Group has also organized two successful conferences for "men within the Churches who are aware of the urgent need to promote gospel based feminist values."[42]

Women for Change is "an ecumenical, feminist, study and discussion/support group. Some issues already reflected on include: restrictions on women's spirituality; the effect of exclusivist language upon our image of God and ourselves; the ordination of women."[43]

Almost all of the women's spirituality groups throughout the country are ecumenical, and many of their members are not affiliated with any church. However, there are some specifically Catholic groups.

One is *The Catholic Women's Federation*. "Its membership is open to Past Pupils of Unions of Catholic Girls' Schools, other organisations of Catholic women and individual Catholic women. It does not engage in party politics, but has the following aims and objectives: continuing education of its members by promotion of social action, with special reference to the family; encouragement of members to participate in community services; collaboration with other women's organisations at home and abroad on matters of mutual interest."[44]

Another Catholic group is *Sisters for Justice,* which is "open to sisters from all religious congregations who share a commitment to empowering the poor to take control of their own lives and to bringing about a more just society, based on Gospel values."[45]

Although most of these groups follow their own specific agenda, nevertheless certain key occasions have been organized where the cooperative energy of all have found a common focus. Such was the International Women's Congress held in Dublin in 1987, organized by Irish feminists, and attended by approximately twelve hundred women from fifty countries.

Following up on the International Congress, a group of women came together to focus specifically on Christian feminism, and later sponsored a one-day seminar on the exploration of related issues. The group is designedly ecumenical in orientation, but has as its background the challenge of Christianity to liberate all, especially women, from oppression and injustice. Since this first meeting in Dublin, associated groups are meeting throughout the country, and further Christian feminist conferences are planned.

The publication of the feminist journal *Womanspirit* has also been a landmark in the networking of women's spirituality groups. An editorial indicates its policy:

"Womanspirit" is a country-wide resource to facilitate groups and individuals interested in Feminist Spirituality in its most inclusive and holistic sense. That means that while it is Christian in its origin and primary orientation, "Womanspirit" wishes to promote and nurture a creative and mutually enriching dialogue between women of all traditions and spiritual journeys. . . .[46]

Church-Related Issues

Although certain church-related issues, such as the ordination of women or women's participation in church affairs, may be part of the ongoing dialogue within some of these groups, it is significant that no Catholic women's group has yet been formed with the specific aim of campaigning for the ordination of women. The 1984 National Survey results showed the unwillingness of sixty-two percent of Irish women to support women's ordination; thus there appears to be no grass roots groundswell to keep the issue alive. It is, however, of interest that some Catholic women have joined the ecumenical pro-ordination group, "Women and Churches." At their meetings in Corrymeela Reconciliation Center in Northern Ireland, Catholic women reflect on the ordination issue together with their sisters in the Anglican, Lutheran and other churches.

The question of women's ordination is frequently debated, related articles are written, lectures delivered, and media programs produced. In most of these the Catholic Church prohibition is usually explained, often questioned and frequently deplored. Christina Murphy, *Irish Times* columnist, expressed the frustration often heard among women who debate the issue:

I frankly admit to total bafflement by the stance of the Catholic Church —and some Anglican clergy—on the question of admitting women to the priesthood. . . . What great threat to the Church can a bunch of well-intentioned, pious and committed women present? Apart, that is, from the threat to the supremacy of the all-male caste now running the Church?[47]

In view of the apparent total blocking of the issue on the part of church leaders, many Catholic feminists are of the opinion that, instead of channeling energy into the issue of ordination, women ought to concentrate their efforts on the struggle to achieve more influence, freedom and participation within the institutional church. A resolution of the Sophia Group states: "It is doubtful if, at this stage, the Group should devote itself to the question of the ordination of women, beyond making a critique of the 1976 Vatican document."[48]

In addition, many women who may disapprove of the current prohibition on the ordination of women would not want to become priests under a patriarchal regime. They would prefer to aim at changing the structures of such a regime in order to make it more sensitive to the needs and aspirations of women.[49]

Even as many women follow their own agenda in doing feminist theology, women's issues are often part of the wider question of lay participation in the church. Some months before the 1987 Synod on the Laity in Rome, a seminar was organized by a group of about fifty Irish lay people, women and men, several of whom were prominent in the media and in public life, to discuss and make public their views on the role of the laity. The event became known as the Pobal (People's) Conference.

During the seminar, a provocative observation was made by one of the participants and was recorded by Kevin O'Kelly in his article, "Fifty Voices":

> It was found possible to make better biblical sense of one aspect of the day's business by turning the debate about clerical domination on its head. Did it really make sense to talk of lay men and women wanting to be included in a clerically dominant church? What we should be trying to do was to include the clergy in what is basically a lay church! Again, a glance around any Sunday congregation would show that it would be more sensible for men to ask to be included in a church made up predominantly of women.[50]

Another article in this Pobal book was entitled, "Women: Part of the Laity." The author, Dr. Margaret MacCurtain, expressed, with appropriate irony, her satisfaction that women have, after centuries, finally "made it" to the ranks of the laity!

The eighties are a plateau stage for women. In the first century, the term "lay person" was the husband of one wife. In the second and third centuries, the term was reserved for the payer of tithes to the Bishop, but the new Canon Law (1983) grants woman a status in her own right.[51]

Different Drums, Different Voices

In Ireland, as elsewhere, individual feminists respond differently to the church in which they were brought up. Mary Cullen describes four modes of women's response to the patriarchal church:

> Some see [the Church] as unequivocally hostile, bent on controlling women's lives and women's bodies in the interests of male domination. . . . Others see it as so permeated by patriarchal thinking that it is useless and counterproductive for women to seek their personal human authenticity in affiliation with the Church. Other feminists believe that, because the Church is still so powerful a force in many women's lives, to ignore it is to betray those women, and that the effort must be made to confront Church authority and teaching structures with feminist analysis. Yet others believe that the Christian tradition in the Gospel records of the life of Jesus does contain the basic elements of a feminist theology as it has developed over the centuries.[52]

The three Irish women quoted below speak with different voices about their experience of the patriarchal church.

Pamilla Kelleher asks:

> How do you leave a Church? And where do you go? Can you have a spirituality integrated into your life without belonging to an institution? For me, my spirituality has to do with my happiness, immortality, my knowledge about myself and the world, my sense of meaning and justice. But as the Church was structured there was no place for me, and I had stepped out of nothing, and found that the Church was fossilized in ritual and moribund in its message.[53]

Another woman, Ursula Coleman, lecturer and writer, tells how she remains within the Church, but at a price:

> There are Irish women and some men who are Christian feminists, and I

number myself among them. For many women who are committed to renewal of and participation in the Church, it is a matter of endurance. Despite belonging to a Church which is such an obviously patriarchal establishment, which has exalted the position and rights of men, thereby depriving women of their right to articulate their experience and to partici- pate in leadership; despite the distortion and imbalance that have oc- curred over the centuries, we believe that the mission of Jesus of Nazareth was to proclaim the mission of liberation for all. Such liberation cannot become reality until those who have become accustomed to status are prepared to renounce their privileges for the sake of equality for all.[54]

Dr. Máire Ni Annracháin, an Irish scholar and university lecturer, questions the commitment of the church to integrate women into signifi- cant areas of its life:

When you ask me to what extent I think the women's movement presents a challenge to the Church, I have to query whether the clergy perceive a challenge there at all; whether they take seriously the need for the femini- sation of spirituality and of various forms of ministry.[55]

Yet another voice was heard in the Sophia Group's response to the Irish bishops' pastoral, "Love Is for Life." The pastoral states:

A Christian feminism will share many of the values and struggles of the world-wide feminist movement, but it will judge them by the standards of the Gospel, and will reject what is contrary to the Gospel.

The Sophia Group, having acknowledged the "reasonableness of this position," went on:

But the reverse side is that the Christian Feminist movement is asking the official Church to reject what is contrary to the Gospel in its own attitude to women. There is a great reluctance on the part of the official Church to admit that there is anything in its attitude to women which is contrary to the Gospel. If the Group could find some way of overcoming that reluc- tance, it would have made a major contribution to the cause of "Christian Feminism."[56]

The "reluctance" seems to be a euphemism for what appears to be a long-standing patriarchal conviction that the problem lies with women, with their demands and their remonstrances. This frame of mind found expression in "Love Is for Life" when the Irish bishops said:

> One of the important challenges facing the Church today is to develop a truly Christian feminism; and in the Church, this task must fall primarily on women themselves, filled with the love of Christ and anxious to play their full part in the life of the Church. They will find inspiration from the figure of Mary, the Mother of the Lord, blessed among women.[57]

Here the bishops place the burden on women, whose model is Mary; let them imitate her and all will be well. However, more and more Irish women refuse to accept that there is a "woman problem"; for them the problem is patriarchy. They, in turn, place the burden on bishops and clergy to examine the discrimination, injustice and negation of gospel values inherent in patriarchy. Only when such an examination and acknowledgement are implemented will there be some hope that we may truly be one people of God.

The difficulties which churchmen will encounter in such a change of heart have been described by Ben Kinnerling:

> The notion of relationship is inherent in the use of the term equality. The relationship which I am going to focus on is that between Church leaders and Christian women, lay and religious. For Churchmen the difficulty of moving towards more intimate relationships is often compounded by their narrow understanding of celibacy. . . . It is important to realize that a lifestyle which precludes close friendships with women produces priests who know little about the humanity of women. . . . In friendships with women, a priest is challenged to accept that women's way of experiencing things, their way of naming reality, their emotional and physical reactions, and their perspectives on moral questions are as valid and close to the truth as are those of men.[58]

Opportunities for forming such friendships as part of healthy personal development have been denied to churchmen from their seminary days, where, in their studies, they have been exposed to the misogyny of patristic writers, and, in their daily experience, have been deprived of the presence of women teachers of philosophy and theology. The world of the Irish seminaries resembles a "total society," where the socialization process offers little to offset the patriarchal structures, ethos and authority of the institutional church. After ordination, such young men have much to unlearn if they are to minister in the spirit of equality referred to in the documents of Vatican II. Mary Cullen writes:

> An adequate response to feminism would require that male ecclesiastics seriously consider the possibility that their own development as human persons might have been impeded by pressures to conform to male stereotypes.[59]

A Call for Clerical Conversion

In 1982 an exceptionally valuable opportunity was offered to the clergy to examine how they might acknowledge, and then attempt to solve, the problem of patriarchy. The National Council of Priests in Ireland (NCPI), in response to a Vatican request for studies of Women in Society, commissioned a working party to draw up a report on "The Role of Women in the Church." The nine members of the working party consisted of women and men, lay and religious, and they presented their report to the Annual General Meeting of the NCPI in 1982.[60]

Some extracts from the report will indicate how clearly the working party had analyzed the problem of patriarchy within the Irish church, and how explicit were their recommendations for a resolution. The first section of the report describes the present state of women within the church:

> The Catholic Church excludes women from the ordained ministry and, more importantly, from deliberative participation in its decision-making structures. In the western world the Church stands out as the only major institution which structures participation on the basis of sex. The practice of the Irish Church fully reflects this institutional exclusion of women. . . . Moreover, in our opinion, the official Church will not be able to do anything about this until it begins to examine its own attachment to these stereotypes and goes beyond them to search out, with women, a more authentic meaning and mode of expression of the person's inner structure and his or her potential for life. . . .[61]

The working party regretted the loss to the church of the valuable contribution of women: a contribution which clerics could ignore only at a significant cost to themselves as males, and at a cost to women, whose alienation is growing.

The report ended with specific recommendations to the clergy:

1. That, as a matter of urgency, they re-examine their own manner of relating to women, including the ways in which they think about, speak to, treat and interact with them.
2. That priests in positions of authority recognise that they carry a heavier burden of responsibility to scrutinize their own attitudes and to set an example to others.
3. That priests and bishops query whether they have negative attitudes to increased participation by women, and ask if and why they feel defensive and threatened.
4. That priests ask themselves the following questions:
   (a) Are women seen by the Church as people in their own right?
   (b) Are women really listened to and responded to?
   (c) Are women often merely tolerated as an unpaid but willing workforce for the performance of menial tasks?
   (d) Do Church structures contradict the dignity of women as proclaimed in Church documents and in the gospel message?
   (e) Since women constitute 50 percent of Church membership, should we not expect them to carry a proportionate degree of responsibility for management of Church affairs?
5. That clerics urgently examine their individual and collective attitudes which are in fact alienating many women from the Church.

The hope of many Christian feminists in Ireland is that, even now, some years later, the dust may be blown off the NCPI report, and its recommendations implemented. If the implications of this document were to be taken with the seriousness and sense of urgency they deserve, the ensuing radical adjustments to the status quo would have the historical significance of the Magna Carta.

Notes

1. *Eurostat* (Luxembourg, 1988), 16.

2. Jenny Beale, *Women in Ireland: Voices of Change* (Dublin: Gill and Macmillan, 1986), iii.

3. Basil Chubb, *The Government and Politics of Ireland* (London: Longman, 1982), v.

4. John A. Weafer, "The Irish Laity: Some Findings of the 1984 National Survey," *Doctrine and Life* 36 (May/June 1986). Also: John A. Weafer, "Continuity and Change in Irish Religion," *Doctrine and Life* 36 (Dec. 1986).

5. Michael Fogarty, Liam Ryan and Joseph Lee, *Irish Values and Attitudes: The Irish Report of the European Values Study* (Dublin: Dominican Publications, 1985), 47.

6. Anne O'Connor, "Listening to Tradition," in *Personally Speaking,* ed. Liz Steiner Scott (Dublin: Attic Press, 1985), 74–76. Also: Donncha O'Corrain, "Women in Irish History," in *Women in Irish Society: The Historical Dimension,* eds. Margaret MacCurtain and Donncha O'Corrain (Dublin: Arlen House: The Women's Press, 1978), 1–2.

7. Gearoid O'Tuathaigh, "The Role of Women in Ireland under the New English Order," in MacCurtain and O'Corrain, eds., op. cit., 26.

8. Margaret MacCurtain, "Women, the Vote and Revolution," in MacCurtain and O'Corrain, eds., op. cit., 52.

9. Ibid., 53.

10. Ibid., 56.

11. Grainne O'Flynn, "Our Age of Innocence," in *Girls Don't Do Honours: Irish Women in Education in the 19th and 20th Centuries,* ed. Mary Cullen (Dublin: Women's Educational Bureau, 1987), 82.

12. *Bunracht na hEireann* (Dublin: The Stationery Office), 136.

13. J.H. Whyte, *Church and State in Modern Ireland, 1923–1979* (Dublin: Gill and Macmillan, 1980), 172.

14. Papal encyclical *Rerum Novarum* (May 15, 1891).

15. Pius XII, "Address to Women of Catholic Action" (Oct. 21, 1945).

16. Mary Cullen, "Knowledge and Power: Patriarchal Knowledge in the Feminist Curriculum," in Mary Cullen, ed., op. cit., 136.

17. Tony Fahey, "Nuns in the Catholic Church in Ireland in the Nineteenth Century," in Mary Cullen, ed., op. cit., 17.

18. Anne V. O'Connor, "The Revolution in Girls' Secondary Education in Ireland, 1860–1910," in Mary Cullen, ed., op. cit., 31.

19. Joseph J. Lee, "Women and the Church since the Famine," in MacCurtain and O'Corrain, eds., op. cit., 41.

20. J.H. Whyte, op. cit., 20.

21. *Schooling and Sex Roles: Recommendations and Summary Findings* (Dublin: Employment Equality Agency, 1983).

22. D.H. Akenson, *A Mirror to Kathleen's Face: Education in Independent Ireland, 1922–1968* (Montreal and London: McGill-Queen's University Press, 1975), 137.

23. Jenny Beale, op. cit., 3.

24. *Report of the Commission for the Status of Women* (Dublin: The Stationery Office, 1972).

25. Ailbhe Smyth, "The Contemporary Women's Movement in the Republic of Ireland," *Women's Studies International Forum,* V. II, N. 4 (New York: Pergamon Press, 1988), 333.

26. Anne Speed, quoted by Ailbhe Smyth, op. cit., 333.

27. Jenny Beale, op. cit., 11.

28. "Travelers" is the accepted term to describe a group of generally nomadic families, formerly referred to as "gypsies" or "tinkers." They number about five thousand, and because of their "different" lifestyle they are often discriminated against by the "settled" community.

29. *Women's Studies Bulletin,* 1 (Autumn, 1984).

30. Margaret MacCurtain, "Women Winning Through," in *The Tablet* (March 16, 1985).

31. Tony Fahey in Mary Cullen, ed., op. cit., 7. Also: *Irish Catholic Clergy and Religious, 1970–81* (Maynooth: Council for Research and Development, 1983).

32. *Vocations Report, 1987* (Maynooth: Council for Research and Development, 1988).

33. Jenny Beale, op. cit., 177.

34. Ibid., 178.

35. Donal Flanagan, "Nuns, the Silent Majority," in *Ireland Today* (Nov., 1972).

36. Sr. Kathleen McDonald, NDS, "Women Religious and Bishops: Some Experiences," in *Religious Life Review* (V. 22, N. 100), 22.

37. Sr. Maire Corbett, "Sisters in Parish Ministry," in *Intercom* (Feb. 1989).

38. Eleanor Cunney, "Dear Bishops. . ." in *The Furrow* (March 1988), 22.

39. Margaret MacCurtain, "Women Winning Through," in *The Tablet* (March 16, 1985), 272.

40. Mary Condren, *The Serpent and the Goddess: Women's Religion and Power in Celtic Ireland* (San Francisco: Harper & Row, 1989).

41. *Womanspirit* (V. 3, N. 1, Autumn 1988), 18.

42. Sophia Group Statement of Aims (1989).

43. *Womanspirit,* op. cit., 3.

44. Catholic Women's Federation Statement of Aims.

45. *Womanspirit,* op. cit., 33.

46. *Womanspirit,* Editorial (V. 3, N. 2, Winter 1988).

47. "Why It's Time for Women Priests," in *The Irish Times* (Aug. 17, 1988).

48. Sophia Group Statement of Aims (1989).

49. Ibid.

50. Kevin O'Kelly, "Fifty Voices: A Report from Bellinter," in MacReamoinn, ed., op. cit., 68.

51. Margaret MacCurtain, "Women: Part of the Laity?" in MacReamoinn, ed., op. cit., 61.

52. Mary Cullen, " 'How grossly do they insult us!': Feminism's Challenge to Patriarchy," in *The Furrow* (Sept. 1982), 579.

53. Pamilla C. Kelleher, "The way my experience has shaped my spirituality," in *Womanspirit* (V. 3, N. 2, 1988).

54. Ursula Coleman, "Christian Feminism," public lecture delivered at Milltown Theological Institute (March 14, 1984).

55. Personal communication.

56. Sophia Group Statement of Aims (1989).

57. *Love Is for Life,* op. cit., 46.

58. Ben Kimmerling, "Women in the Church," in *Doctrine and Life* (V. 37, May/June 1987), 272.

59. Mary Cullen, " 'How grossly do they insult us!' " op. cit., 58.

60. "The Role of Women in the Church: A Report of the Working Party Established by the National Council of Priests in Ireland," in *The Furrow* (Sept. 1982), 579.

61. Ibid., 581.

Ann Breslin, Ph.D., born in Ardara, Co. Donegal, Ireland, attended University College, Dublin, where she specialized in modern languages and education. Her doctorate, conferred by the University of Chicago, was based on research carried out in the field of moral education. Dr. Breslin, a Sister of St. Louis, was always keenly interested in liberation theology, and in this context became involved in the women's movement as an expression of liberation from the oppression of patriarchy. She was a member of several women's groups in Ireland, and frequently gave workshops on topics such as "Women and the Church" and "Feminist Spirituality." As Director of the Irish Catholic Bishops' Center for Research and Development, Ann Breslin had many opportunities to heighten her awareness of the various attitudes of Irish women toward the Catholic Church in that country. Ann's own liberation from her courageous encounter with cancer came with her death at St. Louis House, Monaghan, on March 23, 1991. May this valiant woman rejoice in the fullness of God's freedom and peace!

7

New Catholic Women in Italy

Giulia P. Di Nicola*

The laity is looking and hoping for a situation of more freedom from clericalism and dogmatism in moral matters. Lay people don't want to be so "oppressed." I wish I could find a kinder word.

—A SCRIPTURE TEACHER IN ROME

Women must give time to studies, because, unless we are well prepared and are soundly formulating theology, we will never have a voice in the church.

—A WOMAN WORKING IN RELIGIOUS PUBLIC RELATIONS, ROME

I AM APPROACHING the topic of "New Catholic Women in Italy" from a socio-anthropological perspective.[1] The reader will better understand the argument that I make if she or he is familiar with my book *Uguaglianza e differenza. La reciprocità uomo donna (Equality and Difference. The Man–Woman Reciprocity*. Città Nuova: Rome, 1988), in which I present, at some length, my own reflections on cultural differences. This essay, however, will deal specifically with contemporary Italian feminism.

To fully understand the problem of women in the church in Italy, it is necessary first to realize its interconnectedness with both the process of secularization and the development of feminism in general. The concepts of equality and difference are insufficient in themselves to explain or to justify the man-woman correlation. As I have suggested in *Uguaglianza e differenza,* the anthropological "unidualita" ("one-duality") is already described in the Bible: "God created man in his own image, male and female he created them" (Gen 1:27, RSV).

* Translated by Dario N. Abram, S.J.

We must also recognize that any person's description of a social situation is colored by that person's own pre-comprehension, and it is important that this be acknowledged as well. In my own case, the interpretation that I make comes from my personal experience with a faith that is both inherited and freely chosen. At the same time, it is an interpretation that claims the freedom to be critical and, of necessity, to compare the facts of the tradition with the facts of religion as well as with the demands of my own conscience and contemporary culture. Thus it is that, in a spirit of continuity and with gratitude for the inheritance that I have received, my inquiry looks, without fear, directly at our unresolved problems and the ambiguities that are inherent in them.

In a study such as this, a "problematic" perspective is indispensable in order to avoid definitive conclusions which, at this point, I believe, would be premature.

Women and Religion in Italy

In order to have an accurate sense of the place of religion in the lives of Italian women, it is helpful to look at the Shell Survey of 1973, dealing with the condition of the Italian woman and her role in society.[2] The survey was addressed to a diverse and representative sample of women which included all ages, religions, and social-class categories. To a question regarding the significance of religion in their lives, 35.5 percent answered "sufficient"; 29.7 percent, "a lot"; 20.3 percent, "very much"; and 85 percent declared that religion, for them, was of "crucial" importance. However, a survey done by Doxa on Italian religiosity shows a continuing pattern of unequal religious practice between the sexes; within one week, forty-five percent of the women and only thirty-one percent of the men attended church once.[3]

The large number of women who assert the importance of religious experience is quite in harmony with Italy's historical and cultural heritage. Women, it seems, are more perceptive of the call of the Spirit; their religious understanding, while perhaps unspoken, is profound. Surveys further confirm that, among the young, the greatest percentage of those who believe in God are women.[4]

Most of the women mentioned above maintain strong and habitual ties with tradition and ritual. A study by Burgalassi, published in 1980, confirms this traditional type of feminine religiosity.[5] The atheistic sub-culture is predominantly male (ninety-two percent to eight percent female). The "indifferent" sub-culture is seventy-seven percent male and twenty-three percent female. The sub-culture of the "official Catholic Church model" registers thirty-six percent male to sixty-four percent female, and the "sacral sub-culture," typical of a rural environment, maintains the same percentages, while in the "prophetic sub-culture," thirty-nine percent of the total sample are female. From this survey, one can identify a religious population that is more traditional and composed largely of women, while men are characterized by non-religiosity or by a charismatic type of religiosity which reflects new values as well as uncertainties and ambivalences.

We also find some similarity between Catholics who practice occasionally (those who attend mass once or twice every three months, 12.1 percent male and 12.2 percent female) and young people who are members of associations. A research study by *Centro Italiano Femminile* (CIF, *Italian Women's Center*) shows the alienation of these women, even Catholic women, from magisterial teachings in the area of morality.[6] The research of G. Milanesi indicates that young women involved in religious groups are no different from young men in the same groups. Both think that friendship and existential-personalistic values are more significant than those of work, study and institutional religion.[7] Young women not involved in such groups are more likely to resemble the traditional feminine cliché, though what is striking among these women is their total rejection of religion, possibly due to their espousal of atheistic feminism.[8]

In the presence of variables such as youth, contemporary culture and social participation, masculine religiosity and feminine religiosity tend to resemble one another.[9] But one can say more: the changes in values and behaviors of today's young people seem to be in harmony with the culture of a "feminine" religion, one in which institutional aspects of dogma, norms and laws are less important than those values which have to do with the inner person, values such as personal fulfillment and interpersonally significant and beneficial relationships. And if this is the case, then we can affirm that, not only on religious grounds, but on working, social and cultural grounds as well, there is a tendency toward a centrality of feminine values which, considered weak in the past, are today being rediscovered in a new form and are considered to be basic to the contemporary human experience, for men as well as for women.

A Typology of Italian Catholic Women

From a social-cultural point of view, there is a strong feeling in Italy today that we are in an era of post-patriarchal religion. It is an era which heralds, in a negative form, a critique of the androgenistic-centric God; in a positive form, a search for new references to replace the old ones and for which we do not yet have clear definitions.

It would be simplistic to speak of Catholic women in Italy without keeping in mind the many varieties which are found within the feminine category. And even in attempting to establish typologies of these women, one discovers that it is not easy to capture the range of feminist influences on a qualitative level. Nor should one too quickly identify the mass-going women (messalizzanti) as "satisfied Catholics."

Empirical data in this regard is scant and is incapable of recording that which is much more significant: the unspoken, the word shared in confidence, the only-hinted-at, the indirect indication. The data that we do have give excessive importance to religious practice, distinguishing practicing and committed Catholics from those who do not practice. Yet these data do not examine motivations on a qualitative level: the differences between practicing Catholic women who are satisfied and those who are not, between those who practice and strictly observe the official morality and those who practice but live the separation with other than ecclesial norms for their private and public lives. And even among Catholic women who are dissatisfied, one cannot easily determine the influence of the feminine, or woman, question because of a certain reticence among women in treating this topic explicitly. We must, in the present situation, be willing to work with "soft" data and with questions which are without clear answers.

"Satisfied" Catholic women represent a segment of the female population which does not identify the difficulties of relationship with the church on a conscious level. On the contrary, the average woman, conscious of so many injustices in society and enjoying few spiritual consolations, is loath to criticize that church which has represented and continues to represent her reason for hope. The relationship between intellectual reflection and religious categories is such that conflict between them can cause great instability and ego confusion. Because this is so much feared, there is a tendency by those lacking in psychic and cultural flexibility to avoid such conflict.

Women in Service to the Church

Catholic women engaged in parish service are unpaid and work part-time, according to their availability and their skills. Women are so involved in 288 dioceses, 28,618 parishes, and 3,541 Permanent Pastoral Centers. Some do janitorial and kitchen work; others are engaged in CCD (religious education) and adult evangelization, and prepare candidates for the reception of confirmation and eucharist. Women are occasionally involved in conferences, local radio and television programs, and editing of parish or diocesan papers. They are regularly involved in consulting and courses for marriage preparation. Some women volunteer daily or weekly for service in parish offices and, at the invitation of the pastor, provide group support for excursions, encounters, spiritual retreats and pilgrimages. Their participation on parish or diocesan councils is only at the invitation of those responsible for such bodies: pastors, diocesan delegates or vicars. All these women, for the most part, offer their services voluntarily, are driven by great generosity and faith, and enjoy amicable relationships with their pastors and other members of the parish community. Their involvement provides them great psychological gratification and the prestige that comes from collaboration with the parish priest. So their work, while not permanently or formally defined, is often satisfying to them on a personal or group level. And the parish priest often tries to repay them with whatever help he can give and by offering moments of communal recreation and friendly support in their times of need.

In addition to the works mentioned above, which are unpaid, there are women teachers in theological institutes administered by dioceses as well as women who teach religion in state schools. Women work in diocesan curiae and as clerks in Vatican offices; some are employed as newspaper reporters (*Osservatore Romano, Avvenire,* diocesan papers). While these women add to the numbers of women represented in the pyramidal configuration of society at large, and provide certainly a large *base* of women, there is a progressive diminution of women as the profes-

sional ladder rises. And while it is noteworthy that women are clearly
more numerous than men as students in theological institutes, 83.2 percent women to 16.8 percent men, even here it is rare that one finds
female teachers or women who are qualified to teach at university level.

Living the Contradictions

In describing the religiosity of Italian women, one must admit to a persistent number of women who are characterized by a type of psychological dependence, a "fundamental desire to remain children (bambine),
attached to a protective figure, of which the mother figure is usually the
first and most important."[10] While the numbers of such women are
diminishing, they represent an unfortunate version of "altruism" and
"unselfishness" and are always in search of reassuring words and "safe"
guidance, usually from the male. The lack of an adequate cultural mediation between faith and social process accentuates in many women a
sense of guilt, educated as they are to "conceive passivity as a virtue,
sexuality as sinful and controlled by others, carefully taught to fear to
remain alone, to annoy others. . . ."[11]

Such women, if asked, will always and everywhere defend the magisterium and the church's structure. But one must distinguish between
conscious acceptance and that acceptance which represents the felt inca-
pacity to control historical changes, understood in a confused manner,
or even to express them in "logos" (thought and speech). And there are
other women who, though they have their doubts, do not express them
—to others or even to themselves—for fear of abandoning their faith for
ideologies which would not satisfy them on a personal level.

So there is this fearful silence, dissatisfied yet stifled. Women remain
within the Catholic experience because it is their lived experience, yet
they are inwardly separated from the church's official positions. One can
apply to the experience of such women the expression "psychological
immigration," used by John Paul II in his encyclical *Sollicitudo Rei Socialis,* for those who feel frustrated by rules that deny the creative subjec-
tivity of the citizen.[12] Slowly the conscience grows less sure than it seems
to appear from its firm pronouncements, strategic answers or embarrassing silences.[13] And, more than a blind belonging to or an open confrontation with the institution, one can witness a silent yet real separation in

which women remain within the institution while, at the same time, following their own way.

Appropriately, Gaiotti observes: "It remains sufficiently true enough that, unlike other foreign experiences, the Italian [women's] movement must still be characterized as 'latent'."[14] Perpetuating this dormant state is the vicinity of Rome, which, understood in a geographical as well as in a psychological-cultural sense, is deeply influential in Italy's Catholic tradition. The plethora of questions having to do with such subjects as divorce and abortion are presented in Italy as issues of comparison-conflict between clerical and secular politics, between conservatives and progressives, or even as a collision between Catholic and secular-Marxist cultures. These dichotomies have greatly contributed to the defensive posture of the Catholic Church in Italy.

An internal, critical movement of Italian Catholic women has therefore not yet been able to manifest itself in a definitive organization, though occasional collective actions have occurred. Certainly, it would be very difficult to imagine an Italian woman in the role of the American feminist, Babi Burke, of Fort Lauderdale, Florida, who attempted to celebrate mass in St. Peter's on December 4, 1985. The Italian Catholic feminist movement has preferred, rather, to strengthen its contacts with movements in other countries, collaborating with international and ecumenical organizations in France, Belgium and Switzerland. This has enabled Italian women to avoid collision with the institution and its own sterile forms of lamentation. It is notable, however, that it was Italian women who presented the following demands at the meeting of the World Union of Christian Women in Wislihofen, Zurich, in March of 1981:

1. The readmission to sacred ministries, according to the modality and finality requested by the present pastoral letter.
2. The canonical right to the numerous services effected today as temporary positions in the local churches.
3. Recognition of a greater autonomy for [mother] superiors and general chapters. Right to vote and to speak equal to [male] colleagues and always in collaboration with the bishop.
4. Greater autonomy to bishops in pastoral matters and the possibility of experimentation.
5. Greater presence of lay personnel, both men and women, in ecclesiastical tribunals.

6. That maternity be as fully determined (given the same authority) as paternity.
7. Elimination of anachronistic discriminations, even the juridical (prohibition of altar girls, male privilege in the administration of baptism and the distribution of the eucharist).
8. That the faculty of theology, in conjunction with modern sciences, reflect on the secular conditioning that discriminates against women, especially in areas of nature and culture.
9. A reexamination, according to contemporary scientific progress and post-conciliar reflection, of the image of woman in anthropology and Thomistic and Augustinian theology.

In 1985, church people in Italy collaborated with *Pax Romana* (MIIC), an international movement of Catholic intellectuals, on a seminar entitled "The Participation of Professional Women in Development and in Changes in Society." In addition to social and political problems, the seminar addressed the role of women in the church. While some progress was made in this regard, it was noted that professional women "do not give a significant and specific contribution to the life of the Catholic Church" because, except in some exceptional cases, the principal duties of women have been limited, more or less, to janitorial and domestic services.[15]

Women Religious in Italy

Our panorama of Italian Catholic women would be incomplete if we did not take into consideration the congregations and communities of female religious, which are rich both in potential and in their own unique frustrations, the expression of which is not always easy within cloistered structures. It is no longer possible in Italy to speak of "excluding" the nuns, of their ignorance of ecclesial problems, or of their being fully satisfied with the current state of their spirituality, obedience or service. Yet, among them one recognizes a great variety of types, from those manifesting pronounced ecclesial sensibilities to those more committed to suffering and to giving themselves generously to the cause of Christ.

In 1984 there were in Italy 152,689 women religious in 629 religious congregations and 15,019 religious communities. There are 255 women religious for every 100,000 Italian people (male and female), and 782 women religious for every 100,000 women in the population. In the past twenty-five years, we have registered both a high and a low in the numbers of women religious: from 1950 to 1955, there was an increase of four percent; from 1960 to 1965, a four percent increase; from 1965 to 1970, a holding pattern; and, finally, from 1970 to 1974, a diminution of five percent. Specifically, 27,000 women religious are involved in activities related to education; 37,000 work in schools; 15,000 are engaged in hospital and health services; the rest are engaged in internal governance and administration or are old and ill.[16]

Convents have not remained "waterproof" to the "rains" of Vatican II, to the educational needs of their members, to changing legislation, or to the relationship of their institutes with the new generation of women and with feminism.[17] International contacts and increasing communication with the outside world have brought demands for a new theology and for a reconstruction of spirituality, as expressed by Italy's *Unioni Superiori Maggiori (Union of Major Superiors)* as well as within those faculties of science engaged in the education of women which are administered by Salesian women religious (*Auxilium* Rome).[18]

The Persisting Problem

Even though one may prefer not to depend on cultural clues, clandestine hints or ambivalent language, one can still say with some confidence that Italy bears the wound of the unresolved question of the woman in the church.[19]

> Between an unacceptable radical conflict and an appeal to good will, there remains a void. . . . It must be said simply and with full responsibility that there is always present the danger of violence, and an uncontrollable violence, or of a silent abandonment [of the faith]. . . . The woman's question remains the exception, unspoken and unresolved, in the acceptance of the modern. . . . Woman's democratization is only a pretext . . . a stumbling block . . . a scandal.[20]

The problem reemerges continually—in commissions, seminars, conferences, study groups and theological dissertations.[21] While such events are often diocesan controlled and therefore sifted through orthodoxy, they still offer an index of a pain that is not appeased. At times there are concrete actions of happy, ecclesial disobedience which, while taking care to avoid sanctions, enable the participation of women even in the liturgy.

The problem is certain to grow in the near future, paralleling the growth of Italian women's social, cultural and political consciences. There is an increasing demand for scholarship by Italian women and a greater insistence on substantive content. While the number of women readers of "women's" periodicals remains stable, women readers of daily newspapers increased by four percent between 1985 and 1987 (ISEGI survey). And according to the ISTAT Bulletin of 1986, Italian women read more books than do Italian men.[22] The emerging mentality of Italian women challenges dogmatism and is more attentive to human rights and to collaboration and reciprocity in the church. It is a continuing challenge to the rigid, hierarchical conception of the man-woman relationship in church and in society.

Women's Associations and "Progetto Donna" ("Project Woman")

In social and ecclesial organizations in which both women and men participate, one can often, through confronting current world issues, indirectly address anti-feminist prejudices as well. There are ecclesial movements arising from an intuition, a spirituality or a personal charism which, while they do not deal directly with the woman question, are committed to the work of religious renewal and evangelization and have great respect for the lived experience. There are also movements that more directly address the raising of consciousness regarding the actual needs of the society and of the church.

Italy in the 1980s witnessed a slow yet consistent emergence of woman-related organizations, activities, scholarship and publications. To name a few:

Centro Italiano Femminile (CIF, Italian Women's Center), publishing Cronache e opinioni (News and Opinions).

Associazione Christiana Lavoratori Italiani (ACLI, Christian Association of Italian Workers), publishing Quaderni de azione sociale (Social Action Exercise Book).

Azione Cattolica Italiana (ACI, Italian Catholic Action), publishing Presenza pastorale (Pastoral Presence).

Groups of *Promozione Donna (Promotion Woman)*, especially those in Milan and Brescia, publishing *Progetto donna (Project Woman)*.

Movimento Italiano (delle) Casalinghe (MOICA, Italian Movement of Housewives).

Movimento Femminile Democrazia Cristiana (Women's Movement of Christian Democrats), publishing *Donna e societa (Woman and Society)*.

Federazione Universitaria Cattolici Italiani (FUCI, Italian Catholics' University Federation), publishing *Ricerca (Investigation)*.

In the past few years, the work, in terms of scholarship, has been intense, including seminars by *Italian Catholic Action* and the document produced by the *Women's Coordination Commission* of the *Christian Association of Italian Workers* on the occasion of the 1988 Congress sponsored by the *Italian Catholics' University Federation* which involved both men and women.

Promozione Donna of Milan is a particularly active group in which Maria Dutto has, for the past fifteen years, engaged in work of great sensitivity with critical and constructive scholarship, confronting the institutional church while striving to avoid both sterile vindictiveness and patriarchal benevolence. *Promozione Donna* stresses that women's work in the church is both temporary and tends, in general, to reflect the secular reality. Men are always found in the upper echelons, in the clergy, or, if lay, in administrative or specialized occupations; they are seldom involved in evangelization. *Promozione Donna* asks for a pastoral that is not only *for* but *with* women, who will collaborate with the clergy in creating a religious style, language, and content more representative of the strong presence of women in the church.

Progetto donna (Project Woman) is a periodical which was begun in Brescia in 1982 and is managed by Tina Leonzi, with strong support by Catholic women. Together with the Milanese group of *Promozione Donna*, *Progetto donna* offers a revised scholarship of the Catholic world of women based on Betty Friedan's "second phase" of feminism.[23] The group addresses Friedan's four themes of "second phase" feminism: the advancement of scholarship, women's management of maternity and demographic issues, the crisis of women's continued marginalization, and women's concerns for the "third world" and for planetary survival. The Italian women believe that it is the very recovery of the family and maternal affection that will allow Catholic women to take up the feminist challenge and to recapture the earlier intuition of the women's movement.

Progetto donna is disseminating the above themes through extensive scholarship and through debates at annual conventions which are reaching not only Catholic women throughout Italy but many other women as well. At the first of such conventions, "Italian Feminism: Second Phase" (Brescia, October 1983), Wilma Preti spoke:

> We who have rejected the methods and the battles of much of feminism recognize, nevertheless, the value of its work and research and its potential to change reality. And we hope that we ourselves can know and do as much as they in the future. But we also recognize that there are those who are suffering much—isolation and delay—in the "first phase" (and we clearly refer to the Catholic area), and it is this to which we must contribute today.[24]

While the above has attempted to describe what is happening officially or publicly, much of the diaspora of the 1970s is still in the underbrush. All of these initiatives, both official and grass roots, have crossed one another at many times and in many places, often in responding to cues given by the magisterium itself—for example, in documents such as *Familiaris Consortio (Apostolic Exhortation on the Family,* November 22, 1981) and *Mulieris Dignitatem* (Encyclical on *The Dignity of Women,* August 15, 1988), and that announcing the Marian Year.

The Question of Ministry

It is true that, once we recognize the movement of women as one of the "signs of the time" (Pope John XXIII), first affirmed at Vatican Council II[25] and repeated many times since, the importance of women's participation on all levels of social and political life becomes a "given." What remains in the shadow, however, is the full participation of women within the institutional church. This inconsistency remains one of the thorniest issues for Catholic women everywhere.

The question of equality *within* the church has revolved primarily around women's access to religious ministry; it is a question which has developed in Italy much more gradually and more quietly than it has, for example, in America. It was because of the pressure of this "woman question," especially in North America, that Pope Paul VI, early in the 1970s, created a mixed (male-female) commission of study-research on women in the church. The commission was charged with responding to the questions, though many were prepared to discount the response even before the work of the commission was begun.[26] Though the commission judged that the New Testament does not provide any decisive arguments either for or against the ordination of women, this conclusion was never published. Instead, there was the promulgation of the papal encyclical *Inter insignores* (January 28, 1977). While the first part of the document generously affirms the advancement of women in the social and political arenas, there follows a firm justification of women's exclusion from the priesthood, insisting, however, that this exclusion is not to be seen as a discrimination against women.

If the intent of the encyclical was to put an end to any further discussion of the matter, it was soon evident that this intent was not to be realized, especially in North America.[27] One might even hypothesize that the document had a "boomerang" effect—that its unequivocal "no" served to strengthen rather than to weaken the question. Even in Italy there continues to be hope among women, priests and theologians that the question, with more flexible and less confrontational strategies, can be more satisfactorily addressed in the future, even though this be a long-term process.

The 1987 Synod on the Laity, according to participants, was a positive experience on both spiritual and ecclesial levels. As diligently recorded in the press, however, the Synod was marked by contrasting opinions and a continuing sense of embarrassment on the issue of women in the church.[28] Reaffirming the equality theme of *Mulieris dignitatem,* the fathers nonetheless stressed the order of ministries, unearthing yet again the symbolism of bridegroom and bride. All of this recalls the necessity of probing more deeply, more adequately, and more positively the question of reciprocity, the significance of sexuality in anthropology and theology, and the contributions of women's theology.

The recent *Christifideles Laici* (Apostolic Exhortation on the Laity, "The Lay Members of Christ's Faithful People," December 30, 1988) urges the full participation of women in the life of the church. Without touching the question of ministry, the document favors the presence of women at all levels of management and decision-making (but is not power at stake in this very disparity?) The document reads:

An example comes to mind in the participation of women on diocesan and parochial pastoral councils as well as diocesan synods and particular councils. In this regard the synod fathers have written. . . . Women, who already hold places of great importance in transmitting the faith and offering every kind of service in the life of the church, ought to be associated in the preparation of pastoral and missionary documents and ought to be recognized as cooperators in the mission of the church in the family, in professional life and in the civil community. (C.L. No. 51)

And the 1987 Synod on the Laity reiterates, in Proposition 47:

Women . . . must be associated with the preparation of pastoral documents and missionary initiatives and must be recognized as cooperators in the church's mission in the family and in the professional and secular-civil communities.[29]

While these official statements are obviously a step in the right direction, we must ask ourselves if we are not, once again, at a stopping point rather than at a point of departure for reaching effective equality. If the participation of women, even if it is influential, remains subordinate to priestly ministry, it will function as merely consultative; the final decisions will continue to be made by others and in different places than those in which they have been discussed.

In recent years, Italian women have concentrated less on ministry and more in other areas: a new commitment of women in theological studies,[30] a feminism that is more ecumenical and more open to other marginalized peoples, and a convergence of interests around universal themes of ecology and non-violence.

Rejection of the Institution

There are many who fear that eventual priesthood for women will eliminate the important real and symbolic differences between women and men and will substantially alter that which is most desirable in male-female reciprocity. In other words, there is fear that a concept of simple equality between the sexes will only strengthen clericalism in the church, and at the very moment in which women seek to be eschatologically free of that hierarchy which so clearly expresses the present institutional reality. This fear is fueled by the bitter experiences of women-pastors in other denominations. In this regard, the Ecumenical Council of Churches (COE) has registered in all Christian denominations a denouncement of both sexism and clericalism. Clearly, the presence of women pastors does not eliminate the problem of a church's "male mentality," as attested to by the difficulties in the U.S. Methodist Church, where women have been pastors since 1956, and in the Lutheran Church of Sweden, which has had women priests since 1958. Joined to these observations, there is a diffuse belief, among both men and women, in the great importance of new models of ministry, models which will avoid the traps of clerical caste, enforced celibacy and the routinization of hierarchy.

We are proceeding, then, in the direction of rethinking ministry itself, not in contradiction to the struggles for equality, but to acquire a more global perspective and to make necessity a virtue by reformulating the question and moving forward with the new formulation. In a word, many Italian women are abandoning the struggle for ordination to priesthood and diaconate in order to avoid the traps mentioned above and to call attention to the anti-evangelical nature of the ecclesial system. Even in Italy we share the conviction of Mary Hunt when she states: "The new models of the church, especially the basic Christian communities of Latin America, clearly demonstrate that what is necessary is the development of a new style of ministry for a new model of church."[31]

In Italy there are only a very few small, basic communities of women who reenact the liturgy by sharing prayer, mutual support and engagement in the works of justice.[32] According to *W.A.T.E.R.* (Women's Alliance for Theology, Ethics and Ritual, Maryland, U.S.A.), however, such groups are numerous in other countries, where women (and sometimes men) assemble in private homes to share a meal and a celebration and to seek to relocate themselves in the center of the Christian tradition. Neither a sect nor a "new" church, and not without some pitfalls, this is a movement which seeks to recover, from a woman's perspective, the centrality of the early Christian experience, translating the particularities of women's experiences today (the change of seasons, personal problems, times of transformation, births, menstruation, retirement) from life to liturgy.

For Italian Catholic women, the principal challenge is that of avoiding a conflictive relationship with the institutional church. Nor are there other denominations which are free of similar institutional defects. For some this suggests the "solution" of a parallel church of women, no longer in communion with Roman Catholicism. It seems clear that the basic problem of the centrality/marginality relationship of men and women will not be solved by putting women in the place of men, and the question of institutional mediation, which is the key interpretation of this essay, would only be put aside; it would never be resolved. Perhaps it is for these reasons that A. Zarri, dealing with questions on *Mulieris dignitatem* in Louvain, responded: "The problem of priesthood for women postpones the problem of what it means to be a priest. If, as Roman theology has it, the priest in his essence is different from a lay man, then we [must] reject the priesthood."[33]

Is the demand for priesthood typical of a feminism whose aim is equality? In any case, such diverse movements as *Women/Church* (U.S.A.), *Femmes et Hommes dans l'Eglise* (France), and those intellectual movements, even in Italy, which would go beyond the institution all face a similar challenge—that of understanding the essence and the meaning of reciprocity.

The Central Role of Culture

I wish to conclude these reflections without proposing solutions— which would be premature, in any case—but with some comments on the inadequacy of the current debates in the church as compared with modern anthropology (according to which everyone is simultaneously both man and woman) and with the modern concept of personalism. The current issue of ministry for women demands a rethinking of the meaning of ministry as the vicarious expression of God as both male and female. There is need, therefore, for study and research, not only on women's specificity, whether within or outside of the male's universality, but also on ways to adequately express the one/duality of the human being, created in God's image in equality as well as in difference.

Unity/plurality and equality/difference are conceptual knots within which we must preserve the dynamics of reciprocity. At the same time, we must avoid rigid definitions which would constitute impediments to the process of personalization, both in oneself and in others.[34] It is for these reasons that we must avoid vindicating or premature conclusions. For without an unhurried movement of ideas and without a basic consensus, many of the so-called liberations can simply become new traps, in the service of efficiency, profit, or rationalism; and many decisions, ill-considered, become destructive of ecclesial unity.

In Italy the question of the woman tends to proceed more in the area of cultural deepening than in that of juridical vindication. The question thus becomes a powerful stimulus to rethinking the world of humankind in general. And in this problematic of theo-anthropological inquiry, women's culture acts as the critical and restless conscience which, even when it is not able to speak positively, can serve to unmask the various forms of contemporary idolatry.

The believing woman must engage in the regeneration of culture on at least four fronts:

1. On the secular front, engagement is a matter of gathering together and developing common aims with other women, avoiding prejudice and rejection of others while, at the same time, keeping the faith. Believing women can help to revive that fertile reciprocity between culture and spirituality which has produced so many good fruits in human history, fruits which remain embodied in the great cathedrals and universities of Europe. Each woman must thus freely claim her own history and culture, rather than acquiesce to themes chosen by others. Believing women can no longer allow themselves to be constrained by inferiority complexes and fears of failure or contained by the rejection of the secular culture, on the one hand, or by strictures of the magisterium, on the other.

2. On the Catholic front, the work is no less difficult, for here we face the opposition of conservatives, the denial of official church recognition, the poverty of theological studies, and the distrust of other Catholic women who resist all questioning of their traditional world. All of these have acted as a curb to the formation of a network of solidarity among Italian women, a network which could confront and dialogue, which could give public and media voice to the cause of women, and which could coordinate women's scholarship and writing. Special work is needed to overcome prejudice against women within ecclesial structures and within public universities, where women faculty and students are often faced with macho and hostile academic systems.

3. On the cultural front, the task for women is well expressed by what D. de Rougemont has written of the European "man":

We see [European man], in his pure model, as a man crucified between two opposites that he, himself, has defined: immanence and transcendence, the collective and the individual, service to the community and liberating anarchy, security and risk, the rules of the game which are for all and the vocation which is only for the one. I say "crucified" because European man, as such, does not accept being reduced to one or the other of the two terms that he has given to himself. He tends to assume them [all] and to remain in their tension, in a balance that is always being threatened with eternal agony.[35]

4. Finally, there is the task of perseverance, neither succumbing to a faith of the "simple-minded" nor abandoning to the magisterium our inheritance of the faith. *Christifideles laici,* the encyclical on the laity, is especially helpful in this regard, when it directly solicits the contributions of women:

> . . . women have the task of assuring the moral dimension of culture, the dimension, namely, of a culture worthy of the person, of an individual yet social life. . . . How great are the possibilities and responsibilities of woman in this area at a time when the development of science and technology is not always inspired and measured by true wisdom, with the inevitable risk of "dehumanizing" human life, above all when it would demand a more intense love and a more generous acceptance (No. 51).

In the prolific crisis of meaning affecting the entire arch of knowledge today, beginning with the question of women, we must face all risks to engage in research and work that is Catholic and, at the same time, feminist. All that we know from history must be reconciled with a clear interpretation of revelation. We must seek new horizons without cutting away from the roots of our heredity, which roots have so clearly been nurtured by women. It is their very responsibility for cultural tradition that causes women today to be unsatisfied with easy solutions, with simplifications which ignore complexity, and with the slogans of the marketplace, even at the cost of women's being suspended in a void and unsettled by the pseudo solutions that abound.

If the full content of the women's question is yet unclear, at least the question itself is being brought to light with great clarity, especially since the promulgation of *Mulieris dignitatem.* This document, a reflection on and of women, challenges us to reject those modern, individualistic understandings of woman which so often translate into a search for success, career, and money and deny the value of *being for* others, which is the basic value of the feminine. The document goes on to affirm that, as scripture persuades us, we cannot have one hermeneutic of man as all that is human without an adequate appeal to all that is female. Again, *Mulieris dignitatem* is clear: ". . . the 'woman' is the representative and the archetype of the whole human race: she represents the humanity which belongs to all human beings, both men and women" (No. 4).

Notes

1. Sociology does not enjoy a good reputation as regards the relationship between women and the Catholic Church. At the Synod on the Laity in November 1987, it was felt that a clear distinction had to be made between theology/ecclesiology and sociology. The distinction is expressed as a division between that which is revealed, truth, and that which is the fruit of history and of collective conscience, opinion, and therefore is changeable. If one follows this line of reasoning, God's way and humankind's way are, at most, always parallel, and one who opts for God therefore puts oneself outside of history.

2. Shell Survey, published in *Bollettino Doxa,* 1973, 222–223.

3. Indagine Doxa, "La frequenze alla chiesa e le opinioni degli italiani nei confronti dell'episcopato italiano," in *Il Sabato,* S. 845, October 10, 1984.

4. See the study of P.G. Grasso, *Gioventu e innovazione* (Rome: A.V.E., 1974) 293–321.

5. S. Burgalassi, ed., *Dove va la cristianita italiana?* (Bologna: Dehoniane, 1980).

6. For the results of the XX National Congress on this topic, see "Realtà donna tra utopia e progetto," *Cronache e opinioni,* No. 11, Rome, December 12–15, 1985.

7. G. Milanesi, *Oggi credono cosi* (Turin: L.D.C., 1981).

8. M.T. Bellenzier, "Religiosità al femminile?" *Note di pastorale giovanile,* No. 3, 1983, 27–29.

9. G. Brunetta speaks of a tendency toward "religiosity as a couple." See G. Brunetta, "Frequenza alla messa, alla comunione, alla confessione," in *Aggiornamenti sociali,* No. 1, 1986, 51–65.

10. C. Del Miglio, "Religiosità e donna," AA.VV., *Presenza femminile nella chiesa,* Atti, Gruppo Promozione Donna, Milan, 1982, 11–12.

11. Ibid.

12. John Paul II, *Sollicitudo rei socialis,* February 1988, 24.

13. On the provincial level, an inquiry of six hundred women participating in various religious groups is significant. The findings were presented at a meeting which took place in Bergamo on May 24–25, 1985. To the question, "Can women, in your opinion, receive the sacrament of holy orders?" thirty-four

percent answered affirmatively. To the question, "Can women, in your opinion, have the responsibility of a parish?" fifty-five percent answered affirmatively, and to the question, "Do you think it is proper for a woman to become a theologian?" seventy-seven percent answered affirmatively.

14. P. Gaiotte De Biase, "Donne e questione cattolica," *Appunti di cultura e di politica*, No. 2, 1988. 4–10.

15. R. Goldie, "Laicita femminile nella chiesa," AA.VV. *La donna nella chiesa e nel mondo* (Naples: Dehoniane, 1988), 74–84.

16. E. Colagiovanni, "Le religiose italiane," *Ricerca sociografica* (Rome: USMI, 1984).

17. I recommend to the reader a beautiful book which is a personal testimony to her sufferings by a sister who left religious life: M. Masutti, *Tornero tra la gente* (Turin: Claudiana, 1986). See also A. Cagiati, *Intervista alle suore* (Turin: Marietti, 1977).

18. See the official records of the International Convention that met in Rome in August 1988, which can be found in *Verso l'educatione della donna oggi* (Rome: L.A.S., 1989).

19. See the interview with C. Riva in *La Repubblica*, November 16, 1985. The interview with G. Lazzati, on the other hand, speaks of an "open" problem: see *Il Messagero di S. Antonio*, No. 18, 1985, 32–35.

20. P. Gaiotti, p. 9.

21. Notable in this context is the *Instituto Costanza Scelfo Barbeiri* of the Faculty of Theology in Palermo and the work done there by Cettina Militello.

22. AA. VV., *Parole Crociate*, Official records of two conventions on women and information, Rome, 1986.

23. Betty Friedan, *The Second Stage* (New York: Summit Books, 1981, 1986).

24. W. Preti. "Femminismo italiano; seconda fase," *Progetto donna*, No. 5, 1983, xvi–xxviii.

25. *Gaudium et spes*, Nos. 9 and 29.

26. The delay in the work of the commission reduced its competency and made it no longer necessary to speak of priesthood. Of the ten men and fifteen women appointed to the commission, five of the women sent their resignations, accompanied by letters of explanation, to the pope. See "Des femmes in appellent aux pasteur de l'Eglise," *Pro mundi vita*, No. 108, 1987.

27. If the statement was received in an embarrassing silence in Italy, there were numerous protestations in America. See, especially, Swiedler, ed., AA. VV. *Women Priest: A Catholic Commentary on the Vatican Declaration* (New York: 1977). The Canadian bishops returned to the issue in 1983 and 1984 (see *Documentation Catholique*, No. 63, 1983, 1082; No. 64, 1984, 1184; and No. 69, 1987), as did the bishops of Federal Germany in 1981 (*Documentation Catholique*, No. 63, 1981, 1819). In the U.S., there was a twelve percent increase in the

number of women supporting the feminist position in the months immediately following the promulgation of *Inter insignores.*

28. For media reaction to the Synod, I limit myself to citing the article "Donna, al massimo sarai chierichetta," *Corriere della sera,* October 28, 1987. For a fuller treatment of the issue, including preparation for the Synod, see P. Vanzan, "Problematiche femminile alla vigilia del Sinodo sui laici," *La Civiltà Cattolica,* March 7, 1987, 457–468. See also *Il Regno-Documenti,* No. 584, 1987, and A. Scola, "Fedeli laici, quale futuro?" *Vita e Pensiero,* No. 1, 1988, 2–3, which notes the problematic character of the woman question left unresolved by the Synod.

29. *Il Regno-Documenti,* 708.

30. Among the wealth of writings available in this regard, see P. Vanzan, "La donna contesa. Origini e prime forme del femminismo," *La Civiltà Cattolica,* II, 1983, 24–39; "La donna nella Chiesa: Indicazioni bibliche e interpretazioni femministe," *La Civiltà Cattolica,* I, 1986, 431–444; and "Problematiche femministe alla vigilia del Sinodo sui laici," *La Civiltà Cattolica* I, 1987, 457–468.

31. M.E. Hunt, speaking at a conference sponsored by The Grail, Tiltenberg, Holland, December 1987, on the topic, "Femmes-Eglise dans une perspective globale."

32. For liturgical and cultural activities of base communities, see AA. VV., *Le scomode figlie di Eva* (Brescia-Rome: Communita Nuovi Tempi, 1989).

33. S. Giacomini, "Il veto di Wojtyla non ci preoccupa perché l'immagine di Dio non ha sesso," *La Repubblica,* September 25–26, 1988.

34. For reflections on the topic of communal personalism, see A. Danese, *Unità e pluralità. Mounier e il ritorno alla persona* (Rome: Città Nuova, 1984) and *La questione personalista* (Rome: Città Nuova, 1986), which reprints on pages 150–167 the content of my own essay on "Uomo e donna nel personalismo di Mounier."

35. D. de Rougemont, "L'esprit européen," *Rencontres internationales de Genève,* 1946, *Neuchâtel,* 1947, 144.

Giulia Paola Di Nicola was born in Chieti, Abruzzo, Italy. She specialized in pedagogy at the University of Aquila, and in philosophy at the University of Rome, where her doctoral research was based on the young Hegel's treatment of the history of society and religion. Dr. Di Nicola is currently a researcher in sociology in the Faculty of Political Science at the Università di Studi G. D'Annunzio of Chieti. She has lectured and engaged in research in France, Belgium, Germany and Switzerland and is deeply involved in feminist research, publication and social action. Her writings include *Donne e politica. Quale participazione?* (Rome: Città Nuova, 1983); *Gli emarginati* *dalla politica. Crisi della rappresentanza* (Chieti: Solfanelli, 1985); *Ugua-glianza e Differenza: La Reciprocità Uomo-Donna* (Rome: Città Nuova, 1989); *Antigone. La figura femminile della transgressione* (Rome: CIF, 1990); with A. Danese, *Simone Weil. Abitare la contraddizione* (Rome: Dehoniane, 1991) and articles in journals published in Brescia, Rome, Paris and Malta. Dr. Di Nicola's husband, Attilio Danese, is a researcher in political philosophy and studies personalism and Mounier at the University in Chieti. They have two teenage sons.

8

New Catholic Women in The Netherlands

Catharina J. M. Halkes
and Annelies van Heijst*

Many centuries ago, William the Silent, Dutch prince of Orange, firmly
opposed Spanish Catholic predominance. That fight took eighty years
before William's efforts were crowned with success. In modern times,
many Dutch women fight for their rightful places in society and in their
church. They are no longer silent. Their labor is effective. The article
which follows will attest to this.

THE TITLE GIVEN for this essay, "New Catholic Women in The Netherlands," suggests both its theme and its structure. First of all, we should
say something about the unique history of Dutch Catholicism in order
to provide a context for understanding present-day renewal in the Dutch
Catholic Church (Section I). Then we will pass on to the history of Dutch
Catholic women in which we will depict their attempts to start an organization of their own (Section II). Third, we will consider the "new aspect"
theme of this book. In doing so, we will distinguish a first period of
renewal, 1960 to 1975 (Section III), and, after that, another period in
which the renewal of many Roman Catholic women is progressing at
great speed under the influence of feminist thinking and feminist theology (Section IV). In Section IV, we will also discuss the specific role which

* The first part and the commentary of this essay were written by Catharina Halkes, the
second part by Annelies van Heijst. Both authors share responsibility for the entire essay.
Translations by Maria van Doren, I.C.M., and Paula Copray. Edited by Paula Copray.

Dutch women religious have played during these historical periods. Finally, we will conclude this article with a brief commentary (Section V).

I. The History of Dutch Catholicism

In the Eighty Years' War (1568–1648), the provinces in The Netherlands, especially those in the north, were finally successful in resisting Spanish predomination over their country. This victory had a significant effect both on the social position of Roman Catholics in The Netherlands and on their relationship with Rome. That is why we can observe three characteristics that make up the Dutch Catholic identity.

1. *The "Protestantizing" Characteristic.* The Eighty Years' War was not only the revolt against foreign tyranny, but it was soon to become a war between the Roman Catholic and Protestant religions. The reformation, especially the radical Calvinists, became deeply rooted, and it was the Dutch Calvinists, together with their leader, the prince of Orange, who soon took the lead in this revolt. The peace treaty of 1648 meant not only the political triumph of the northern provinces over Spain, but also the triumph of Calvinism over Roman Catholicism. And as the Calvinists entered the corridors of political power, they also, according to international practice at the time, determined the "national" religion. The remaining Dutch Catholics became a "minority" and were subject to various forms of discrimination: they were excluded from public office and from government assistance to the poor. Subsequently, many upper class Catholics, in order to secure their careers, and many working class Catholics, in order to guarantee their financial support, gradually became Protestants. The Catholics became largely middle class, and they were no longer prominent in the areas of culture and science. They tended to turn to business for their livelihood.

Freedom of religion was not recognized in The Netherlands until the beginning of the nineteenth century. In order to regain their lost liberties, the Dutch Catholics first sided with Dutch liberals, but, after 1860, they greeted the Protestant political parties as their allies. This gave birth to strongly confession-oriented party politics through which the Dutch Catholics regained their self-confidence and their pugnacity. Even to this day, this confessional coalition remains the strongest political party in The Netherlands.

2. *The "Romanizing" Characteristic.* Loyalty to Rome became very

important; without a hierarchy of bishops, the Dutch Catholics, as in many other "mission" areas, came directly under Roman jurisdiction. They became, in effect, "Romans." Moreover, in reaction to discrimination by the Calvinists, it was only natural that Dutch dependence on Rome and Dutch obedience to Rome should reign supreme. When Rome spoke, Dutch Catholics obeyed, fulfilling papal decrees to the letter, providing papal zouaves (guards) when Rome was in trouble, and sending countless missionaries throughout the world. The Netherlands thus was the most obedient "child" of the Roman Church.

Meanwhile, in 1853, the Dutch episcopal hierarchy had been restored, and Catholic self-consciousness gradually emerged. Dutch Catholics began to organize themselves in all aspects of public life, not only in schools and hospitals, but in social clubs, class organizations and the like. This denominational segregation aimed at building up a Catholic power position and, at the same time, preserving the people's faith, for this denominational segregation was meant as a defense against the evil and "godless" world. Thus, a strongly conventional Dutch Catholicism appeared, constantly resisted, though with little success, by a more open-minded Catholicism. It was not until the late 1950s that a breakthrough could take place. An episcopal letter of 1954, resisting any breakthrough, was "accepted" as usual, but it was not lived up to in actuality.

3. The "Secularizing" Characteristic. The Second Vatican Council, proclaimed by Pope John XXIII, not only opened the doors and windows in Rome; it did so especially in Roman Catholic Holland. And while the doors and windows in Rome are pretty well closed again now, Dutch Catholics prefer living in a "draft" to sitting on the lee side. Dutch Catholics have matured and have learned to think critically; they want to assess the many Roman decrees on their value and truth and they have called in their personal consciences. This reversal can also be explained as being a reaction to a Roman tutelage that had lasted too long. It cannot be denied, however, that an undercurrent of conservative Catholicism is still perceptible. These Catholics want to maintain their traditional obedience to Rome.

Catholic renewal in Holland today stresses the importance of learning to live among a pluralism of faith convictions, of seeing the church as "a people on the way." Such a church should have democratic structures, and it should be "in process," searching, encountering and growing. Yet, again, it is characteristic of the Dutch Catholics to try to apply and make real the renewal of Vatican II, and that with a speed not witnessed in any other country. This became especially clear during the six plenary sessions of the Dutch Pastoral Council in 1969–71, where it was evident that a strong spirit of ecumenism pervaded all of Catholic Holland, with observers from different denominations attending the council and contributing to the exchange of ideas. However, this springtime of the Dutch Roman Catholic Church was short-lived. In the 1970s the winter of Roman discontent was not long in coming: very conservative bishops were appointed. Frosty times were ahead. The bloom was nipped in the bud.

II. The Awakening of Catholic Women

The background given above is important for an understanding of the history of Catholic women in The Netherlands. The earliest organizations of Catholic women date back to the time when denominational segregation was in full bloom, and these organizations had all the characteristics of this particular era. It was a priest, Alfons Ariëns, a pioneer in social work, who made the first move. He had a special concern for the drinking problem among textile workers. Convinced that he needed the help of women in his endeavors, he founded the League of Mary in 1895. This was followed by the official start of the Dutch Catholic Women's Union (1912–13), which itself followed the establishment of the International Catholic Women's Union in 1910.

The Dutch Roman Catholic Women's Union focused on the formation and development of Catholic women as persons, as mothers, as social beings. The golden age of the Women's Union was in the 1920s. During this decade, its membership grew steadily and was further increased in 1931, when some eighteen thousand new members, including forty-six congregations of women religious, joined the union.

Then, as now, the union included women of all social classes, even encompassing a group of women initially intended to become a political pressure group. Today, after more than seventy-five years, a new wind is blowing in the union, influenced especially by all the events of the 1960s. Today's Dutch Catholic women want to function critically and creatively in both church and society. As always, there is a pioneer group pressing for renewal, while the majority is slow in following. But things are moving! At the same time, naturally, there is a counter-current that wants to stress the old values and to reclaim the slogan so long cherished by so many women: "Equal But Different."

III. The Beginnings of Renewal

Vatican II and Its Aftermath

In The Netherlands, both Catholics and many others, ecumenically interested, were deeply involved in Vatican II and all that followed the council. Among them were a small group of involved women who have slowly but steadily grown in number. In 1963 some of these women wrote a letter to Pope Paul VI, pleading for lay women as well as lay men to be invited to the council as observers. Although the official response was diplomatically vague, some lay women were present at the third session of the council, among them a Dutch woman, Rie Vendrik. In 1964 a book was published by Catharina Halkes, a Dutch theologian. Its title, *Storm After the Silence,* proved to be prophetic. Though still pre-feminist, the book was a strong call for the emancipation of women, for a new view of female/male relationships, and for equal participation and shared responsibility by women and men, both in church and in society. The publication of *Storm After the Silence* awakened and activated many Dutch women who had not been motivated before.

At about the same time, Catharina Halkes was engaged as co-director of an experiment started by one of the Dutch bishops, a program of weekend formation for lay people to train them for pastoral work. This institute started in 1965 with twenty-four students, including eighteen lay women, two women religious and four men religious. The project was inspired not so much by an anticipated shortage of priests, but by a deep conviction that "pastoral work" is not a special category *within* the church, but a characteristic feature of the church itself. The church will bear fruit only if it is "pastoral": the whole point is that the church should be present in the world. As a result of the professional pastoral formation provided by the institute, these lay people, predominantly women each year, assumed new responsibilities in the church. Their awareness of themselves as "being" church grew. They were "God's people on the way."

In 1967 two important events occurred. The first was the World Congress for the Lay Apostolate in Rome, which passed a resolution on

"Women in the Church," asking for serious theological study of the role of women in the sacramental order and in the church as a whole. The Congress further requested the inclusion of women on all papal commissions and the consultation of women on the proposed revision of the Code of Canon Law, especially on those articles directly related to women.

The second event was the foundation of a Catholic Working Group in The Netherlands, a group which played a critical role in the growing process of church renewal in The Netherlands. The Dutch Catholic Working Group became part of the St. Willibrord Society, the National Ecumenical Advice Committee of the Dutch episcopate. It was a small group, consisting of three women and three men, of whom René van Eyden, Akke van Dam and Catharina Halkes did most of the work. The group stated that the negative results of patriarchy in the church were still apparent. It urged changes in women/men relationships which are not merely external and numerical, and it stressed the necessity of a new attitude and appreciation, which could only grow out of an inner conviction, of regarding women and men as equals.

It is true that the issue of women's ordination was much on our minds in the 1960s. Since the 1920s, women in the more liberal (Protestant) churches in The Netherlands had served as ministers, and, during the 1960s and 1970s, the two major Protestant denominations had admitted women to the ministry. Many of them thought at that time that the struggle was over, but this proved to be a mistake. The issue was not only the admission of women into the ministries of the church. This would only solve the problem partially. Catholic women felt that this was only the tip of the iceberg. Nowadays, Dutch Catholic women are convinced that their problems with the church are much more fundamental. Still, the dialogue on women's ordination has been important—a sign of stirring awareness.

The discussions which took place around the report of the Dutch Pastoral Council (1969–71), "Toward a Fruitful and Renewed Functioning of Ministries," greatly advanced the process of consciousness-raising. A council subcommittee studied the issue of women and ministry, and this resulted in a recommendation both on optional celibacy for priests and on women in ministry, saying "It is necessary for women to be incorporated as soon as possible in all church duties."

The Catholic Working Group, which carefully reviewed all documents issuing from the various commissions established by the Dutch

Pastoral Council, began to look for ways to operationalize the recommendations on women in ministry which had been made at the council. A "pastoral letter" was formulated by members of the Working Group, three of the seven bishops and four theologians (all men, as there were few Dutch women theologians at that time), and submitted to the bishops' conference.

After several meetings, with the bishops arguing for a less progressive "concept," and the Working Group delegates being unwilling to further weaken their text, the idea of a "pastoral letter" was finally abandoned. Both parties ultimately agreed on a compromise: the "pastoral letter" was to become a "discussion note," to be published by the Secretariat of the Bishops' Conference. In their meeting on June 26, 1973, the bishops decided to officially recommend this "note" on "The Place of Women in Pastoral Service in the Church" for further study. "This does not mean," they added, "that we agree with everything in the text. We choose this method to keep the discussion open as widely as possible. The Working Group delegates who formulated this note are responsible for the text." The text was finally promulgated on March 8, 1974—in retrospect, a symbolic date.

The members of the Working Group resigned in 1977, but only after promoting the establishment of two national Working Groups: a section on "Women in Church and Society" within the Dutch Council of Churches, and a Working Group on "Women in the Church" within the Dutch Roman Catholic Church. These two groups have become points of convergence for Dutch women, and were to be the initiators of countless activities.

Both of the above groups have two important characteristics: both are nationwide in their reflection and action, and both keep open the lines of communication with their respective churches. As part of the Council of Churches, "Women in Church and Society" is involved in all the council's ecumenical initiatives, such as the Conciliary Process, the Dutch Day of the Churches, and the Ecumenical Decade, "Churches in Solidarity with Women." The Catholic group focuses more specifically on the situation of women in the Roman Catholic Church, and has regular official consultations with a delegation from the Dutch Bishops' Conference. Thus, women are in a position to press for renewal directly with church authorities. When they are not successful, at least there are channels for communication and information. Women cannot be stopped; they are moving.

IV. New Catholic Women in The Netherlands

When writing on "new Catholic women," it becomes clear to us that feminist theology has been the first and most important element in this renewal. That is why we wish to concentrate first on feminist theology.

Feminist Theology

It is not easy to determine to what extent there has been an interplay between academic feminist theology and what we now call the "woman and faith movement." It is obvious that some interplay was there from the very beginning. The issues included in the so-called "women's studies theology" are always influenced—though not always to the same extent—by the experiences of women at the grass roots. Likewise, the issues of "women's studies theology" have had an impact on the discussions and positions taken by women at the base.

It is Catharina Halkes who, with her students, introduced feminist theology at the University of Nijmegen in 1974. Being both pastorally prepared and coming from years of active work with denominational organizations of women, Halkes opened the doors within the theological faculty to this new discipline. The first feminist theology course at Nijmegen, from 1975–76, was a study of North American feminist literature, including the works of Letty Russell, Rosemary Radford Ruether and Mary Daly.

Since the mid-1970s the teaching of feminist theology has spread rapidly in Dutch theological faculties and universities. In Utrecht, René van Eyden and a group of active women students took the initiative in reflecting on feminist theological topics. Other courses sprang up throughout the country promoted by women students and academicians such as Fokkelien van Dijk-Hemmes and Denise Dijk. Because of the pioneering work done by the University of Nijmegen, a special chair for feminist theology was established there in 1983. Since 1988, this chair has been occupied by Dr. Mary Grey.

Looking back over the last three decades, we see a flourishing network of organizations and relationships in the field of feminist theology. The university working group, Feminism and Theology, has more than two hundred members from various backgrounds, including students, university teachers, church workers and researchers. A study assessing the years 1976–86, "Van Zusters, Meiden en Vrouwen" ("On Sisters,

Girls and Women"), shows that feminist theology has now been incorporated into virtually all academic programs in The Netherlands. Still, this
does not mean the end of the struggle to legitimize feminist theology.
When universities face financial cutbacks, the teachers of feminist theology are the most likely to be dismissed. And the "location" of feminist
theology, as an independent discipline or as an aspect of other courses,
remains ambiguous.

In its earliest phase, feminist theology had an iconoclastic character.
Initially, it focused on unmasking the misogyny apparent in the texts of
scripture and tradition. Church structures and institutions were also
decried for the absence of women within them. Today, influences of
Marxist analysis and of the European Socialist Movement are more
evident in Dutch feminist theology, where being politically committed
and working for justice in both secular and religious spheres are one and
the same thing for many.

Criticism and deconstruction go hand in hand. Women were soon to
realize that a mere demolishing of old images would not do, and that
they should not get stuck in "accusing" and "being the victims." There
proved to be a demand for inspiring church women with whom they
could identify and for a rewriting of church history in order to dig up
many precious women who had got under the sand. It was a necessity
also deeply felt by women at the margin and even by those already
outside the church.

The Woman and Faith Movement

The Dutch Woman and Faith Movement has attracted both women in
the church and women outside the church. Most participants, however,
are women "at the edge" of the church; women are "border-crossers"
both in church and in culture. Three institutions have played major parts
in making the experiences of women more available and in popularizing
the ideas of feminist theology: the media, the national and regional
educational institutes, and the two national working groups already
mentioned: the Ecumenical Council of Churches and the Catholic
Council for Church and Society, together with their many regional and
local groups.

As early as 1976, a Dutch radio station of Christian signature provided a platform for feminist theology in a radio series entitled "When
Women Deliver the Word." The program evoked considerable re-

sponse, notably from the educational institutes that investigated women's needs and offered a course to meet those needs. A need most frequently mentioned was the desire to exchange experiences with other women and to look critically at the patriarchal character of scripture and tradition.

At the same time, discussion groups, some of which developed into action groups, sprang up throughout the country. By 1989 every diocese had its own Woman and Faith group, although many groups had lain in very different cradles. Some groups originated at the invitation of the bishop, whereas others developed in spite of considerable opposition. Conservative bishops did not think their dioceses needed such a group —but the women carried their plans through by themselves. So models of "women/church" grew in a diversity of ways, sometimes on good terms with the bishops, sometimes without consulting them; sometimes within the institutional church, sometimes completely outside.

A milestone in the Woman and Faith Movement was a three-day conference on "The Church and World Institute" at Driebergen, held in 1987. The conference was attended by more than two hundred women from various denominations and from all walks of life. It was a conference that resulted in the *first ecumenical women's synod*. For the first time in church history women made their own decisions about their spiritual lives without male interference. Seventy elected delegates voted on more than fifty recommendations which were then to be forwarded to their respective church leadership departments. It struck that, for the very first time, Dutch women—whether they were more traditional or more radical and/or feminist—underwent together a process of thinking and growing awareness that resulted in a growing unity, which is of the utmost importance when living in an ecclesiastical climate with a "divide and rule" policy. These links were made permanent in the form of a network.

An ever-increasing number of Dutch women desire solid theological formation, both in general and in the area of feminism. In 1983 such a formation was initiated in Nijmegen by a course continuing for six semesters. This group included women and men and met weekly for theological formation. Since that time, the waiting lists for the course have lengthened. Many of the applicants are middle-aged and feel the need of considering their own life experiences and existential choices with a critical eye in the light of newly acquired knowledge. In 1987 a similar course was begun in the province of Limburg.

Further evidence of women's interest in theology was the attendance at the 1987 conference sponsored by the group "Theology and Society." Designed to study Elisabeth Schüssler Fiorenza's book *In Memory of Her,* the conference attracted more than six hundred women and thirty men, the largest number ever gathered specifically to honor the work of a contemporary woman theologian.

With ecclesiastical structure in The Netherlands hardening and with less space for lay theologians in church functions, the number of theology students is decreasing. Opposed to this is the fact that thousands of Dutch women remain committed to a variety of courses. Through these meetings, new forms of community are developing which may be important for "being church" in the future.

Pastoral Ministry

The ordination of women is "marked down" on the feminist agenda. Theologically speaking, all arguments for the admission of women to the priesthood have long been gathered. But today, in the present patriarchal structure, few Dutch women want to be priests. Still, women perform a wide range of church services, often unpaid and as volunteers, and primarily in the roles of care-givers. The steady decline of priests in The Netherlands leaves much work for the women who are available: welcoming new parishioners, visiting the sick and the elderly, preparing children for their first communion. These are the works mostly done by volunteers between the ages of forty and sixty-five, whose children have left home and who want to make themselves useful. Though the executive and administrative functions on the parochial and diocesan levels are still in the hands of men, some women are finding themselves with significant responsibilities in everyday church management, a situation unheard of even ten years ago. In this respect, the "emancipation" of women in the church is still one-sided. Women are moving carefully toward some executive and administrative functions, whereas men are seldom joining the women in the communicative and care-giving functions.

While the number of women whose work for the church is unpaid has doubled in the last decade, there are some women church workers who are salaried. From time immemorial there have been women housekeepers in parish rectories. Their activities vary greatly. Sometimes they are involved in organizational activities as well. Then there are parish assistants and pastoral workers. The function of the parish assistant is a helping one; the pastoral worker has a theological formation and can work independently. The relations between these two groups are not always smooth, for their specific competencies are not always clearly defined. One of the reasons might be the fact that housekeepers and parish assistants are usually women religious and, as such, they are held in higher esteem than lay women by the parishioners.

The role of the male or female pastoral worker is a rather recent innovation. The year 1973 saw the first men appointed as pastoral workers. In 1975 there were thirteen women among the 154 pastoral workers. In 1988, the number of women pastoral workers had risen to 115. The most recent data for The Netherlands are 2,457 priests, 70 deacons and 327 pastoral workers.

Women pastoral workers and women pastoral assistants are not always radical feminists. Their first concern is to give the church a human face. Often they are swamped with organizational tasks and are challenged to keep parish activities going with limited resources, both human and financial. Moreover, they and their colleagues on the parish team have to cope with ever-increasing opposition from the conservative hierarchy.

In a number of dioceses, the official rules governing pastoral workers have become more strict. This implies that the practices of baptizing, anointing of the sick and presiding at word-communion services are being restricted anew, though not in every diocese. In effect, all sacramental priestly functions and the main responsibilities of the pastoral ministry have been returned to priests and, partly, to male deacons, ordained since the mid-1980s. Dioceses are also increasingly concerned, both financially and emotionally, with the newly founded seminaries. Almost every diocese now has new forms of seminary education for priests: church priorities have again become clerical ones.

What of the attitude of the faithful toward women pastoral workers? As in the past, though less now, the faithful have some initial difficulty in accepting them. The Roman Catholic Church has no old-time tradition of women priests. And, suddenly, the parishioners see a woman where they have always seen a man. However, once the faithful get used to women pastoral workers, they are usually well-accepted. For one thing, the "clerical distance" between the pastoral worker and the faithful is completely absent. Moreover, women pastoral workers often see themselves more in the service of the faithful than of the institutional church.

Many initiatives have been taken by women in the fields of spirituality and celebration, notably in formation centers such as that of the Grail Movement in Tiltenberg, where many new forms of liturgy have been developed. Other centers focus more on society, for example "de Vuurdoop" ("Fire Baptism") in Tilburg where young theologians work together with those who are socially marginalized. In parishes, too, women organize celebrations with explicitly female themes, to which celebrations everyone is welcome. Generally speaking, movements such as the goddess and witch movements have aroused little enthusiasm among Catholic women in The Netherlands. On the other hand, "holistic" spirituality meets with a warm welcome. Outside the established churches, there is a widespread and therapeutic variety of various forms of "holism," eastern religions, and reincarnation and Christian-mystical spiritualities.

The Papal Visit and the Eighth-of-May Movement

If we are asked what brought the Woman and Faith Movement into the limelight, we must answer, strangely enough, that it was the visit of Pope John Paul II to our country in 1985, or, rather, two related incidents involving women which roused considerable attention.

Several weeks before the pope was to arrive, Cardinal Simonis barred Catharina Halkes from speaking in the presence of the pope. The Union of Catholic Women had asked her to give an address on the occasion of the papal visit. This veto, sounding as if we were back in the dark middle ages, met with an uproar within—and, even more, outside—the Roman Catholic Church. In protest, two women's organizations, the Catholic Women's League and the Dutch Women Religious, decided to abstain from attending the meeting with the pope.

What in Catharina Halkes' speech made it so revolutionary that it could not pass the papal ears? Listen to the most "rebellious" passage of her text:

It is high time for women to take up the church positions that are rightfully theirs, to share responsibility on all levels of faith and church struc-

tures. . . . The pope, in general, speaks to or about women in relation to
motherhood and family. He would be a more refreshing source of inspiration for many of us, especially for young women, if he could point out the
many human possibilities which women might realize at this moment.

Was it the text itself or was it the assertive and feminist image of Mrs.
Halkes that frightened the church authorities so much? Mrs. Hedwig
Wasser, too, caused quite a stir by adding some personal observations to
the text she was to deliver before the pope, a text that had been carefully
prepared for her by the Dutch Mission Council. She said:

> Do we gain faith-credit if we bring the liberating message of the gospel
> with a warning finger instead of stretching out a helping hand? If there is
> no room but only a closed door for those who live together without being
> married, for the divorced, for homosexuals, for married priests, for
> women? Do we gain faith-credit if bishops stand above us rather than
> among us, people-on-the-way? . . . Many of us, in critical faithfulness and
> Christian obedience, have become disobedient to the church because of
> recent developments within the church. But we all *are* the church!

A storm arose! A storm of applause from people who felt oppressed
within the church, and a storm of indignation from the papal-faithful.
This act of resistance—though viewed apart as very modest—assumed
the dimensions of an international row. All this raised the question:
"What sort of church do we have if women speaking out freely can
shake the church to its foundations?"

Reactions to both events greatly differed. For many whose relationship to the church was already tenuous, it was an occasion to sever their
ties completely. For others, it became a moment for organizing, for
bringing together all those of one mind to lend each other a listening
ear and to show "the other face of the church." Accordingly, on the
eighth of May in 1985, thousands of Roman Catholics assembled in
The Hague.

This meeting initiated the Eighth-of-May Movement (EMM), which
has since continued to bring thousands of Dutch Catholics together
annually. They are most impressive meetings which give support and
inspiration to many. Various groups participate: peace and environmen-
tal groups, women's organizations, gay and lesbian people, Christians for
socialism, the League of Married Priests, and many others. The EMM is

not an "organization" with "members." Rather, it is a network in which various people and groups participate. It is attended by many individuals who come for inspiration and encouragement. Today the Woman and Faith Movement is primarily found in the EMM, where people are indeed "moving." But we deal with networks, not with organizational structures. We deal with people on the move, people on borderlines who are so difficult to lay hold on. The same can be applied to women religious. Owing to their special status in the church, they have, on the one hand, a position that asks for special attention; on the other hand, they are involved in the movements mentioned above.

Women Religious

Do we classify women religious in The Netherlands "new" Catholic women, or does their median age characterize them as "old" Catholics? Statistically, Dutch women religious are "old" Catholics. In 1988 there were 17,440 women religious in The Netherlands, of which two-thirds were over age sixty-five. Whereas most of them are members of apostolic congregations, 991 are contemplative, or cloistered, nuns. The total number represents a dramatic decrease from the 1930s, when The Netherlands boasted more than 30,000 women religious. Because so few are entering religious life today, it is expected that the present form of religious life for women will soon die out (see Kaski Report, No. 251, Den Haag, 1988). From this perspective, is it possible to see women religious as renewed and renewing women?

When we consider the profound spiritual renewal that congregations of women religious have gone through, together with the influence they have had on renewal in the Dutch church, the answer must be a clear affirmative. This change of congregational spirituality was in many respects no less than a conversion. The sisters today have left behind them a lifestyle that was alienating them from the world; it was individualistic, overly ascetic, strongly legalistic and authoritarian. Their future is sought in discovering together a new lifestyle characterized by communication and sisterhood, openness and shared responsibility. Though, in justice, we must acknowledge the fruits of the "old lifestyle": disciplined communities of women religious were pioneers in founding Catholic schools and hospitals, in social services, in care centers for the elderly, and in service in the foreign missions.

After the experimentation period of the 1970s, religious congregations were expected to submit their revised rules and constitutions for approval by *men* in the Vatican. The ensuing discussions between women religious and Rome have made two points very clear: whereas the sisters strongly value their affiliation with the institutional church, they have also grown much more critical and more insistent on a much greater degree of self-determination about the way they live their lives. The former point is especially influenced by the fact that many Dutch congregations have an international character; they have convents in different countries, even on different continents. Religious congregations are small institutions within a big institution, the church. Living in an institute, dealing with differences and trying to come to terms: all this is more a part of the religious lifestyle than is the case with lay Catholics. This may be the reason why the sisters have been able to endure the recent "typically institutional" tensions. They hold out longer.

Relations between Dutch women religious and the institutional church have not been improved by the recent appointments of Dutch bishops. Although there are contacts between sisters and bishops on an official level, the gap between them is great and wide. And many a sister personally feels this gap even as a chasm. In nearly every congregation/ order, there is a minority that is quite comfortable with traditional church authority. For them, "renewal" is a threat to the convent life which they chose so long ago. Obviously, this is a potential source of pain and conflict.

But the majority has embarked on a new course, which appears in recent chapter decisions of congregations. And within this large unity there arise small groups or even individuals who embrace the radical consequences of a life devoted to the poor and marginal in our society. This new orientation has its impact on how church is experienced. And, whereas church authorities may not feel happy about it, religious women participate in critically oriented base communities and movements in the church. In contrast to their U. S. sisters, who were openly called to task by the pope for their strong positions and self-determination, Dutch sisters adopt a more cautious attitude. But in spite of this, on the occasion of the papal visit to Holland in 1985, women religious were "reminded" that their first duty was prayer and not their work for the world. The sisters felt this as a correction of the new meaning they had given to their vocation and mission in response to the "signs of the times."

Dutch women religious have been extremely creative in their search for new ways to combine the two elements of contemplation and care. Many sisters joined the peace movement, either in action or in prayer. Others, still vital enough to do so, have turned to work with those who are marginal in society: refugees, drug addicts, heroin prostitutes, foreign women and the homeless. Hundreds have found a new task in pastoral ministry, either as volunteers or as professional pastoral workers.

Experiences of Dutch Women

What are the differences between "old" and "new" Catholic women in Holland? The pre-World War II generation of Catholic women were almost invariably mothers of large families. "One more child on the way every year" was the expectation. Women had little sex information, and contraceptives were forbidden. In the book *Zodoende was de vrouw maar een mens om kinderen te krijgen* (*In Fact Women Were Only Meant To Have Children*), letters from three hundred such women told of their problems and their poverty, but they also described the warmth of a big family. As one woman gave her experience:

> We had seven children in eleven years. But I decided the births of the later children. Some of them were just a year apart. You were hardly recovered from the one when the next was on its way. It really was a life of sacrifice.

Since reliable contraceptives have come on the market, many Catholic women have been using them. Most of the women and their partners have no moral problem with this. When nowadays Dutch women reflect on their faith, sexual morality is not a primary topic; they are more concerned with a new vision of God and about what it means to be human. As one woman speaks:

> God, for me, is not an a-historic being but a dynamic reality, continuously working in the midst of our history today. To me, believing in God means believing in human beings—human beings in their daily, down-to-earth reality with all its problems and misery.

The above are only two voices in the much bigger choir. And there are other voices, speaking specifically about the experience of women with the Roman Catholic Church.

In 1981 the results of a study of Dutch women in relation to the Catholic Church were published in an article entitled "Revelation of Experience." It was clear from the study that many women had had negative experiences with the church administration and with the attitude of the church concerning women. The women's criticism highlighted the tremendous "distance" they perceived between official church teachings and the lived experience of women, as well as the unequal treatment of men and women in the church. The study included the respondents' specific recommendations for change in church attitudes and practices. Finally, there was an urgent request for a scientific follow-up study to this one.

This request was complied with: Kaski (Catholic Social Church Institute), which is regularly involved in religious research, compiled a report based on interviews with more than six hundred women from twelve parishes throughout the country. Its most important conclusion is that certain findings from "Revelation of Experience" were clearly confirmed: in its teaching and practice and in its views of men/women and morality, the church is far removed from the faith experience of ninety-eight percent of the women interviewed. The same could be said of the church's practice and theory (theology), which regard women as subordinate and as complementary to men. This is not consistent with women's self-perceptions or with their personal experiences.

Two trends emerge: on the one hand, many women are increasingly engaged in working for change in the church; on the other hand, more and more women, out of disappointment or indifference, are leaving the church. The latter is especially true of younger women.

Women under thirty-five years of age, the generation which is educating young children, have a strikingly different attitude toward the church than that expressed by older women. The younger women are just not that concerned about the church anymore. It is all the same to them. Is the church losing a whole generation of women? And, if so, what of their children and future generations? Even now, many of the children of these young mothers know nothing of the Old and New Testaments; their faith inheritance has become an "empty testament." The frame of reference of Bible stories, religious images, liturgies and rituals is completely or almost completely lacking. In the long run, this situation will lead to great impoverishment on the cultural level. But it will also have an impact on people's philosophical and religious questions. At the same time, interestingly enough, secular European culture is reviving its old sensitivity to forms—to art (modern as well as ancient art); to conventions (a revival of etiquette); to distinguishing oneself by clothing (women's dress is becoming more "feminine")—whereas the progressive part of the church has said farewell to many, many forms. The young who may be looking for such symbols and traditions mostly find what suits them in conservative religious groups. These are the groups that have conserved the forms. This should be an issue of great concern to those in the Woman and Faith Movement who are beginning to miss having young women among them.

V. Commentary

These last remarks have brought us into the evaluative sphere. What conclusions can we now make regarding the situation of new Catholic women in The Netherlands?

The Netherlands' new Catholic women—those who remain connected to the institutional church—are intensely engaged on every level in the work of church renewal. In this work, however, their orientation is clearly ecumenical, and they want to give shape to this orientation.

In our western society, so deeply characterized by aggressiveness and consumerism, and with an ever-growing gap between the rich and poor, it is the women, women religious included, who labor for the quality of life, for sharing the need of the minima, for realizing justice, peace and the integrity of creation (all major themes of the Conciliar Process). In the early 1980s the focus was still on liberating women and marginal people from the injustices of a patriarchal culture. More recently, feminism has begun to criticize culture itself, and the question more often being asked today is, "Liberation for what?"

In order to preserve the shaky balance between personal autonomy and relationality, it is the small work-and-life communities of women religious which provide inspiring examples of how individual authenticity and solidarity can be combined.

The new concept for a Dutch law that guarantees "equal treatment" will, if accepted, make it easier for lesbian women to "come out" and to function without discrimination in all areas of endeavor, including Christian institutions.

The surprisingly large numbers of women volunteers and the growing number of women pastoral workers in the church make clear that women are more and more the sustainers of the faith community in The Netherlands. If this trend continues, women in the church will be a strong bulwark against the growing conservatism of church authority. We might even venture to say that the Woman and Faith Movement is a birthplace of "Women-Church."

The rapid and strong development of these women's movements and their wide range of activities can be attributed, in part, to some typically Dutch characteristics. We mention some of these:

The Netherlands is a small country with excellent communication and transportation systems. Distances, relatively speaking, are short, and the number of assembly points is great.

Having been emancipated politically, Dutch Catholic women, both lay and religious, gave, in the 1960s, a warm welcome to the process of religious emancipation. Their intense involvement in both Vatican Council II and the Dutch Pastoral Council has brought them to a level of profound maturity.

Ecumenism has flourished as never before, and this is in keeping with the ecumenical development of feminist theology. Moreover, throughout the years, there has been and there still is a good and inspiring contact between Dutch Catholic women and the World Council of Churches.

Again, The Netherlands, being a small country, has always had a strong international orientation. It is a transit country with a transit culture. That is why Holland's own identity may have become less strong, while its frequent encounters with Europe and other countries throughout the world have given wider scope to its vision and have enabled the Dutch to acknowledge their relative limitations.

Finally, in the light of all that has been said, it will not come as a bolt from the blue to the reader to hear of the second Dutch Women's Synod in 1992.

Spring 1990

Documentation

Bekkenamp, Jonneke, e.a. *Van zusters, meiden en vrouwen.* I.I.M.O. Leiden-Utrecht: 1986.

Goddijn, Walter. *Roomsen dat waren wij.* Hilversum: 1978.

(Govaart)-Halkes, Tine. *Storm na de stilte. De plaats van de vrouw in kerk.* Utrecht: 1964. (Duitse vertaling: Frau, Welt, Kirche. Graz-Wien-Köln: 1967.)

————. "Ceterum censeo—Over de vrouw in het ambt." *Kultuurleven* (oktober 1967) 34e jaargang nr. 8.

Hopmans, Corry M. J. "De Rooms Katholieke Vrouwenbond, 1912–1928." Doctoraal-scriptie, Katholieke Universiteit Nijmegen, 1978.

Katholieke Raad voor Kerk en Samenleving. *Openbaring van de Ervaring.* Amersfoort: 1981.

KASKI. *Vrouw en Kerk.* Rapport in opdracht van de Katholieke Raad voor Kerk en Samenleving. Amersfoort, Leuven: 1978.

Kerklaan, Marga. *Zodoende was de vrouw maar een mens om kinderen te krijgen.* 300 brieven over het roomse huwelijksleven. Baarn: 1987.

Nationale Vrouwenraad voor Nederland. *De vrouw in de Nederlandse samenleving.* 's-Gravenhage: 1956.

Thurlings, J.M.G. *De wankele zuil.* Nijmegen, Amersfoort: 1971.

van Eyden, René. "De vrouw in liturgische functies." *Concilium.* 8e Jaargang nr. 2 (februari 1972) 68–83.

————. "Die Frau im Kirchenamt." *Wort unt Wahrheit.* 22e Jahrgang (mai 1967) 350–362.

van Heyst, Annelies. *Zusters, vrouwen van de wereld.* Aktieve religieuzen en haar emancipatie. Amsterdam: 1985.

Verhoef, Will, ed. *Vrouw en macht—Vrouwenmacht.* Verslag van 10 jaar Vrouw en Geloofswerk op Kerk en Wereld, waarin de aanbevelingen van de Oecumenische Vrouwensynode. Driebergen: 1987.

Vrouwen:

Davids, Joke, 40 jaar Katholiek Vrouwendispuut, 1946–1986. z.p.; z.j.

Derks, Marjet, Catharina Halkes en Annalies van Heijst (red.) Roomse Dochters. Katholieke Vrouwen en hun beweging. 1992.

de Waal, Anna, 15 jaar Katholiek Vrouwendispuut, 1946–1961. z.p.; z.j.

Opdat de geschiedenis niet verloren gaat—25 jaar geschiedenis Katholieke Vrouwengilde, uitgegeven bij de viering van het 75 jarig bestaan, Baarn 1988.

Sectie Vrouw en Kerk en Samenleving van de Nederlandse Raad van Kerken. Al gaande zal je kracht vermeerderen—Teksten van en over Zuster Francesco (Antoinette) van Pinxteren. 's Hertogenbosch/Amersfoort: 1990.

Van Onmondig tot Mondiaal, de zin van de katholieke vrouwenbeweging; haar 50-jarig bestaan, Tilburg 1963.

Themanummers Kosmos en Oecumene:

"Nairobi 1975: Assemblee Werelddraad van Kerken." 9e jaargang (1975) nr.
     10–11.
"(On-) zichtbaarheid van vrouwen." 20e jaargang (1986) nr. 8.
"Samenwerking man-vrous." 3e jaargang (1969) nr. 1.
"De Vrous en het ambt." 1e jaargang (1967) nr. 2.
"Vrouw-en-Kerk." 22e jaargang (1988) nr. 5.
"Vrouw en Pastoraat." 5e jaargang (1971) nr. 1.
"Vrouw-maatschappij-kerk." 8e jaargang (1974) nr. 4–5.
"Vrouwen en mannen over oecumene." 20e jaargang (1986) nr. 9–10.
"Vrouwen en de Wereldraad van Kerken." 19e jaargang (1985) nr. 3.
"Wereldlekencongres." 1e jaargang (1967) nr. 8.

Catharina J.M. Halkes holds a doctorate from Leyden in Dutch literature
and philology and in the history of medieval philosophy and mystics. Her
later studies in pastoral theology were done at the Universities of Utrecht
and Nijmegen, and, from 1970 to her retirement as "emeritus" in 1986, she
was a member of the staff of the theological faculty of the Roman Catholic
University of Nijmegen. In 1982 she received an honorary degree from the
Berkeley Divinity School at Yale University, and in 1983 she became the first
incumbent of Nijmegen's special Chair in Feminism and Christianity. She
lectures widely and has published extensively in feminist theology; her latest
book was published in 1989 and is available in both Dutch and English. She
is the mother of a daughter and two sons and has three grandchildren.

Annelies van Heijst studied ethics and feminist theology at the University of
Nijmegen and, as a lay woman, serves as theological advisor to the Dutch
Conference of Women Religious in The Netherlands. In 1985 she published
a study of the history of the emancipation of Dutch women religious, *Zusters, Vrouwen van de Wereld* (*Religious Sisters, Women of the World*). She
has also published numerous articles on feminist theology, and is finishing
her doctorate thesis: *Losing one's self: Feminist subject-positions in postmo-
dernity—a theory of reading.* She was one of the initiators of *Mara*, a periodical focusing on feminism and theology.

9

New Catholic Women in Spain

María Salas
with the Collaboration of Marifé Ramos*

> Are we to deduce from the fact that Christ was a man and that he chose only men that he wished forever to exclude women from the priesthood? Christ also did not choose a single Gentile, and the church never had a problem considering or accepting Gentiles.
>
> —A WOMAN IN BARCELONA
>
> After so many centuries in which churchmen have presented woman as temptation and sin, as the cause of evil, as danger for the male—and all this not centuries ago but even yesterday—why not a gesture of contrition? Why don't we ask for an apology, just as another pope apologized to the "separated brethren"?
>
> —THE EDITOR OF *Foc Nou*

Membership and Practice

ACCORDING TO OFFICIAL RECORDS, in 1987, eighty-six percent of all Spanish adults over fifteen years of age identified themselves as Catholic.[1] Within this large group, women predominate; ninety-one percent of the women identified themselves as Catholic, as opposed to eighty-one percent of the men. Women not only participate in greater numbers, but they also play a much more active role in both the preparation for and the reception of the sacraments. In some parishes, the attendance at

* Translated by Armida Deck and N. Carmina Chapa-Gutierrez

some of the services—daily mass, Lenten conferences, community prayer, etc.—is almost exclusively female.

We have the impression that if, historically, fidelity to religious practice has been greater in women, the rejection of the church by women, when this has occurred, as it has fairly recently, has been all the more radical and violent. The first generation of women who left the church have frequently continued to manifest strong feelings of resentment to the church and have almost taken pride in a very active and, at times, militant opposition. When women abandon the church today, their departure seems to be more gradual and to happen with much less trauma to themselves.

Ministries and Service

Few Lay Ministries for Women

Lay ministry in Spain exists in very few dioceses and only as the exception. Accordingly, few women have been called to minister, and their presence and activities in this regard are largely unknown. Even persons deeply inserted in church life seem to be unaware of the presence of women.

One of the bishops who does recognize women's role and contributions is the ordinary of Bilbao, who defines lay ministry as "a mission or public charge, not just for certain moments, which may be temporary or indefinite." And he has demonstrated his episcopal blessing by assigning such ministries to women in solemn liturgical ceremonies. In some cases, giving even greater significance to his actions, he has requested that the commissioning of women take place at the same celebrations in which seminarians are installed as lectors. It must be noted that, in the current church situation, he could do no more!

The women who have thus been commissioned for ministry are charged with pastoral duties within the parish such as catechesis, health ministry, financial management and Sunday celebrations in the absence of a priest. In the case of such Sunday celebrations, the women ministers conduct the entire liturgy—with the exception of the consecration—including the homily.

In March of 1982, in a parish in Madrid, a group of lay people, including both women and men, was given public recognition for the ministries in which they had been engaged for several years. Though these ministries have been recognized in this parish for some time, still the way has not been opened for similar experiences in other parishes, and this program remains "one of a kind."

If the number of women who have been formally commissioned to ministry is small, the number of women who regularly engage in service to the church is huge. This is a strange distinction.

Women today can carry out some of the services from which they were formerly excluded as long as they do not demand any official recognition of their ministerial positions. The most surprising of these services are those of lector and acolyte; though still prohibited to women by the new Code of Canon Law, some women perform these services daily without the slightest problem. Thus the services of women are utilized, but without official acknowledgment.

The majority of the services performed by women in the church are found in two clearly delineated areas which traditionally have been considered appropriate for women: catechesis and works of charity. As Monique Hébrard says in her book *Les Femmes dans l'Eglise,* it is taken for granted that "catechesis derives naturally from [women's] traditional role; the mother gives life and transmits the faith."[2] And women have always been at the bedsides of the ill and with those who suffer.

There are some 230,000 catechists in Spain today, and, of these, seventy percent to eighty percent are women. Some women have been pioneers in catechetical renewal. In the early post-conciliar years, Margarita Riber, a religious of Maria Reparadora and a catechetical formation expert, wrote a biblical catechesis that has had many printings. Ana Maria Muñoz, a Sister of Jesus and Mary, initiated the use of audiovisual materials in catechesis. Many others have collaborated and continue to collaborate, as we shall see further on, with diocesan and national catechetical teams. And, collectively, an association called JARIS, promoted by women close to the Teresian Institute, is engaged in catechetical research and experimentation and in the production of teaching materials.

Another task engaging many people in service to the church is that of teaching religion in the schools. The number of women in this area is much lower than in parish catechetics, perhaps because a university degree is required. But the presence of women here is nonetheless significant. In primary education, which has the lowest social status and is poorly paid, if paid at all, the vast majority of religion teachers are women. In the middle grades, the opposite is true; until recently, all religion teachers at this level were priests. Now, however, women are increasingly attaining positions in the middle grades, though their working conditions are precarious, with low salaries, no social security and with temporary contracts.

In higher education, of three hundred and fifty professors teaching at the university level in Madrid, thirty-four are women.

While the main responsibility of the religion teachers is to instruct the students in official church doctrine, quite a few of them are also engaged pastorally—for example, in preparing candidates for the sacrament of confirmation—and they attend to the spiritual needs of the students through religious gatherings and celebrations.

Charitable services are sometimes professionally administered, with the help of social workers; at other times, they are offered by volunteers who, for the most part, are women. It cannot be denied that imaginative and creative women have been able to respond effectively to some very serious problems which high civilian authorities were incapable of resolving. Many such actions form part of that hidden history of women which will one day have to be written.

Presently, in some Spanish provinces, the best attention to the needs of the poor and homeless is provided by women volunteers who offer social service programs that are responsive to the times. Again, however, these programs are not included in the category of services supported by the civil administration.

Spain's best answer to the needs of the third world is found in the efforts of "Manos Unidas" ("United Hands"), an organization established in 1960 by the women of Catholic Action. Presently the group collects some 2,500 million pesetas annually, with which it is able to finance 168 projects in Asia, 135 in Africa, and 443 in South America. Only 2.3 percent of the funds collected are used for administrative expenses. The efficiency of "Manos Unidos" has won the respect of the general population, including even non-believers.

New Fields for Action

In addition to roles traditionally assigned to them—catechesis and the works of charity—Spanish Catholic women are slowly taking on new roles which were formerly forbidden to them.

We have already referred to the gradual increase in the number of women in the field of religious education in both public and Catholic educational centers. Another field in which women are advancing is that of spiritual direction. As one of the contributors to this essay reminded us: "Superiors of monasteries and directresses of novices have always assumed responsibility for the spiritual formation of their sisters." This is yet another aspect of that history of women which is still to be written.

The work of spiritual direction—without official recognition, of course—is now done by women religious as well as by lay women, and for a broader public than ever before. Though still few in number, these women direct the Spiritual Exercises, preach retreats and lead courses in prayer. On rare occasions, some of us have had the opportunity to preach, though the number of women who do this regularly is very small, and such preaching is always requested by groups that are exclusively female.

Although there are quite a few women with licentiate and doctoral degrees in theology, the inclusion of women on the faculties of seminaries is very recent and very minimal. In 1987 Dolores Aleixandre, a Religious of the Sacred Heart, was named Professor of Sacred Scripture at the Jesuit University of Comillas. Felisa Elizondo, of the Teresian Institute, is a Professor of Theological Anthropology at the Seminary of Madrid and at the Institute of Theological and Catechetical Sciences. There are perhaps two or three others who do some teaching in diocesan seminaries.

Leadership Positions in the Church

In Spain today there are some dozen women who are administrators of parishes, and they exercise all the functions proper to a pastor, excepting the consecration of the eucharist and the sacrament of reconciliation. The majority of these women are women religious who have received their assignments either personally or collectively, but there are also some lay women chosen for this task.

Women are gradually being incorporated into vicariate teams in the larger dioceses. Most often they are volunteers and serve as secretaries, though little by little they are finding their way onto policy and decision-making committees, sometimes with their own individual responsibilities. In one instance, in 1980, a woman was named as catechetical delegate to a vicariate in Madrid, and her appointment by the bishop was published in the official episcopal bulletin. Though she continued to enjoy the trust and help of her bishop, she resigned in 1985, feeling the absence of welcome and support by the local clergy.

Women can be found in almost all diocesan pastoral groups in parity, more or less, with the men. According to diocesan reports, there are at the present time perhaps thirty women in the sixty-five Spanish dioceses who serve as diocesan delegates or representatives. They work in the areas of family life ministry, vocation ministry, migrant ministry and liturgy; some are secretaries of the diocesan pastoral council.

In the Spanish Episcopal Conference, women are present primarily as secretaries and typists. While some women serve as technical collaborators on policy-making teams, only two women serve in the higher echelons: Rosa de la Cierva, a Religious of the Sacred Heart, has served for several years as technical secretary of the Episcopal Commission on Education and as Director of the corresponding Secretariat, and Rafaela Rodriguez Caso of the Teresian Institute directs the Cinema Department of the National Secretariat on Media in Social Communications.

Working Conditions for Women in the Church

Since they are seldom paid, or paid inadequately, most women perform their ministry or service to the church on a part-time basis. Thus they often have to juggle two positions. Only a minority of the women work full-time in ministry, and still fewer are reimbursed adequately for their services. Most often, the full-time ministers are women religious who are supported by their religious communities.

Scarce economic resources is one of the excuses used to justify the limiting of lay involvement, in general, and of women in responsible positions, in particular. Besides the lack of compensation for lay ministry, there is also an evident lack of esteem for the work done by the laity. It is a pity that some of the services being given with such dedication, especially in small towns and rural areas, are so little appreciated by the priests, who are the principal beneficiaries, that often not even a word of gratitude is expressed. On the contrary, the clergy at times make women the object of ridicule, prohibiting them from occupying more responsible posts while deriding them for being content with the less significant tasks.

More significant roles in ministry for women are frequently achieved only through their own personal initiative. Only in the area of catechetics, because the need is so great, has there been a direct call for women's services. A long-term plan for preparing the laity and giving them responsible positions in the church is sorely needed—and is still missing in Spain. There is no overall collaborative pastoral planning. Women complain bitterly about this. They are sought out only at times of dire need, never because of a profound conviction as to their value in the church or of a desire for coherence with the gospel message, or at least with the documents promulgated by the magisterium.

Some clergy admit this quite openly. In gathering material for this essay, we visited the secretary to one of the Spanish bishops who has entrusted responsible positions to women. When we asked him if the number of women working in the diocese was still the same, he explained that two of the women had been replaced by priests. Shocked, we demanded to know if these women had only been used as substitutes. To our further dismay, his answer was a direct and clear, "Of course!" For once, we remained silent.

Women also complain about how this utilitarian approach leaves the pastoral plan totally at the mercy of the priest in charge, who, often feeling that his "territory" is being invaded, is careful to control just how much involvement is permitted.

At present, ten to twelve women continue to serve as pastors of parishes, and their experiences are varied, from being more or less accepted by their priest-colleagues to constantly receiving unsolicited "wise advice" from clergy as to what they should do and how they should do it. The majority of these women, however, feel well supported by their respective bishops.

In general, Catholic parishes and communities accept these changes much more readily than the prognosticators would have had us believe. The people do not seem overly surprised at the presence of women in new kinds of ministry, nor do the people reject them. And the new generations would be willing to go further. In one parish in which a woman serves as pastor, the children find it strange that a priest from the outside must come to celebrate the eucharist, and they ask their woman pastor: "Is it because you do not know how to say the mass?"

There are, however, some very traditional congregations in which the people prefer that a priest assume the responsibility for all services. There have even been cases of parishioners actually changing their seats in the church to avoid having to receive communion from the hands of a woman.

Finally, we should point out that most of the women who have responsible ministries in the church—like their sisters working outside the church—experience the need to demonstrate a higher level of competency than their male colleagues (some of whom are, in fact, quite mediocre). When we questioned people about the degree of participation by and acceptance of women on male-female parish teams, a typical response was: "She participates a great deal and is well accepted because she acts very sensibly." The men can simply do their job. Women have to be both competent—and discreet.

Theological Formation in Seminaries and Universities

Theological studies are not offered in secular or state universities in Spain, and this lack is sorely felt. The Catholic Church offers theology courses only in its diocesan seminaries and in its own theology faculties.

Until a few years ago Catholic theological education was not available to women, so it was impossible for a woman to obtain a degree in theology in Spain. In 1969 one of the authors of this essay, having been refused admittance to any of the theological programs in Madrid, had to move to Louvain for the several years of her study. More recently, however, the situation has changed for the better. In the last several years the number of women enrolled in theological studies in Spain—whether short-term or within seminary programs—has exceeded that of men in the lower levels.

While assistance for women in theological studies, though sporadic and not always systematic, has become more widespread, there is an interesting related phenomenon. As the number of women in the various theological *programs* increases, their presence at higher levels of theological studies declines significantly. So while there are more women who have studied theology, there are few women with licentiate degrees and even fewer with doctoral degrees.[3]

A study by FERAT in 1987[4] recorded responses from the eleven dioceses which participated: there was a total of 268 theology students, of whom 145 were lay women and 93 were women religious. While the levels of their studies varied, it was obvious that very few were preparing for the doctorate. We must note, however, that this number of women is still surprisingly high, given the few economic incentives which such studies offer, the almost non-existent possibility of promotion within the church, and the lack of recognition of these studies by Spanish civil authorities.

The FERAT study asked students about their motivation for the study of theology. Most responded in personal and vocational terms rather than in terms of monetary incentives or of any desire to obtain high positions in the church. Listed according to the frequency of responses, the students study theology in order to:

1. Give a more solid grounding to the faith and to their experience of the Christian life.
2. Form themselves to engage in pastoral services.
3. Be able to clarify the faith to a critical and conflictual society; give the world a better and more intelligent perspective from the faith.
4. Participate in church renewal by assuming co-responsibility with the clergy and the laity's own responsibility.
5. Engage in a personal search rather than remain content with what others say regarding God and Jesus Christ; accommodate faith and scientific knowledge.

With respect to the obstacles they have encountered, many of the women theology students cited the same difficulties which any lay person might encounter—for example:

1. Programs oriented to clergy and religious.
2. Scanty treatment of the specific problems of secularized society.
3. The absence of a "theology of the people of God." The theology which is taught reinforces the hierarchical structure of the church.
4. Difficulty in harmonizing their theological studies with other disciplines, their work or their families. (They say, "You have to be brave to study theology!")

Women pointed out obstacles which they found precisely because they are women:

1. Paternalistic, distrustful or ironic treatment.
2. A masculine and patriarchal vision of some of the subject matter.

3. The necessity of constantly having to prove that one is a serious
   student rather than someone who is just passing the time.

Some women expressed more external or circumstantial difficulties.
For example they cited the very few women theology professors, the
excessive control over women students and the lack of participation by
women students in the theology faculties. While many appreciate the
welcome expressed to them by several professors and fellow students,
they still feel generally treated as persons who do not "belong."

At the present time Spanish women cannot say that they encounter
obstacles from school administrators when they apply for admission to
theological studies, but it is made clear to them that the programs are
designed for future priests and for religious and not for the laity—even
less so for women. For women, there are the so-called "short courses,"
or courses of a less academic nature. As one clear example, classes for
the licentiate are usually held in the mornings, when family and/or work
obligations make it impossible for women who have earned the B.A. in
theology through night courses to study for the licentiate.

Though hesitantly, some theology faculties are considering allowing
students already holding B.A.'s in theology and licentiates from state
schools to be exempted from some of the course work. In the meantime,
the potential of many women to become excellent theologians and to do
serious theological reflection in the church is being ignored. Yet, as
women demand greater participation in church-related tasks, they are
reminded how important it is for them to be theologically prepared.

The Theology of Women

Perhaps what most characterizes the theology of women in Spain is its
"savoring of the word" and its invitation to others to share in this
knowledge and appreciation. Magazine articles in this vein are written
by women theologians, and though there is seldom any financial remuneration for such works, they give clear evidence of women's interest
and efforts in this area. However, we are not acquainted with a single
theology book (in the academic sense) written by a Spanish woman, for
Spanish women have in no way been prepared for or encouraged in such
endeavor.

Since November of 1985, a group of women theologians in Madrid have met regularly to develop a uniquely feminine theology. While they have not yet published collectively, they have accomplished a great deal in establishing the criteria for such a theology: its language must be simple enough to be accessible to all, it must involve humor, it must be spiritual, expressive of a profound experience of God, and it must be sensitive to the relationship between faith and culture and be open to the interdisciplinary (history, medicine, journalism, etc.).

There are other groups of women who do similar work in feminine theology. Maria Teresa Rodriguez de Lecea, who holds a licentiate in philosophy and is a member of the Council of the Institute of Faith and Secularism,[5] initiated a seminar which met bi-weekly in 1988–89 to analyze and discuss Elisabeth Schüssler Fiorenza's book *In Memory of Her*.[6] Participants included some fifteen women of varied university backgrounds, one of whom, at each meeting, examined a section of the book from the perspective of her particular discipline: theology, history, philosophy or the like. Two Jesuit theologians occasionally join in for these presentations and the discussions which follow.

Women Religious in Spain

According to data published in 1989 by the Office of Statistics and Sociology of the Spanish Episcopal Conference, Spain has a total of 59,155 active (non-cloistered) women religious. They belong to 295 different congregations and live in 5,828 community settings. In 1980 the number of women religious was 63,008. The decline in membership in the past ten years is not so much due to departures from religious life, as was true earlier, but rather it represents deaths from old age. New vocations to religious life, down for many years, have recently been increasing.

Congregations of women religious in Spain engage in a wide variety of services, attending to the needs in their own schools as well as working in hospitals, asylums, rest homes, dispensaries, retreat houses and the like. Today, however, it is much more commonplace to find women religious teaching in state schools as well as working at the parish, vicariate and diocesan levels. It is in these newer settings, beyond the protections and support of their own communities and institutions, that women religious are more frequently challenged to act on their own initiatives.

Yesterday's large communities of women religious, housed in spacious institutional buildings, more often have given way today to small groups living in neighborhood houses, close to the parishioners of the local church. This has effected significant changes, not only in their lifestyle but also in their thinking and behavior. It is still difficult, however, to assess the full impact of these changes on such a large and relatively silent group of women.

From the knowledge of religious congregations of women which we do have, especially after research for this essay, we can verify at least five types of positions among Spain's women religious.

1. There are venerable, older women religious who do not yet have a clear understanding of the Second Vatican Council and the changes which were initiated by the council. Yet, occupying positions of authority in their respective congregations and recognizing in the council "the breath of the Spirit," they have graciously retired in order to enable others to make the called-for changes.

2. There are some women religious who feel that the council has been misinterpreted and that we have been caught in the midst of a process of de-Christianization and are facing catastrophe. They offer their sufferings and prayers for a return to "normalcy." Among them are found some very belligerent groups who work actively for a return to the past.

3. Many women religious, trained to silent obedience, are quietly accepting of the changes, yet without perceiving their deeper meanings or the central issues involved.

4. There are dynamic and renewing groups of women religious, probably the greatest in number, who are bravely undertaking new courses of action. They are happily working at pastoral tasks which seem vital to them and to which they are attracted.

5. Finally, there are women religious who are acutely conscious of being "used" and who try to assess, in both theoretical and practical ways, their real position in the church. When accepting pastoral responsibilities, they ask to be told exactly what their functions will be and they are clear about their expectations of being regarded as the equals of men doing the same work. The difficulty of their situation is gradually gaining appreciation. As a group of Spanish Christians stated at a recent meeting in Madrid: "The unquestionable spirit of service, of graciousness, and of sacrifice which characterizes these consecrated women

should be taken into account by church officials with greater consideration and disinterest."

Women's Attitudes toward the Institutional Church

As might be expected, the attitudes of Spanish Catholic women toward the institutional church cover a wide spectrum, from those who are quite satisfied and express no desire for change, to those who have turned their backs on the Institution and make a clear distinction between their religious beliefs and the institutional church. For the latter, it is often only their friendships with church members which remind them of their former affiliation.

A clear example of the diversity of positions among Spanish women is provided by reactions to Pope John Paul II's apostolic letter *Mulieris Dignitatem* (1988). The day after its publication, when there had hardly been time to digest the dense and lengthy text, commentaries appeared by women who expressed gratitude to the pope for the new possibilities he was offering to them. Yet other women refused to even read the apostolic letter, commenting that it simply had no interest for them or that they did not expect anything from it.

Those Who Are Satisfied

The women who are satisfied with the church today explain this by saying that women are now "more integrated in the institutional church" and that "dialogue is taking place between the hierarchy and the laity in such a manner that women are able to assume an important role, enriching that dialogue with the gifts of their femininity." These women also feel that they have been supported by the recent encyclicals, letters and exhortations of Pope John Paul II, which have further developed the encyclical *Gaudium et Spes*.

Other women, though still dissatisfied with the role of women in the church and less optimistic about change, nonetheless express a general satisfaction with the institution. They feel that they have been given an opportunity to grow in their awareness of themselves and of their own potential. For these women, many of whom are housewives and non-professionals, church activities have provided them with opportunities to meet others with concerns similar to theirs, to attend religious gather-

ings and congresses, and to participate in religious formation courses
which have opened new horizons for them.

Many of these women hold responsible positions in apostolic organizations, are members of pastoral teams, or are otherwise involved in
religious activities. In specifying the sources of their satisfaction, they
note the following:

1. The documents of Vatican Council II, the encyclical *Pacem in
   Terris,* and the interventions of some of the synodal fathers, especially in the Synod of 1971, in which the participation of women in
   the church was openly discussed.
2. Opportunities for women to work in certain situations on an equal
   basis with men, whether clergy or lay.
3. The opening of the doors (though with some restrictions) of theological formation to women.
4. The access of some women to responsible positions in the church.
5. The increasing number of priests who are abandoning their attitudes of superiority and are daring to admit the equal collaboration of women.
6. The pastoral appreciation for women expressed by some of the
   bishops.

A minority of women, which increases daily, still has serious difficulty
in feeling "satisfied" in the church today. To surface these dissatisfactions, they look at the concept of the church as mystery and as the place
where Jesus and the gospel are met. And while they acknowledge the
advances that have been made in regard to women in the church, they
see that these are still quite inadequate and perhaps even counter-
productive in that they create a false sense of openness. The adherence
of these women to the institution is thus fraught with pain and tension.

Many of the women in this latter group are quite active and hold
positions of responsibility in base communities and in parish and diocesan groups. Yet, even though they may be personally assigned to such
positions by bishops who trust in them, they feel, at times, both discouraged and manipulated.

Those Who Are Not Satisfied

The reasons which women give for their dissatisfaction with the institutional church are many and varied. At the heart of their dissatisfaction

are the ecclesial actions which show that women in the church are neither recognized nor appreciated. All of the women's other complaints
originate with this one conviction: "They [the church authorities] don't
listen to us; they don't consult us. They decide for us who we are and
what we think, what we can and cannot do."

Women also feel that the institutional church is strong on theory but
weak in practice. On the one hand, there are the official declarations; on
the other, the day-to-day realities. The sublime dignity of woman is
affirmed in theory while, in practice, the actual woman is undervalued
almost to the point of contempt.

In the 1987 Synod of the church of Bilbao, the problems of women in
the church were discussed as follows:

> At this time, women appear to be second-class members of the faithful:
> silent spectators, obedient collaborators, responsible for the most odi-
> ous tasks of the Church, only slightly heard, and without any access to
> decision-making. [In] the hierarchy, the tribunals, the presbyterial coun-
> cils . . . the men make the decisions. An overwhelming majority consider
> it quite serious that women are forbidden access to ministry, including
> priesthood, without any valid reasons. Many ask themselves whether or
> not women have the qualities to proclaim the word of God and are capa-
> ble of performing such ministries. . . . Women now only carry out tasks,
> even though their numbers as participants continue to grow. Only two
> groups have shown themselves to be against the priestly ordination of
> women, while fifty-five have said that this is necessary. One of these
> groups has even gone so far as to relate this need to the very future of the
> church.

Other serious reasons given by Spanish women for their dissatisfaction with the church:

1. Ecclesiastical language frequently reflects and favors a philosophy
and an anthropology which are dated and clearly masculine. Women are
constantly becoming more sensitive to this and are bothered that the
"complementarity" expected is called for only from women (never mutually): women's intuition, passivity, tenderness, personalism, etc. There is
also the use of false and/or painful images of women: the fertile soil that
receives the seed, Eve as sinner, and others. At times, too, the poetic and
flattering language used by the church in regard to women is patronizing
and uncomfortable for them and seems to reflect a guilt complex on the
part of priests, who feel themselves constrained to pay compliments that

are largely irrelevant. Liturgical language, especially, is in need of revision in order to eliminate sexist terminology which is inappropriate in present-day culture.

2. The hierarchy overstresses "motherhood" and has a tendency to perceive—or even to define—woman according to her functions. Pilar Bellosilla, an auditor at Vatican Council II, who has also held responsible church positions at national and international levels, writes in this regard:

> We are disconcerted by certain assertions such as, "Motherhood should be seen as the primary and unquestionable greatness of woman as well as her vocation," when it would be better said that the dignity of woman as a human person confers greatness and the highest dignity on her specific function of motherhood. . . . Her vocation is not motherhood, but rather self-realization as a person, integrating and assuming completely what is specific to her sex.

3. The institutional church tends to establish sexual moral norms without consultation with those to whom the norms pertain and without weighing the experience of the faithful. Pilar Bellosillo recalls a different experience at Vatican Council II: when such issues came up in the various commissions, the bishops would look to the lay auditors to ask their point of view, since it was the laity who would actually be putting into practice the values derived from the gospels.

4. The pyramidal structure of the institutional church makes it impossible for the laity, and, of course, for women, to have any representation at the top. Virtually all responsible posts are held by clergy, even those tasks which have no relationship to the sacrament of orders: notaries, archivists, business managers, and those involved in the Catholic press, social action, statistics, artistic patrimonies and the like. Consequently, women are automatically excluded from all of this. As one Spanish woman theologian sees it, this happens "because, notwithstanding what is being said, there is still an abundance of priests. If this were not the case, [the clergy] would see themselves obligated to fill only those positions which are seen as exclusively related to the sacrament of orders." This still, however, would not be the most laudable reason for calling women to leadership.

5. The exclusion of women from ordination has been given no satisfactory explanation, though priestly ordination for themselves is of inter-

est to only a minority of women. More radical women question the very model of priesthood which has evolved in the church over centuries. Thus, while many would wish to see this issue clarified with dispatch and with a liberality of spirit, others are disposed to admit that the question itself is not yet mature and that present sociological conditions exist that preclude a simple and satisfactory solution. Still, it troubles women that the current arguments against the ordination of women are so unconvincing.

A woman who holds a responsible post in the diocese of Barcelona has recently written with regard to the Pope's apostolic letter *Mulieris Dignitatem:*

> The men and women who had asked for deeper reasons for the exclusion of women from orders will be disappointed. . . . Are we to deduce from the fact that Christ was a man and that he chose only men that he wished forever to exclude women from the priesthood? Christ also did not choose a single Gentile, and the church never had a problem considering or accepting Gentiles. . . . These are arguments that are still difficult to understand and accept in spite of all the argumentation.[7]

Desired Changes

The reasons for women's dissatisfaction mentioned above provide some indication of the changes in the church which Spanish women would welcome.

Some groups are asking for *radical* change: that the church be structured as a genuine community, in which authority is exercised as service rather than as power, with a more human internal dialogue. In such a setting, the "shepherds" of the church would imitate Jesus' own behavior with regard to women. Some suggest that, with *Mulieris Dignitatem,* this request has already been honored. Yet too many fear that, once again, church theory and practice will become two distinctly different realities. Regardless of their particular positions, however, women's cry for equality is unanimous.

Spanish women are able to give clear reasons for the changes they desire:

1. The majority present their arguments from the point of view of sheer *justice:* women ask that their rights and responsibilities as baptized

members with full rights in the church community be recognized. As Spanish women continue to achieve full rights from the civil government, they can no longer tolerate that the church continues to treat them as minors.

2. There is the argument from the point of view of *coherence:* the church can no longer ask secular society to grant what she herself is unwilling to give. Granted, there are church documents addressing the need to incorporate women more actively and responsibly into the work of the church. But these declarations have not been made operational. Pope John Paul II's last two apostolic letters set forth a series of plans which, though still inadequate, need to be fully implemented.

3. Some argue from the point of view of *fidelity to the gospel message,* which proclaims the basic equality of all human beings as children of one Father who is also Mother. Because we are one in Christ, St. Paul says, there is no longer among us male and female.

4. Finally, there is the argument from the point of view of *enriching the church* through the addition of values considered even today to be "feminine."

Addressing this last point, some of the participants in the 1987 Forum of Religious Phenomena in Madrid tried to imagine a culture with greater feminine input. They hypothesized:

> Thanks to the feminine, elements of force and power [in such a culture] would be less aggressive, more resistant to discouragement, more long-suffering and sacrificing; knowledge would become less rationalistic, more integrated with feeling, less exploitive, wiser. Life would become less stressful, with greater interiority based on subjectivity and the cyclic quality of life. Correlatively, space might become less an object of conquest and more related to living—a home, even a vacuum to be filled with humanity. Finally, acceptance of the "other" and of that which is unknown or hidden would put in doubt the facile simplifications and dogmatisms labeled "masculine." This could lead to a recovery of "contemplative questioning" and to the welcoming of that which is different.[8]

Some groups propose the strategy of occupying all positions in the church presently available to women in order to move forward, step by step, as in a game of chess. In this vein, women at the diocesan Synod of Bilbao, mentioned earlier, summarized the proposals received and the "actions we are prepared to take":

To intensify activity, making commitments and helping according to actual capabilities.

To prepare and to form ourselves theologically in order to grow in maturity and to assume responsibility. To share this formation with other women. To better prepare future generations. To make our voices heard more audibly and to encourage reflection.

To be ready to create another kind of committed and consecrated woman religious outside of the cloister. To petition for a permanent diaconate that includes women. To commit ourselves to full participation, including priesthood.

To create a movement through parish groups who will insist that these questions be addressed.

The Forum for Women's Studies (FEM), an organization to which both authors of this essay belong, has itself developed a series of concrete proposals which have been published in a number of newspapers. FEM proposes:

A serious commitment to study and reflect on the problem of women's participation in the church from the perspectives of anthropology, theology and revelation.

Full recognition of women's complete participation in the life of the church, the voice of women being essential to the church's sacramentality and to its witness.

Greater participation by women in the church's discernment and in policy-making bodies whose work will impact the vital social debates that especially affect women: bio-ethics, violence, the family, etc.

Access to the ministries of lector and acolyte, until now reserved to men, and a revision of other sections of the Code of Canon Law which discriminate according to gender.

The actual implementation of ecclesial writings on the role of women.

Consciousness-raising of seminarians, priests and bishops in regard to these issues.

Reasoned responses and convincing arguments to these proposals regarding women which are *not* acceptable.

The presence of women theologians in all arenas of theological debate
and development.[9]

Organizations Working

There are presently no official church organizations which are specifically dedicated to promoting the changes which Spanish Catholic
women are seeking. There are, however, many informal groups of interested parties who maintain an information network, carry on the debate,
and provide support for individual action.

The two authors of this essay, together with six other women from
the Forum for Women's Studies (FEM), have organized a group which,
though still legally unincorporated, has the goal of sharing information
and perspectives and of studying the possible arenas for collaborative
action.

Many other groups of Catholic women meet in Madrid and in other
regions of Spain. There is, for example, the Collective for Women in the
church in Barcelona. However, the fact that the Collective has neither
official recognition nor a secure infrastructure (lacking, as it does, dues
and subsidies) seriously undermines the organization's networking and
collaborative efforts.

The Federation of Theological Students (FERAT) is an important
organization for women enrolled in theological studies. It provides
moral support and a base from which women theology students can
address the recognition of their rights.

The Confederation of Spanish Women Religious (CONFER) is an
organization that works for the advancement of women religious
through providing courses and assemblies of various kinds. However,
CONFER's desire to respect the pluralism represented in its thousands
of members has precluded its taking any position on the situation of
women in the church.

Another possible avenue for the advancement of Spanish Catholic
women is the recently established publishing house, EGA, which plans
to publish a collection of books on the women's issue from three different sources: original works in Spanish, preferably by women, translations of works from other languages, and works that are unpublished or
difficult to obtain. Some of the Catholic Action movements, insofar as
they educate female members and encourage them to take active roles in

church and society, provide possibilities for change, though this depends on the perspective of the particular group. In many—perhaps most—cases, diocesan Catholic Action groups promote an uncritical and unconditional adherence to the church's official positions. Yet Eva Gomez Pina, who currently heads Spain's Catholic Action, even its male groups, and is highly regarded by the hierarchy, maintains a critical and progressive posture on issues related to women in the church.

Within some of the diocesan lay councils, there are commissions on women which stimulate women's participation in the church and work to remove obstacles to such participation. There are also church groups working for justice and renewal which support the women's cause, even though the equality and participation of women is not their primary objective.

In summary, Spain is just at the beginning stage in organizing to change the anomalous situation of its Catholic women. Nonetheless, the beginning that has clearly been made seems to us the indication of a tremendous energy that can break through at any moment. We hope and trust that this movement will not be deliberately aborted before its birth, since, if it fails to find adequate resources within the church, it may well develop outside the church, with greater virulence and perhaps with the loss of its original roots.

Notes

1. Survey on "Secularization" conducted by the Center for Sociological Investigations, September 1987.

2. M. Hébrard, *Les Femmes dans l'Eglise* (Le Centurian/Le Cerf, 1984), 17.

3. This is true except for the University of Navarra, which is under the auspices of Opus Dei and is graduating many women with doctorates in theology. We were unable, however, to obtain official verification of this.

4. FERAT, Federation of Theological Students.

5. The Institute of Faith and Secularism was founded in 1967 by the Society of Jesus (Jesuits) to continue the spirit breathed into the Catholic Church by the Second Vatican Council.

6. Elisabeth Schüssler Fiorenza, *In Memory of Her* (Bilbao: Desclee de Brouwer, 1989). Recently translated into Spanish by Maria Tabuyo of the theology group in Madrid.

7. Maria Martinell, "Algunos interrogantes," *El Ciervo* 453 (November 1988), 9.

8. The Forum of Religious Phenomena meets annually in Madrid at the

behest of a group of intellectuals and under the auspices of The Institute of
Faith and Secularism. The 1989 Forum addressed the theme "Women, Today
and Tomorrow" and was attended by some one hundred men and women
representing virtually all regions of Spain.

   9. *Vida Nueva* 1609 (November 28, 1987), 32.

María Salas is a journalist who holds a licentiate in philosophy and literature. From 1944 to 1968 she was national vice president of Girls in Catholic
Action and of Women in Catholic Action. She was president of the Commission of Adult Education in the World Union of Catholic Women's Organizations (UMOFC) from 1966 to 1974. From 1970 to 1988 she worked
professionally with a religious publishing house. She has written several
books and numerous articles regarding both women's issues and educational issues. She is presently employed in the field of adult education for a
non-profit cultural association.

Marifé Ramos holds a licentiate in religious studies and theology and will
shortly defend her doctoral dissertation in theology. Since 1975 she has
taught religion at the secondary level in a state school. She is a regular
contributor to the periodical *Religion y Escuela,* and since its beginning she
has been a member of a group of women theologians who meet regularly in
Madrid. She has written several articles on themes related to women in the
church and women in theology. Marife Ramos is married and is the mother
of two children.

10

The Voice of the Turtledove

THE HYPOTHESES which I took with me to the 1985 U.N. Decade for Women FORUM, and with which I subsequently undertook the present study, have, I believe, been confirmed. First, as I had hypothesized, I found a new self-awareness among Catholic women in Europe about their identity as women of faith and about their roles—and rights—in the institutional Catholic Church. My second hypothesis was also validated: there are indeed some notable variations in the ways that this new awareness manifests itself among the different countries and cultures of western Europe. What I did not fully anticipate, however, was how much the similarities among the women in the countries studied would outweigh even some of the very real differences among them. In every case and in every country, the specific parochial concerns which were expressed were most often only echoes of a much larger and commonly shared call by Catholic women, a unanimous and transnational call for an institutional church which gives *full* representation and *full* participation to women. And in this "voice of the turtledove" being heard so clearly throughout Europe, Europe's new Catholic women are connecting with their sisters and indeed with men of good will as well around the globe.

In this concluding chapter, I offer my own summation and interpretation of the essays presented here and of all that I have personally experienced, heard, and read in journeying with my European sisters these past several years. And I presume to describe—for them, for all new Catholic women, and for growing numbers of men throughout the world—that vision of church to which I believe the Spirit of God, through this persistent and ever swelling "voice," is calling the institution today.

"Are There Any Catholics Out There?"

While the specific focus of this study has been on new Catholic *women* in Europe, and the methodology has been descriptive and qualitative rather than statistically quantitative, it is useful to cite, in summary, a recent study by Andrew Greeley and Michael Hout in which they propose to dismantle what they refer to as "the secularization myth," a myth which, they note, has been frequently applied to northern Atlantic countries in particular.[1] Basing their research on both the International Study of Values (ISV)[2] and the International Social Survey Project[3] as well as additional sets of data from Britain, the U.S., Australia, Italy and West Germany, Greeley and Hout find no evidence to support the often heard claim that gradual secularization has occurred over the past twenty years (forty years in the U.S.). They maintain that the decline in Catholic practice in the early 1970s was not the result of "secularization" but was more likely, as seems clear to them in the U.S., a reaction to *Humanae Vitae,* the 1968 papal encyclical on birth control. Greeley and Hout describe this abrupt change in religious practice as a "one-shot" decline which "righted" itself almost fifteen years ago, as Catholics became more comfortable with following their own consciences regarding the use of contraceptives while continuing to practice their faith. The researchers explain the subsequent return to the sacraments by what they call a "loyalty" factor, or "tenacity of affiliation." "Quite simply," Greeley and Hout maintain, "Catholics like being Catholic and are not about to give up their heritage."[4]

It is instructive, in this context, to look at the current data on the eight countries we have studied here regarding the percentage in each country who are listed as Catholic (according to the most recent, 1986, figures of the *Statistical Yearbook of the Church*) and the corresponding percentage of men and women over thirty-five (from Greeley and Hout, 1989) who attend mass at least once a month:

Country	% Catholic	% Attendance
Belgium	89.28	60
England (G.B.)	9.27	60
France	84.61	45
West Germany	46.38	67
Ireland	75.14	95
Italy	98.07	53

Country	% Catholic	% Attendance
The Netherlands	38.54	67
Spain	97.88	77

While these figures, at first glance, are not nearly so damning as the popular imagination would suggest, it is important to note the "at least once a month" criterion used by Greeley and Hout; this is a far cry from the every-Sunday Mass "obligation" which defined the "good Catholic" in the past. In my own research, which concurs with that of Greeley and Hout in this regard, I soon came to realize that the "obligation"—or even the desire—to attend Mass weekly is simply not as strongly felt as it used to be. Especially evident in Italy and Spain is the phenomenon of the "special occasion" or "four seasons" Catholic, the Catholic whose church-going is limited to baptisms, first communions, weddings and burials. Other women, who in speaking with me readily identified themselves as "Catholic," nonetheless seemed to make little connection between their religious identity and their church-going, which might be quite infrequent, if at all. Some of my respondents considered themselves fortunate to have found in certain parishes, usually small ones, faith communities that are affirming of them and congenial to them as women, and this gives them hope that such is at least a possibility for others. And there are, of course, new Catholic women who remain intimately connected with and actively involved in their local parishes. These are most often the religious educators and the parish workers, sometimes "official" and salaried, but more often "unofficial" and unpaid, and, in all cases, greatly taken for granted. In general, however, the old sense of weekly mass "obligation," for the variety of reasons mentioned in the essays, is not strongly felt by Europe's new Catholic women.

Greeley and Hout also address the general decline of religious interest among young people, which they find evident cross-nationally, a decline which is likewise addressed with great concern by a number of our women essayists. Greeley and Hout tend to describe this decline as a "moratorium" on rather than a definitive abandonment of religious interest. According to their data, "young people increase their church attendance as they marry and have children at the same rate in all sixteen countries studied."[5]

While one might like to believe, as Greeley and Hout seem to imply, that this present pattern of young-adult return to the faith will continue in the future, I would suggest that there are other factors presently at work in this regard which are not yet manifesting themselves statistically and which might dramatically affect this expected post-youth return to Catholic practice. In Europe these factors include, among others, the growing disenchantment of young, democratic-minded Europeans with an institutional church which is seen as increasingly monarchical in its operating style and as clearly unrepresentative of large numbers of Euro-Catholics.[6] Even more critical, in my estimation, is the growing disaffection of young European women, many of them *already* wives and mothers, with a church institution which is totally male-dominated and which they see as continuing to relegate them, as women, to the dark ages of uncomplaining servitude and unquestioning procreation. Young people today, in Europe as in the U.S., are not so tractable as they were even a generation ago. And it is on young women, still the primary transmitters of the faith to their children, that the very future of the church may well hang in the balance. Among countless other European women with whom I spoke personally, Halkes and van Heijst address this concern quite specifically in their essay on "New Catholic Women in Holland."

Certain generalizations can be made about women and traditional religious practice in all of the eight countries studied here. Practice is consistently higher among women in rural and suburban areas than in the larger urban areas. Practice is higher among older women than among younger women, as noted above. And, as is true in the U.S., far more women than men are regular church-goers. While few of the broader surveys on religious practice make the male/female distinction, the preponderance of women attending church is documented in a number of national studies, and one has only to church-hop through Europe, as I did, to verify this fact. In my own eye-count at scores of European church services, women outnumbered men by an average of three to one. In the pews, that is. With rare exceptions, such as "Eucharist in the Absence of a Priest," the altar remains the exclusive preserve of ordained men. The irony of this sexual segregation of altar and pews is writ large for all to see in church after church after church, where women are the large majority of worshipers and men retain exclusive control of the worship services.

In my own youth we used to speak, sadly, of those who, for a variety of reasons, from divorce and remarriage to having been castigated in the confessional, were "ex-Catholics." It is a term I rarely heard in Europe.

Some, of course, have definitively "left the church" on principle and some of these—women, often—with a great deal of hostility, but, for the most part, "once a Catholic, always a Catholic" still seems to maintain, despite the infrequency of church attendance. Nor is there any evidence that Catholicism in Europe has any substantial competition from other major religious denominations or traditions; Catholics do not seem to be leaving the church to join something else. As Greeley and Hout suggest, Catholics do not too readily tend to divest themselves of their Catholic heritage. But, I repeat, to what extent can we be sure of this in the future? In addition to less frequent mass-going in general, we are left with the hard fact of a continually declining Catholic practice among the youth and young adults, and I suggest that, in our rapidly changing world today, it is extremely sanguine, if not extraordinarily naive, for the reasons suggested above, to confidently await their return to religious practice as the parents of young children. Their "moratorium" may be much longer than projected, or, indeed, it could be a permanent departure and secularization might prove not to be such a myth after all. Add to this the fever-pitch frustration of many Catholic women of all ages with a moribund ecclesial institution and their continuing and insulting disenfranchisement within it, and we may well be dealing with a different set of membership/practice data by the century's end.

Where, then, does one find hope for desperately needed ecclesial change, for the evolution of an institutional church which offer both authentic leadership and a Christian community which is fully inclusive of and inviting to all its people, especially the young, and most especially women? The answer, I propose—if an answer is truly desired by institutional leaders—can be found in the experiences, in the insights, and in the example of Europe's new Catholic women, who, even now, are keeping the faith alive at its deepest roots.

The Labor Force Is Female

Imagine a European-wide, month-long work stoppage of all women involved in service to the church. Typewriters and computers go silent, nothing can be retrieved from files, religion classes are canceled, sacramental preparation ceases, altars remain unadorned and the supply of clean sacred linens is exhausted while dust gathers on the pews, the elderly and the sick are bereft of pastoral visitation, clergy meals go unprepared, liturgies are not planned, the poor are not fed, the stranger is not welcomed. For all practical purposes, the institutional church grinds to a screeching halt.

Such an exercise in imagination can be highly instructive. For, without dismissing committed clergy and male workers in the church, the exercise enables one to realize, in a strikingly illustrative way, that the everyday church in Europe—as elsewhere—runs primarily on woman-power. This is evident in all of the essays on the eight European countries studied.

Like the U.S., western Europe has experienced a dramatic decline in its number of priests and seminarians.[7] In an upbeat article on the Catholic Church in western Europe, Jack Dick, an American lay theologian and author at The American College in Louvain, reports that, between 1970 and 1989, the number of priests decreased more than 34,000 (from 264,692 to 230,487) and that, of those remaining, fifty to seventy percent, depending on country and diocese, are over sixty-five years old. At the same time, he notes, the Catholic population has increased by more than twenty-six million.[8] With regard to the permanent male diaconate, Dick observes: "With the exceptions of Belgium and Germany, where there has been a degree of acceptance and ministerial effectiveness, the situation in western Europe remains ambiguous," and he raises the question, "Why ordain some men to do what many men and women can and are already doing?"[9]

Indeed, it is lay men and women who are the "worker bees" in the European church today, and, according to my research in the eight countries studied here, the vast majority of these workers are women, including women religious. Yet the status of these women in the church is more "ambiguous," by far, than that of the permanent deacons on whom Dick comments. Most of the religious service of women continues to be part-time and done on a volunteer basis. Even for women employed on a full-time basis, pay scales are seldom commensurate with their education and abilities, their roles tend to be vaguely defined, involving little if any clear authority for the women, and their job security often depends on the disposition, if not the digestion, of their current pastor or clerical supervisor. However, according to the women I interviewed, the most painful part of their work for the church—and I heard this again and again—is their "voicelessness." Few of them are granted formal representation on governing boards and in decision-making bodies, even when their theological education and professional training are superior (though, perhaps, for the very reason that they are superior!) to their clerical counterparts. While the work they do is obviously needed and important to church ministry, they too often feel devalued as persons, their talents and generosity exploited by the institution.

Yet, while many women have opted out of church work as either a thankless or a fruitless task, or possibly both, many more perservere and their numbers, in most countries, continue to grow. For most of them, their response to my "Why do you do it?" was given in terms of their genuine care and concern for the people they serve, regardless of the difficult circumstances of their service. Some responded in terms of a baptismal "call": "It is what Christians do." Still other women see their work for the church as an essential sign of hope—for themselves as well as for others—that the conversion of the institution is possible, and they painstakingly work for such a conversion "from within." Catholicism is their heritage, they say, and no institution is going to take it away from them!

It is a tribute to the women who "hang in," despite the difficulties, that some changes are being made to accommodate the church in western Europe to its vanishing-clergy syndrome. While the degree of change varies from country to country as well as among dioceses within each country, and the pace of change seems grindingly slow or even nonexistent to women in certain areas, a number of the countries studied, especially those on the continent and in the north, seem to be taking on the challenge of the future much more realistically and much more foundationally than many dioceses in the U.S. So much for our American superiority complex!

In Belgium, for example, where some five thousand laypeople are involved in a variety of pastoral ministries, professional training centers for lay pastoral leaders, among whom many women can be counted, have been in place since the mid-1970s, and a woman heads the National Justice and Peace Committee, a presidential role reserved in the past exclusively to European bishops.

Interestingly, just a few miles across the English Channel from Belgium, the pace of institutional adaptation and change is significantly slower. The Catholic Church in England suffers, no doubt, from its minority position in a predominantly non-Roman Catholic country, not to mention its ever tenuous relationship with the Church of England—

which ordains women! However, while Catholic women continue, as
before, to be concentrated in religious education and other traditional-
for-women ministries, some advances are evident. Officially or unoffi-
cially, more women are involved in counseling and spiritual ministries,
they are increasingly active in non-ordained liturgical ministry, and there
has been a considerable increase of women on parish councils as well as
their greater participation on deanery councils and diocesan and national commissions.

In France, where priestly vocations are down by half, eighty-five percent of the country's 200,000 catechists are women, and some dioceses
have become responsive to the calls of these women for more formal
preparation and training. Many dioceses have also instituted the role of
permanent church worker, involving an official appointment to ministry
(of many women) by a bishop or local pastor. And seventy-five percent
of all French dioceses are now holding "Sunday Assemblies in the Absence of a Priest," which are said in general to be more popular than
those presided over by the occasional visiting clergyman!

The implications of the recent reunification of Germany, East and
West, as regards the Catholic Church have yet to be fully grasped. In
East Germany, where Catholics have been only an estimated eight percent of the population, feminist consciousness and involvement is presently more apparent in society at large than in religion. On the other
hand, West Germany, which is predominantly Catholic and which has a
long-standing clergy shortage, also has a twenty-year tradition of "lay
theologians," the majority of whom are women, working in pastoral
ministry. Called "pastoral referents," they receive the same theological
education as seminarians, are usually full-time and salaried, and are engaged in virtually all non-sacramental parish services. Women also predominate as "pastoral workers"; these have less formal training and tend
to serve on a volunteer basis. Though I was told that the use of pastoral
referents has recently been discouraged by the German Bishops' Conference and by some of the clergy, many church leaders see them as the
most creative way to deal with the dearth of ordained clergy.[10]

As in England, the pace of institutional change in Ireland is a bit more
sluggish than it is on the continent. The reason here, however, unlike
England's, may be due to Ireland's very Catholicity as a nation; the
decline in priestly vocations has not yet taken its toll on the Irish church.
Women continue to fill the pews, while their more active participation

in liturgy is minimal. Yet, in addition to their traditional roles as religion teachers and caregivers, some new ministries for women are modestly emerging, specifically in counseling and retreat ministries and in adult religious education. But as one woman wryly commented: "We don't have any bishops crying out for women theologians or for women to work in the parishes."

Very Catholic Italy, like Ireland, has not yet had to come to grips with a dramatic decrease of ordained clergy. Accordingly, the involvement of women in church service there tends to be mainly traditional: domestic and secretarial work, religious education and adult evangelization, and the preparation of candidates for the sacraments. Some women are members of parish or diocesan councils or are employed in Vatican offices and in religious media, though inevitably in safely subordinate roles.

Despite continuing internal problems, many related to the recent papal appointments of conservative bishops there, The Netherlands retains its place in the vanguard of post-Vatican II Catholicity. And women desiring to work in the church have sometimes been among the beneficiaries of this Dutch legacy, as when a number of progressive bishops ordered a 50-50 balance between men and women on parish councils. While the greater part of Dutch women's work in the church remains part-time, volunteer, and traditional—in teaching, counseling and domestic service—an increasing number of women in The Netherlands are seeking theological education and pastoral training and are working full-time, albeit with problems regarding role definition and a just wage, in church ministry.

In Spain, another very Catholic country, women continue to be heavily involved in their traditional church ministries of religious education and works of charity, and "lay ministry," as Salas and Ramos tell us, "is largely unknown." It is important here, however, to note several surprising breakthroughs, as the bishop of Bilbao's publicly commissioning women to ministry in the same ceremony in which he installs seminarians as lectors. Some of these women preside at "Sunday Celebrations in the Absence of a Priest," though this is by no means a common practice in Spain. There are also some dozen women serving as administrators of parishes, and Spanish women are increasingly involved in spiritual direction and on diocesan pastoral commissions, the latter more or less equally with men.

Women in the Halls of Ivy

Europeans do not tend to make the academic distinction that Americans do between "religious education" and "theology." In Europe, if one studies or teaches about the Catholic faith, at whatever level, one studies or teaches "theology." We have spoken earlier about the extensive involvement of European Catholic women in youth and adult religious education and about the growing number of pastoral training centers in many countries for the preparation of lay teachers of religion. Let us look now at European Catholic women in the "halls of ivy," university, or, as we say in the U.S., "higher" education.

In Europe, one is struck not so much by the numbers of women with university degrees in theology (these are far fewer than in the U.S.) but by the quality of these women and by their energy and productivity. Until recently, few university theology departments have been open to women students, though this situation is gradually improving, more in some countries than in others. A woman must be highly motivated and perservering to get into such a program in the first place, and she must be a survivor to complete her studies and win a degree, especially if she is working in an area of feminist theology, in these traditionally all-male (predominantly all-clerical) bastions. According to my respondents, Catholic women seeking a terminal (doctoral) degree in theology are most likely to be found at the University of Louvain in Belgium; at Heythrop in England; at Paris, Lyon or Strasbourg in France; at Tübingen, Munich, Kassel, Berlin, Frankfort, or Münster in Germany; at Nijmegen or Utrecht in The Netherlands; or at universities in the U.S. or Canada.

For Catholic women, however, an even greater challenge than earning a doctoral degree in theology is obtaining a university professorship, and few hold such positions. For a professorship in theology, Catholic theology faculties require, in addition to a doctorate, the famous (or infamous!) "habilitation," which involves a research project beyond the dissertation and the ultimate approval of a bishop. So, while some women may teach as assistants or lecturers, few, if any, ever become full professors. In this regard, a strange anachronism obtains in Germany, where, according to a 1933 concordat between Hitler and Rome which is still in effect, theological faculties are paid by the state, with the church having the ultimate sanction regarding those to be hired. The real "sticking point" of the concordat, however, is its mandate that eighty-five percent of those approved must be clergy, leaving little opportunity for lay men theologians and even less for lay women. To date, only one woman in Germany has been granted a professorship—in canon law—and the country has suffered a severe "brain drain" involving a number of its outstanding women theologians who have left Germany for professorships in other countries.

Still, there is great interest in the study of theology among European Catholic women, and the percentage of women students in the theology programs that are open to them is increasing everywhere. In a number of countries there are growing numbers of women who are receiving the same theological education as seminarians, without, of course, the expectation of ordination or even that their training will be fully utilized in service to the church. In all of this, one must be struck by the tenacious adherence to the Catholic faith which continues to be manifested by so many European women and, even more, by the wealth of potential that they represent for the European church when ecclesial barriers are finally removed.

Women Religious/Religious Women

Even more so than in the U.S., the overall decline in membership of European communities of women religious has been a dramatic one; in some communities, the numbers have decreased by half in the past thirty years. According to the 1986 *Statistical Yearbook of the Church,* there were, in the eight countries studied here, a total of 293,826 professed women religious and 3,236 novices, with the largest numbers in Italy (114,149 professed, 1,144 novices) and in Spain (55,195 professed, 729 novices) and the smallest in Belgium (7,853 professed, 107 novices). In 1986, Rev. Paul Byrne, then Secretary General of the Conference for Major Religious Superiors in Ireland, counted 14,000 women religious in that country and observed that, if the present trend of deaths, departures and few religious vocations continues, there could be none in the year 2050.[11] The average age of professed women religious in most European communities today is sixty or above, and many if not most of these are retired. As in the U.S., the European communities having the greatest success in attracting new members tend to be the contemplative orders and the more traditional, "habit and horarium" congregations, though I was told in Germany that the Dominicans, Franciscans and Benedictines seem to be getting vocations, "perhaps because of the clarity of their spirituality." There are also a number of new groups such as the Missionaries of Christ, founded in Munich in 1956, who are requesting from Rome the designation of secular institute rather than that of the more restrictive religious congregation. I expect that the future will see other such new communities which, while honoring the traditional commitment to consecrated celibacy as a still valid vocational choice for new Catholic women, will, at the same time, enable their members time to enjoy greater self-determination and less separation from the lives and experiences of the rest of their sisters in the faith.

The renewal of religious life mandated by Vatican II seems to have been translated somewhat differently in Europe than it was in the U.S., where, among their other renewal activities, U.S. sisters began to swell the ranks of colleges and universities and, for a time at least, became much more "degreed" than Catholic women in general. This rush for higher education, except in a certain few religious communities, was not a notable characteristic of the renewal of religious life in Europe, due in part, no doubt, to the resistance to women students on the part of the universities themselves, especially in theology faculties. Perhaps as a result of this, European women religious have not played the same role in the development of Catholic feminism and feminist theology in Europe as U.S. women religious have played in the States.[12] Nor have they had to pay the price, by way of Vatican investigations and censuring, that has been exacted of U.S. women religious (see note 3 in Chapter 1). In fact, as some of my respondents have suggested, the discomforting attention paid by the Vatican to U.S. women religious may very well account for some of the timidity of European sisters about challenging the institutional church and taking public stands.

Yet, in many ways, I found the European women religious with whom I spoke more comfortable than many in the U.S. about their precarious present and uncertain future. I attribute this, in part, to the Europeans' keener sense of history (they have so much more history to be sensible about!) and to their enviable ability to take the long view of things. For example, a sister in The Netherlands told me, very matter-of-factly, that her community was now dying and would soon no longer be in existence. When I asked how she felt about this, she replied: "Well, you know, the church always survives. Religious groups throughout history have come and gone as needed, and the church continues. The faithful will find what they need."

While many of Europe's traditional religious communities may be declining or even dying, a number of signs were evident to me that the European church is indeed "finding what it needs"—in the amalgamation of some smaller religious communities into new associations, in the opening of other communities to lay associates and co-workers, who share in the spirituality and the spirit if not the vows of the community, and especially in the activities and involvements of its new Catholic women in general, including women religious. While they are rarely in the forefront of the feminist movement, one finds Catholic sisters in Europe today engaged not only in their traditional works but serving on pastoral teams and in deanery and diocesan offices, offering retreats and spiritual direction, and reaching out in new ways to the needy and the marginalized. They are living among the poor, working with prostitutes and the addicted, with abused women and immigrants. And, more than ever before, they are working in conjunction with other women, where a new kind of "sisterhood" is emerging.

Catholic women in Europe, including the sisters, are finding and developing varieties of "religious community" both among themselves and with others—in prayer and Bible study groups and in base communities, in organizations focusing on world peace, social justice and ecumenism, and in groups committed to the development and promotion of feminist theology, critique and social change. Such communities, the women tell me, are the sources of their spirituality today; they find in them the rich wellsprings which are essential to the nurturance of their personal and communal faith. "Women religious" or "religious women"? The distinction seems to matter less when all new Catholic women stand together in their faith, as is happening more and more in Europe today.

Feminist Theology: A Movement Rooted in Faith

A major topic at the 1987 Vatican Synod on the "Vocation and Mission of the Laity in the Church and in the World" was the role of women in the church, on which Cardinal Tomás O'Fiach of Ireland commented: "Feminism can no longer be considered middle-class madness or an American aberration."[13] The remark is a tribute to new Catholic women everywhere. Single voices have become an international chorus which is finally being heard even in the halls of the Vatican. But Rome's hearing the voices is one thing, its effectively listening to them is another, and

Catholic women, though they may be sustained by Christian *hope,* cannot yet afford to be *optimistic* about their prospects in the institutional church. Yet it is the very faith of these women that sustains them, not in optimism but in Christian hope.

Hand in hand with liberation theology, feminist theology is leading the church, albeit kicking and screaming, into the modern world. And feminist theology, if in fact it ever was, is no longer the exclusive preserve of American women. Granting that U.S. feminist theology, especially that of Rosemary Radford Ruether and Elisabeth Schüssler Fiorenza (herself a German), has often served to "prime the pump" in Europe, more European Catholic women are now making their own distinctive contributions to the discipline and to the struggle.

The essayists in this volume have each made significant contributions to the advancement of feminist theology and of women, not only in their own countries but often in international and ecumenical settings. While the names of certain individual Catholic women theologians are well known in Europe, like that of Catharina Halkes in The Netherlands, a pioneer of the movement, and Elizabeth Gossman in Germany, a well-known author who now teaches full-time in Japan but retains a home in Munich, much of the theologizing of Catholic women is done collaboratively with Protestant women theologians and, in at least one noteworthy instance, with men. Denise Peeters describes the work of this latter group, Femmes et Hommes dans l'Eglise (Women and Men in the Church) in her essay on "New Catholic Women in Belgium."

In all of the countries studied, there are groups working in feminist theology or for the advancement of the feminist agenda in the church, most often both of these combined. In England, The Catholic Women's Network, discussed extensively in Alexina Murphy's essay, has been an especially effective means of connecting smaller groups of Catholic feminists and encouraging their work, while L'Action Catholique Général des Femmes (Women's Catholic Action) has been an important vehicle for Catholic feminine thought and the promotion of women's issues in France. The Milan-based Promozione Donna has made significant contributions to feminist theology and institutional critique in Italy, as has the scholarly and widely read periodical *Progetto Donna (Project Woman).* In The Netherlands, both the Women and Faith Movement and the Eighth-of-May Movement have been powerful instruments of consciousness-raising and theological development, especially for women. In addition to their involvement in the international Femmes et

Hommes dans l'Eglise, mentioned earlier, the concerns of Belgian Catholic women are addressed by a variety of other national groups, including the Dialogue Caucus of Catholic Women's Organizations, which addresses itself directly to the country's Catholic bishops. Many Irish Catholic women are actively engaged in the Catholic Women's Federation, Sisters for Justice, and the Christian Feminist Conference, the last of which focuses specifically on Christian feminism. In Spain there are several groups of women theologians who meet regularly in order to develop a "uniquely feminine theology," though there are, as yet, no national groups with this agenda. Many new Catholic women in Germany, as described in the essay by Hedwig Meyer-Wilmes, are active in traditional Catholic and ecumenical organizations, but others are finding greater satisfaction in their own feminist associations such as Action Group—Feminism and the Churches and Women's Network in the Church. There is also in Germany much feminist interest in "The Church from Below," which, as a non-institutional forum for progressive Catholics, in many ways resembles the Eighth-of-May Movement in The Netherlands.

It is important to repeat, in discussing the organizational involvement of Europe's new Catholic women, that many of these involvements are ecumenical and international. These include the European Society for Women's Research in Theology, which is itself part of the European Feminist Network, the World Council of Churches' sub-unit on Women in Church and Society, the World Union of Catholic Women's Organizations (WUCWO), Pax Christi International, Woman-Church, and Femmes et Hommes dans l'Eglise. Because there are so many European countries in such close proximity to one another, internationalism is a "given" for European women theologians and activists, and offers a rich, interfaith and intercultural dimension to European feminism. Noteworthy, too, is the global perspective that is resulting from such exchange, as European women connect with their sisters on other continents and in the third world.

While each European country might express its feminist agenda somewhat differently, Catholic feminist theology in Europe is everywhere a theology of basic human rights, maintaining the co-equality, both ideologically and in practice, of women and men in society *and* in the church. In the countries of southern Europe and in Ireland, equality in marriage is still a major issue for most women, which no doubt accounts for the much more positive response on the part of Italian and Spanish women than that given by other European women to the papal encyclicals *Familiaris Consortio* (1981) and *Mulieris Dignitatem* (1988). But to the question "What do European Catholic women *want?*" there is an amazing similarity in their responses, as the essays herein and the results of my own interviews have revealed.

"If the Pope Granted You Three Wishes—"

"If the pope granted you three wishes—no holds barred—what would those three wishes be?" This was the question I regularly asked toward the end of my interviews with European Catholic women, inviting them into a world of sheer fantasy and hoping to give us all a good time in the bargain. And a good time was had by all! Not so incidentally, however, the semi-humorous query elicited some clear and focused answers to the more general and often asked question, "What do European Catholic women *want?*" To illustrate, here are some of the answers I received, as the women addressed their "wishes" to the pope:

> I would like to have my "habilitation" in theology recognized.

> I would like to see a woman's council, part two of Vatican II.

> Let the Church foster the inculturation of the gospel into local traditions.

> Overcome the devaluation of women. Let orthopraxis be of more concern, orthodoxy less.

> Go on a journey where you sit down with people and really listen.

> Address the ordination question not as a dogmatic question, which it is not, but as the canonical question which it is.

> Have more courage. Democracy instead of hierarchy is the key for me.

> Stop harping on sexual issues.

> See women as equal partners in the church, called by Christ in the same ways as men.

> Give equal representation to women in all church bodies; this would involve the ordination of women.

> Spend more time with men like Bernardin (U.S. cardinal) to help you get some things together.

Give Vatican City back to the Italians and live in a bishop's house.

Stop making so many pronouncements about women and women's ordination and encourage a climate of moderate, temperate experimentation. Let's do it for a while and see if we like it!

Resign!

Ordain women. The exclusion of women is heretical.

Change seminary training. Parish priests contribute so much to the frustration and oppression of women.

Let's see a new surge in the field of ecumenism.

Dialogue. I feel that you are afraid and forget that people are created in the image of God.

Be as catholic as I am. I accept the universe of men; you do not accept the universe of women, who are half of all humanity.

Give us complete freedom for the next five years, then ask us to evaluate what has happened.

Be more sensitive to questions raised by young people all over the world.

Give more attention to *real* issues like poverty, human misery, war and peace.

Let the church be less triumphalistic.

I cannot even imagine three wishes. I stopped going to church ten years ago. I felt ill at ease at mass, a cult which is based on discrimination.

Change the church's hierarchical structures to a community as Jesus would have wanted it to be.

Remove some of our bishops. They are roadblocks to the development of the Catholic Church.

Open priesthood to women. Women need to be linked to jurisdiction, authority and leadership positions.

Issue no statement without considerable lay expertise on the matter.

Find someone to help you see the depth of your patriarchal ways.

Challenge women in their possibilities other than maternity.

Understand that the fact that Jesus was a man does not mean anything about the possibility that women are the incarnation of God as well.

Give every priest a six-month sabbatical so that he may get a new vision of the church; the church must do more than mere maintenance.

Admit that the just war theory is wrong.

Allow new spiritualities to arise without excommunicating or marginalizing people. Examples? Creation theology and other prophetic spiritualities reflecting the global aspirations of humankind.

Give us hope and cheer.

Live as a woman for a length of time so that you can experience sexism.

Change the entire way that bishops are appointed.

Be more involved with the special concerns of the poor and oppressed groups.

Be more sensitive to the voice of the Spirit speaking through the women's movement throughout the world.

The Voice of the Turtledove

The number seven, appearing fifty-four times in the book of Revelation (in which also, incidentally, a *woman* represents a *people*) signifies fullness, perfection; it is a symbolic number which appears throughout the book of Revelation. At the risk of sounding apocalyptic, I would like to propose that the new vision of church which Europe's new Catholic women (and many new Catholic men as well) are striving to realize, as evidenced by all that has been said above, is sevenfold. It is a vision which calls for Conversion, Revisioning, Representation, Reorganization, Simplification, Globalization, and Experimentation.

1. *CONVERSION*. Granting that true conversion is always the work of the Spirit, one must first let the Spirit in, and this opening of oneself to the Spirit is—except, perhaps, for Paul's unintended tumble from his horse—a voluntary human activity. My hunch is that the hierarchy's seeming inability to open itself to the Spirit-filled voices of its new Catholic women is due primarily to that all-too-human deterrent, fear. This fear is easy to understand when one considers the paradigm, or worldview, into which the hierarchy of the church has, for so many centuries, been socialized and now perpetuates as "gospel." It is what I call the paradigm of dominance, a worldview that is assumed to be the correct worldview, indeed the only one, premised on an obsolete, dual-

istic understanding of reality: spirit/matter, right/wrong, dominance/ subordination, good/bad, white/black, and even wisdom/ignorance. Consider, then, how unthinkable it must be for the powerful in such a paradigm to open themselves to the powerless, to allow that those "below" might also have some purchase on rightness, goodness and wisdom. Yet is not this what the gospel is all about? Honoring "the least" among us, giving ear to the wisdom that comes "from the mouths of babes"? And does not the gospel also counsel, "Do not be afraid"? I propose that conversion of current church leadership is of primary importance, above all else, for the validity and vitality—even for the very survival—of the Catholic Church in the world today.

2. *REVISIONING.* Intrinsic to the fear of conversion on the part of the hierarchy is their overriding fear of losing that very power which has become so much a part of their self-definition. According to the paradigm of dominance, which is the modus operandi of the hierarchy, if one is not "in power," then one is "powerless," that is, the object of someone else's power. And one simply does not allow this! One does not simply "hand over" the institutional church to the laity and to women! What those steeped in the paradigm of dominance have difficulty understanding (dualistic thinking strikes again!) is that power does not have to be win-or-lose, an all-or-nothing game. That—just imagine!—power can be shared! That all persons can be empowered! That there is a whole other paradigm, a paradigm of partnership, where there are neither winners nor losers, but all are enabled (the root of "power"—"posse"—"to be able") to achieve an ever fuller and more dignified humanity. This, it seems to me, is what Europe's new Catholic women, together with their sisters around the world, are asking: not power *over*, which would simply be a rearrangement of the old paradigm, but partnership *with*, a new paradigm, a communion of co-equals, trusting one another and celebrating one another's gifts in a common service of the faith. This, quite simply, is the revisioning needed. And should one be surprised, when reflecting on such revisioning if the gospel and the first Christian communities come to mind?

3. *REPRESENTATION.* Genuine partnership requires full and equal representation on the part of all parties involved. In the institutional church today, "consultation" is called representation, and the consultation engaged in is typically mere tokenism, a patronizing bow by the powerful to the "objects" of their deliberations, which deliberations are ultimately resolved in clerical privacy. I am reminded of what a

student once told me about how decisions were made with the superior of his religious congregation: "I discern, he decides!" Or how a group of Catholic laity describe their relationship with the church: "All work and no say!" The dignity of all Catholics both as human persons and as members of the church is, in and of itself, their authority to speak, to be heard, and to have their voices honored as an integral part of church governance. When this right becomes reality, church documents on marriage will truly represent the voices of those who are themselves married, those on women will reflect the wisdom of women themselves, and those on the Catholic laity will issue from the hearts and experiences of the laity. It is increasingly evident that Europe's new Catholic women will be satisfied with no less than this from the church they wish to serve and to save for future generations.

4. *REORGANIZATION*. Obviously, if all that has been said above is to come to pass, the "purple pyramid"[14] of the present ecclesial structure must be reexamined and reshaped. It was interesting to me that few of Europe's new Catholic women, if given the chance, would actually eliminate the papacy. Some of the women spoke of a pope as an important visible symbol of a world church and of the universality and unity of the faith. In a late-night "what if?" session in The Netherlands, it was suggested that the pope might be like the Dutch queen, an honored and much beloved symbol of unity and identity, but with little political control—"the people have the power!" While most agree that some kind of organization is essential, it is difficult if not impossible to blueprint, from our present vantage point, the particular structure which would best serve the church in all four corners of our world today. Certainly, though, in the vision of Europe's new Catholic women, the structure would be one which is not an end in itself, which is not self-serving, but which exists only for the service of the faith and of the faithful. It would be fully participative, engaging women and men, old and young, and recognizing and empowering the gifts of all. All would be fully represented in decision-making, more so if the decisions envisioned will affect them specifically. No leadership role would be prescribed—or proscribed—on the basis of sex.

A word here about women's ordination and the erroneous, if widely held, belief that Catholic women would be "satisfied" if only they could be ordained to the priesthood. It is not nearly so simple as all that. Few, if any, of the hundreds of women represented in this study expressed any desire for the ordination of women *in its present form;* they want no part of the prevailing clericalism. However, since ordination today gives entree to the only official church ministry and is, at the same time, the only access to roles of canonically legitimated leadership and authority in the present church, the exclusion of women from ordination stands out as a powerful symbol of the institutional church's celibate-male domination. As such, it must be specifically and directly challenged if the institutional church is to be opened up to the faithful, if the pyramid of ecclesial power is finally to be re-formed, and if much greater winds of conversion and change are to blow.

5. *SIMPLIFICATION*. For a worldwide institution such as the Catholic Church to hold itself in existence and to flourish, some forms of structure and organizational management are essential. But any complex organization, of whatever ilk, also suffers from the dangerous tendency to be seduced and preoccupied by its structure as such, and thereby to feed on itself, creating an ever more labyrinthine monolith which ultimately becomes its own raison d'être. When this occurs, the original and usually simple inspiration which called the organization into being in the first place becomes obfuscated or is lost completely. The Catholic Church has not been exempt from this tendency to over-institutionalize, and thus to lose the essential and non-hierarchical content of biblical faith amid Holy Offices and papal commissions, amid theologies developed to support institutional decisions, amid the maze of bureaucracies and birettas in the Vatican. The new Catholic women we have heard are calling for a *simpler* church, an institution that is efficient but minimal in its bureaucracy, an institution which is clearly the voice of its membership, an institution that visibly reflects in the world today that radical impulse of biblical faith which first brought it into being. Again, there is no pat formula for dismantling a monolith, but the process quite possibly begins with the conversion of its current managers and their openness to the representation of the faithful in an authentic spirit of Christian community.

6. *GLOBALIZATION*. Most interpreters of Vatican II, notable among them the German theologians Karl Rahner and Hans Küng, have observed that this council, among its many other contributions, marked a rite of passage for the church, from the *Roman* church that it had been for so many centuries (though not from the beginning!) to a *world* church, a church of many nations, many cultures and many voices, a church of tremendous diversity even in its essential unity. I have found that Europe's new Catholic women are uniquely cognizant, appreciative

and supportive of this new vision—and reality—of the church. While many of the women's concerns are local and are unique to their own cultures and particular ecclesial constraints, their ideal of the church of tomorrow is not circumscribed by purely parochial concerns. It is wide and all-encompassing; their sense of sisterhood-with-brotherhood is global. These new Catholic women call the institutional church to a deeper appreciation of its unity-in-diversity, to a greater respect for cultural differences, to a more courageous commitment to inculturation, and to a new listening to the Spirit as it speaks to all of us from the four corners of the world. They call, too, for an institutional church that is truly ecumenical, able to reverence and to dialogue with other Christian traditions and with other great world religions. Europe's new Catholic women call for a vision of the church that is, both in theory and in practice, an authentically global vision.

7. *EXPERIMENTATION*. There was a TV commercial in the U.S. some years ago (I have forgotten now the product it was touting) that urged viewers to "try it, you'll like it!" Conversely, by implication, if you don't "try it," you'll never know! Europe's new Catholic women would like to see the institutional church "try it"—to risk a bit of experimentation in ridding itself of some of the bureaucratic baggage that has become so dysfunctional not only for its administration of the church but for its very reputation, which is less than glowing in many parts of the world today. There is a fine line between being sensible and being stodgy, and the institutional church is erring today in the extremes of stodginess, as the world—and the lived faith of the Catholic community —is passing it by. Granted that the vision of church proposed in these seven points is idealistic (visions always are!), we cannot allow that the vision is unrealistic or even unattainable. At the same time, we do not suggest that these are changes which can be made overnight. But they *are* changes which *can* be made—or at least tested—through experimentation. Why not try a council on the laity which is conducted *by* the laity? Or, for a change, have Catholic women write their *own* pastoral on women? Or ask young people sometime what *they* need to make the faith meaningful to *them*? Why not at least "listening sessions," as the courageous U.S. Archbishop Weakland has recently provided on the volatile issue of abortion? Put a few women in charge—really in charge —of Vatican commissions. Ordain some women in priestless areas. We all might like it! Experimentation requires the wisdom to know that change is needed and the courage to act on that wisdom. Experimenta-

tion is essential if the institutional church is to enter the next millennium as a respected voice of the gospel and of the Catholic tradition in the contemporary world.

Conclusion

One cannot really conclude an unfinished story. I have proposed in these pages, primarily through the good graces of the women essayists from the European countries studied, that the Spirit of God, the "voice of the turtledove," is presently heralding a new age for the Catholic Church, not only in Europe but throughout the world. One must often read between the lines (or listen between the notes!) for the turtledove's voice to be recognized here, for the notes of hope are frequently interrupted by the sad sounds of departing footsteps and the even harsher sounds of anger and frustration from those who remain. Nor can we discount the current gathering of the forces of reaction and the closing of ranks in Rome. But conversion often occurs "in extremis," and that may well be the state of the institution in the months and years immediately ahead. A structure which methodically undermines its own foundation cannot long endure. Ultimately the foundation itself must again be honored; the cornerstone must be retrieved. And the "converted" structure is all the better for it.

In the meantime, hope endures in the people of God who see, even through darkness, that something profound is indeed happening—that a new age in the history of the Catholic Church lies ahead, that the authentic and beloved tradition will be recovered in a renewed community of faith. And it is this hope which is especially nourished by the thousands of Europe's new Catholic women, who continue faithfully (though at times with a faith which exacts a high price) to claim their Catholic identity and to serve the people of God in the name of that faith. It is nourished by the women religious whose commitments remain firm and their ministries magnanimous, and by the feminist theologians who are uncovering for the church lost treasures in the "science of God." It is nourished by the organizations and associations of women throughout western Europe, who toil relentlessly that the Spirit in their own voices be finally recognized. And it is nourished by the men who stand with them and share in the vision of the Church converted.

And so, in the name of the Catholic Church (in whose name I am not

yet officially authorized to speak!), I thank these new Catholic women—
and their brothers who are the church's new Catholic men—and say to
them all, "You are not alone. Listen! The 'voice of the turtledove,' even
now, 'is being heard in our land.' Let us hear it and rejoice!"

Notes

1. Andrew Greeley and Michael Hout, "The Secularisation Myth" (London: *The Tablet,* June 10, 1989) 665–67.

2. The International Study of Values (ISV), conducted in 1981, analyzed data from Spain, France, The Netherlands, Belgium, West Germany, Denmark, Italy, Ireland, the United Kingdom, the United States, Canada, Australia and New Zealand. It is scheduled to be replicated in the early 1990s. Further information is available through Pro Mundi Vita, Louvain, Belgium.

3. The International Social Survey Project, which conducts annual studies, is made up of a consortium of survey institutions worldwide. Further information is available from the Zentralarchiv für Empirische Sozialforschung, University of Cologne.

4. Greeley and Hout, 665.

5. Greeley and Hout, 666.

6. A 1989 study by the Sample Institute in Molln (Schleswig-Holstein) indicated that some 37.7 percent of West German Catholics are dissatisfied with Pope John Paul II's performance as head of the Catholic Church. Among young Catholics, those under thirty-five, the percentage dissatisfied was 50.5.

7. Though some recent data indicate a slight increase in the number of men applying to seminaries in western Europe, it is difficult to know as yet what this means: whether the trend will be temporary or enduring, if it represents the conservative backlash apparent in some quarters, etc.

8. Jack Dick, "Euro-Catholics Are Just Like Us Only Different" (*National Catholic Reporter,* May 4, 1990) 1.

9. Dick, 1.

10. After Vatican II, there was even some talk among German bishops of ordaining pastoral referents, an idea that was quickly quashed by Rome. In recent years the Vatican has taken care to appoint more conservative bishops to German posts, a practice especially decried in "The Cologne Declaration" (January 7, 1989). Signed by 163 German-speaking theologians from Germany, Austria, The Netherlands and Switzerland, "The Cologne Declaration" speaks out against what the theologians observe as disturbing changes in the post-conciliar church: "a creeping extension of exaggerated hierarchical control; progressive undermining of the local churches, suppression of theological debate, and reduction in the role of the laity in the church; antagonism from above which heightens conflict in the church through means of disciplinary measures."

11. From an interview with Catherine Moore in Dublin for *The Sunday Press* (April 6, 1986) 11.

12. It has been of more than passing interest to me that, of all the women recommended to me as being the most knowledgable and the most qualified to write about "new Catholic women" in their respective countries, the only woman religious so recommended was Sister Ann Breslin of Ireland.

13. Quoted by Dolores R. Leckey in "The Synod of '87: A View from the Aurelian Wall" (*America,* February 27, 1988) 208–09.

14. This colorful expression refers to the purple robes and organizational structure of the church hierarchy. It was coined by Sister Lillanna Kopp, one of the 1970 founders of my non-canonical religious community, the Sisters for Christian Community. Kopp elaborates on the "purple pyramid" in her study of the trends of change in Catholic sisterhoods, *Sudden Spring: 6th Stage Sisters* (Waldport, OR: Sunspot Publications, 1983).

Anne Brotherton, SFCC, a Sister for Christian Community, was born in Augusta, Georgia. She received her doctoral degree in sociology in 1974 from Fordham University, specializing in the area of comparative institutions. From 1974 to 1978 she was Director of Nonviolence Education at the Martin Luther King, Jr., Center for Social Change in Atlanta, Georgia. In 1978 she was appointed to the faculty of the Jesuit School of Theology at Berkeley, a member school of the Graduate Theological Union, where she is currently tenured as Associate Professor of Sociology and Ministry and Director of Experiential Education. Her present teaching includes theological reflection seminars on social justice and courses in "Christian Feminism: A Paradigm for Peace" and "The Socio-Theology of Catholic Marriage." She has published articles and lectured widely on experiential education, ministry, social justice, Christian feminism, non-violence and peace.